Praise for
The Evolved Nest

"In this groundbreaking volume, Bradshaw and Narvaez seamlessly weave back and forth between Animals and humans in order to describe the deeper mechanisms, common to both, activated in the evolved nest that optimize the socioemotional growth of a developing organism. Writing in an evocative, passionate, and at times poetic style, they offer numerous fascinating intimate portraits of the early beginnings of the evolved nest across not only humans but a broad spectrum of species, and thereby their shared capacity for engagement, self-regulation, play, love, and consciousness. . . . This book is an absolute pleasure to read, yet at the same time it provocatively challenges us to rethink our relationship with and moral responsibilities to the other species with whom we share the planet."

—ALLAN N. SCHORE, PhD, Department of Psychiatry and Biobehavioral Sciences at UCLA's David Geffen School of Medicine

"Taking us on a timely and vital tour of our evolutionary history of cooperative child-rearing, Narvaez and Bradshaw provide a crucial documentation of how our ancestral history is [more] one of collaborating as a larger identity than the lessons modern culture portrays of solo-self in isolation, not only in childcare, but in our larger life journeys. With this perspective, we are given a pathway back to the truth of our larger experience of self, one deeply woven not only in these bodies we are born into, but also in the relationships with humanity and Nature that are waiting for us to reclaim our joyful belonging to all life on Earth."

—DANIEL J. SIEGEL, MD, *New York Times* best-selling author of *The Whole-Brain Child*

"Human exceptionalism—the belief that humans are fundamentally different from and superior to all other species—is used to justify our exploding population and attempts to bend all of Nature to our will. It has taken a terrible toll, not just in terms of mass extinctions and ruination of ecosystems, but also on our own emotional well-being. In this finely crafted book, Narvaez and Bradshaw show that our refusal to accept and cherish the commonality we have with other beings is undermining our ability to raise children to be happy and socially functional adults. If only we paid attention to how other Animals do it."

—DR. REED NOSS, past president of the Society for Conservation Biology

". . . a breathtakingly comprehensive, insightful, and singularly creative understanding of the intimate connections between humans and Animals necessary not only for life itself but also for thriving. Readers will learn that any positive future for humanity rests on mutually beneficial relationships with the diverse Animal species that share our planet and our destiny."

—RICHARD M. LERNER, Bergstrom Chair in Applied Developmental Science and director of the Institute for Applied Research in Youth Development at Tufts University

"One of the greatest misconceptions of the dominant worldview is that humankind is essentially different from the rest of the natural world. In this masterpiece of reconceptualization, Narvaez and Bradshaw reveal the deep commonalities in the developmental systems of both humans and our nonhuman Relatives."

—JEREMY LENT, author of *The Web of Meaning* and *The Patterning Instinct*

"Profound, wonder-filled, and deeply reasoned . . . *The Evolved Nest* will reveal to you a new and empowering path forward to relating to those you love, society, and the natural world we are part of."

—DACHER KELTNER, director of the Berkeley Social Interaction Lab and author of *AWE*

"*The Evolved Nest* should be required reading for people of all ages globally because the future of our fragile, magnificent, and interconnected planet depends on the goodwill and love of *everyone* living *everywhere—people of all cultures*. And there is no better cohort on which to focus than youngsters, because they are the future."

· —MARC BEKOFF, author of *Rewilding Our Hearts*

"Narvaez and Bradshaw have written a beautiful book that seamlessly integrates knowledge from the natural world with anthropology, psychology, and even sophisticated neurobiology. The wisdom they have extracted from the complexity of development and evolution is deep and refreshing. *The Evolved Nest* has much to teach academics, society, and parents about how to support the rearing of a healthy child."

—C. SUE CARTER, PhD, professor of psychology at the University of Virginia and Distinguished University Scientist at the Kinsey Institute, Indiana University

"For all who understand that we are a part of Nature—in raising children as in so many other ways—*The Evolved Nest* is a fascinating and lively way to begin learning about how human childcare fits into the vast spectrum and deep evolutionary history of the caring that is central to community."

—MELVIN KONNER, MD, PhD, Samuel Candler Dobbs Professor of Anthropology, Program in Neuroscience and Behavioral Biology at Emory University

"This beautifully written, scientifically rich book takes us into the caregiving worlds of other Animals, all the while constantly challenging us to learn from their wisdom the radical changes needed in how we raise and nurture children. Humans around the globe have disengaged themselves from essential evolutionary and ecological lessons critical for sustaining fulfilling future lives for all inhabitants of our increasingly threatened planet."

—GORDON M. BURGHARDT, professor of psychology at the University of Tennessee

"In *The Evolved Nest*, Narvaez and Bradshaw compassionately remind us of our evolutionary and contemporary connection with the diverse social systems of nonhuman species that populate the Earth. . . . They remind us that to optimize the development of our young, we need to look for commonalities with our phylogenetic ancestors (Mammals) and cousins (Birds) to learn the powerful lessons of evolution that have been encoded in the 'evolved' nest."

—STEPHEN W. PORGES, PhD, Distinguished University Scientist at the Kinsey Institute, Indiana University; professor of psychiatry at the University of North Carolina; and author of *Polyvagal Safety*

"The metaphor of the evolved nest makes clear the basic need of all Animals, including humans, for a supportive context. Scholars and practitioners alike will be informed and inspired by the interweaving of remarkable insights drawn from across many Animal species."

—L. ALAN SROUFE, professor emeritus of child development at the University of Minnesota

". . . simultaneously brilliant and breathtaking. . . . Through exploring the lives of Animals and their patterns of care, this book reveals much about humans and interconnectedness."

—DOUGLAS P. FRY, PhD, author of *War, Peace, and Human Nature; Beyond War;* and *Nurturing Our Humanity*

"Narvaez and Bradshaw's brilliant, soul-nourishing stories of human and Animal families are a welcome journey home."

—LISA REAGAN, editor of Kindred Media and cofounder of Kindred World

"In their book, Narvaez and Bradshaw offer an approach to learning what Gregory Bateson refers to as 'the pattern which connects mind and Nature.' They provide teachings that stem from observing our nonhuman relations, showing how they exemplify a life-sustaining kinship worldview that guided us for most of human history. If we heed what they say, it could do so again."

—WAHINKPE TOPA (FOUR ARROWS), aka Don Trent Jacobs, PhD, EdD, coauthor of *Restoring the Kinship Worldview* and author of *Teaching Truly*

The
Evolved
Nest

The Evolved Nest

Nature's Way *of* Raising Children *and* Creating Connected Communities

Darcia Narvaez, PhD *and* G. A. Bradshaw, PhD

FOREWORD BY GABOR MATÉ, MD, CM

North Atlantic Books
Huichin, unceded Ohlone land
Berkeley, California

Published by
North Atlantic Books
Huichin, unceded Ohlone land
Berkeley, California

Cover design and illustrations
by Jasmine Hromjak
Book design by Happenstance Type-O-Rama

Printed in the United States of America

The Evolved Nest: Nature's Way of Raising Children and Creating Connected Communities is sponsored and published by North Atlantic Books, an educational nonprofit based in the unceded Ohlone land Huichin (Berkeley, California) that collaborates with partners to develop cross-cultural perspectives; nurture holistic views of art, science, the humanities, and healing; and seed personal and global transformation by publishing work on the relationship of body, spirit, and nature.

North Atlantic Books's publications are distributed to the US trade and internationally by Penguin Random House Publisher Services. For further information, visit our website at www.northatlanticbooks.com.

Library of Congress Cataloging-in-Publication Data

Names: Narváez, Darcia, author. | Bradshaw, G. A. (Gay A.), 1959- author.
Title: The evolved nest : nature's way of raising children and creating connected communities / Darcia Narvaez, PhD and G.A. Bradshaw, PhD ; foreword by Gabor Maté.
Description: Berkeley, CA : North Atlantic Books, [2023] | Includes bibliographical references and index. | Summary: "A resource that reconnects us to lessons from the animal world and shows us how to restore wellness in our families, communities, and lives by exploring different animals' parenting models"-- Provided by publisher.
Identifiers: LCCN 2022054753 (print) | LCCN 2022054754 (ebook) | ISBN 9781623177676 (trade paperback) | ISBN 9781623177683 (ebook)
Subjects: LCSH: Child rearing. | Human behavior. | Familial behavior in animals. | Animal behavior.
Classification: LCC HQ769 .N248 2023 (print) | LCC HQ769 (ebook) | DDC 649/.1--dc23/eng/20230313
LC record available at https://lccn.loc.gov/2022054753
LC ebook record available at https://lccn.loc.gov/2022054754

1 2 3 4 5 6 7 8 9 KPC 26 25 24 23

To Earth

Contents

Foreword

In the arrogance of what we like to call our civilized culture, we tend to see ourselves as superior in intelligence and accomplishment to our evolutionary cousins, the other Animals with whom we share the Earth. We even look down with pride on brother and sister humans whom we are pleased to dismiss as "primitive," such as Indigenous people and, more especially, the few, small remaining hunter-gatherer groupings that still cling to a tenuous existence in the face of the relentless march of "progress." This is what the anthropologist and author Wade Davis calls "cultural myopia," the sense that "other peoples are failed versions of ourselves. Or that they are ancient, vestigial creatures, destined to fade away, quaint and colorful humans who wear feathers. These are living, dynamic people who have something to say."[1]

This gem of a book, modest in length but vast in erudition and insight and rich in mind-boggling scientific observation, will leave the reader both humbled and grateful. Subverting our egoic self-satisfaction, it illuminates how humanity has forgotten its own nature, even as it has abandoned and turned against the Nature that formed and sustained us over millions of years. In doing so, our authors, psychologists Darcia Narvaez and G. A. Bradshaw, also point the way to redemption. No fanciful social utopianism here; only a profound understanding of what our core needs are, right from conception, and what we have to learn from the ancestral human and Animal ways of being as they were formed in the crucible of Nature.

The salutary subversiveness of *The Evolved Nest* is that it shows our commonality, in the deepest emotional sense, with fellow creatures such as Parrots, Elephants, Whales, Wolves, Penguins, and even Octopuses. The capitalizations are the authors' device for reminding us of the essential personhood and psychological complexity of these other beings whom we assume to be so different from our own genus, *Homo*.

Unlike humans still connected to Nature, most of us don't think of ourselves as sharing emotional dynamics with other Animals. Yet from the point of view of modern neuroscience, when, say, Indigenous peoples ranging from Alaska to the Amazon refer to Animals as relatives to be honored, they are accurate. Neuroscientists have pointed out that we share evolutionarily bestowed primary emotional processes with a wide variety of species. The brain circuits humans share with other creatures—as this book elegantly illustrates with examples that more than once left this reader in a state of wonder—include caring love, joy, play, panic, and grief. Witness, for example, the heartrending story of a young Elephant who twice in her short existence suffered the loss of a mother figure. As the authors reveal, we share with Animals the capacity for consciousness, feelings, thoughts, and dreams. An Octopus with a neural substrate for cognition, self-awareness, and consciousness? Yes.

The emotional dynamics generated by these cerebral circuits serve well-being, compassion, self-regulation, confidence, and other healthy qualities, as they are meant to; but only if they are evoked by the proper circumstances— that is, only if their development is supported by the evolved nest. "Evolved nests," Drs. Narvaez and Bradshaw tell us in their introductory chapter, "are developmental systems tailored to nurture psychological, social, and physical needs in a species-unique manner." For humans, they later elucidate, the evolved nest is the set of processes and structures that provide children with the social and ecological microenvironment perfectly tailored for optimal growth and health. To put it bluntly, we have lost the plot in the pursuit of economic and technological advancement. This has been a traumatic development in the history of our species, one whose ramifications we are experiencing all too keenly in the epidemic of ill health, mental disturbances, aggression, social divisions, and other plagues that beset present-day societies. It is no slur on human ingenuity nor a denigration of modernity's truly miraculous inventions and achievements to argue, as our authors do, that we have much to learn from our hominin forebears and from the Animals whose evolved nesting practices they document so eloquently.

Did you know that an Elephant newborn is greeted by the gentle stroking of a posse of other mothers? That Emperor Penguins share gestational duties between male and female and that the safekeeping of their offspring, as of young Whales, is a communal task? That Wolves, even if childless, will lactate to feed the young ones when the clan's needs call for that? In case after case, this book teaches us how Nature has inculcated collaboration, empathy, a communal ethic, and mutual support as the necessary legacy of each species for the optimal development of their fledglings. This is true for humans as well—though one would hardly know that from observing how we gestate, birth, and raise our infants and young children today. With the loss of the evolved nest, we have become alienated from the benign child-nurturing instincts with which Nature has imbued us over eons. For example, we are the only species who, by design and according to the prescriptions of "experts," allows infants to cry without responding to their distress in order to "teach" them to sleep—thereby impairing their brain development and jeopardizing their future mental health, as Darcia Narvaez has shown elsewhere. Nor, in Nature-based human cultures, are the young hit, harshly punished, or isolated from caregivers as a way of bringing them to heel. On the contrary, the authors note later in this volume that "any aggressive actions in the toddler years are greeted with playful response, as everyone knows that young children are not yet fully empathic or aware of their actions' effects."

Having lost its evolutionary niche, our species is inflicting its distress upon our fellow creatures, as Dr. Gay Bradshaw already documented in her remarkable work on post-traumatic stress disorder (PTSD) in Elephants. This book, too, abounds in lamentable examples of Animal cultures—such as Wolves in Yellowstone National Park or even in the Alaskan Denali wilderness—being traumatized at the hands of Westernized humans who, unlike most Indigenous people, have no concept of being part of Nature, having become severed from their own nature by the traumatic demise of the evolved nest.

As a result, there is almost as much sadness as beauty in this exquisitely crafted book. Yet our authors leave us on a positive note: they have written here not a dirge, after all, but a paean to Existence, to the possibilities inherent in us, despite our losses, and a call for a future informed and reinvigorated by what the past and everlasting Nature can teach us.

—*Gabor Maté, MD, CM*

A Note on Terminology and Sources

Our goal is to bring together insights and reflections from Western science, Native science (*sensu* Cajete),[1] other Animals, and our personal experiences as threads of a common fabric for the purpose of restoring peace and well-being for all life. To retain the integrity of sources, we have sought to quote voices directly as much as possible (*sensu* Younging),[2] and in keeping with others working at ontological crossroads, we "humbly pay homage to the traditions discussed in this paper, knowing there is not one representational reality to that which is presented, recognizing the limitations of our own abilities in even discussing these ways of living-thinking-being."[3] Because the challenges of interdisciplinary work include the dynamic use of language and concepts, where meanings can vary across disciplines, cultures, and time, we list how key terms and concepts are used here.

Ancestral context: the common lifeway characteristics in which humanity (*Homo*) spent 95–99 percent of its existence universally as nomadic foragers, and which still exist today among contemporary foragers.

Capitalization: Reflective of usage prevalent among many tribal peoples, as well as neuroscience's findings that treat species' differences like those of cultures,[4] we capitalize Animal names (e.g., Gray Wolf) in keeping with capitalization of the names of human nations (e.g., Tewa). "Animal" and "Plant" are capitalized to underscore this understanding. Although such categories retain a dualistic perspective that splits phenomena into pieces and therefore reflects a particular human cultural view—one contrary to the framing of this work and the sciences covered—this convention is used for clarity of communication. Ultimately, the work and view here draw from nondualistic frameworks, such as Buddhism and quantum mechanics, that regard names and words such as "Animal" as vestiges of dualism, not definitions.

Carer: For many species such as Mammals the *initial* and *primary* carer is the mother. For other species such as the Emperor Penguin, the *initial* carer is the mother because she develops the egg, but the *primary* carer after birth is the father. Many Animal cultures such as African Elephants have a constellation of carers, a community of adults (referred to as *allomothers* or *alloparents*) and younger family members. Subsequently, across human and nonhuman cultures, carers can range from primary carers (e.g., mothers) to supportive carers (e.g., allomothers or alloparents), all of whom ensure continual support and security. The same convention holds for the use of **mother, father, parent,** and other familial terms that are not always constrained by gender.

Companionship care and nestedness: *Nestedness* describes specific socio-ecological experiences (e.g., soothing perinatal experiences, breastfeeding, touch, play, responsive care) rooted in relational attributes of attentiveness, responsive care, love, and moral commitment provided by carers and others in the conspecific and broader natural community. Nestedness is tailored to each species' needs, but principles are common across phyla. *Companionship care* refers to the broader context of relationships beyond conspecifics based on the needs and sensory capacities of the species. These vary by particular ecology and Umwelt (an Animal's unique perceptual and sensory experience of the world); hence, companionship care varies by species.

Dominant culture: the Westernized worldview that considers humans as separate from, superior to, and having self-proclaimed dominion over Nature. The dominant culture is one that normalizes disconnection from Nature, body, relational attunement, and ecological embeddedness.

Earthcentric and **Nature-based:** generalized terms for people and cultures whose ethics and principles align with those of (nonhuman) Nature and who understand themselves as partners with Nature, not separate from or superior to it. Earthcentric and Nature-based lifestyles are regenerative, rather than extractive and consumptive, as in the case of the dominant culture.

Familial terms: Instead of using species-specific scientific names (*sensu* Carl Linnaeus) for Animal offspring, we generally use "child." Animal families are regarded as comparable to human families.

Indigenous: This term can be applied to everyone as indigenous to the Earth, but the term is usually applied to contemporary cultures, many of whom are (self-) referred to as tribal, Native, or First Nation Peoples (see below). The Indigenous or kinship worldview is generally reflected in and embraced by Nature-based cultures and considers the cosmos unified, sacred, and moral.[5]

Native Peoples, First Nation Peoples, tribal people: members of groups that associate themselves with a particular landscape from which emerged a unique language, deep observational wisdom built over generations, and respectful traditions for living in mutual wellness with nonhuman Nature. This would also include living at a particular place on Earth where the people would know and respect Nature through practices of mutuality and respect. Because of settler-colonial genocides, forced migration, banning of cultural and linguistic traditions, and other violence, many First Nation Peoples have been displaced and now reside in lands different from where their ancestors lived.

Nature: used in contrast to "human," but with the understanding that humans are members of Nature.

Nomadic foraging communities: migratory groups of five to fifty multi-aged humans who do not domesticate Animals or enslave Plants, do not overly collect possessions, and are generally egalitarian.

Pronouns: Generally, gender-neutral pronouns (e.g., they, them, their) are used throughout except when necessary for clarity of communication and meaning, such as referring to a female mother (e.g., she/her) or a male father (e.g., he/him), or to distinguish one individual (e.g., baby) from another (e.g., mother) in the same sentence.

Science: Science is generally understood as a systematic analytical process and gathering of knowledge. Physicist F. David Peat writes that in **Western science,** "It is not so much the questions themselves that are the problem, but whole persistent desire to obtain knowledge through a particular analytical route. . . . There are times when it is better to listen than to ask, better to feel than to think, more appropriate to stay with a silence than to seek answers in speech."[6] **Native science** is broader and more inter-disciplinary than Western science, informed and formed through an under-standing of the cosmos as comprising constant change, motion, and flux, an interconnected, animate, spirit-filled place. As Gregory Cajete (Tewa), direc-tor of Native American Studies at the University of New Mexico, writes: "Native science is born of a lived and storied participation with the natural landscape. To gain a sense of Native science one must participate with the natural world."[7] It is "a reflection of creative participation, a dance with chaos and her child, the creative spirit."[8] In Native science, coming to know something involves personal transformation.

Settler-colonizer culture:[9] the ongoing (dominant or dominating) system of power, based on capitalism, that continues the genocide and repression of Indigenous peoples, their languages, and their cultures. Settler-colonists consider themselves and their culture superior to Indigenous cultures and identify with the concept of "progress." Settler-colonialism seeks to displace, replace, and obliterate Indigenous cultures and societies.

Western/Westernized: a culture and worldview that originated in Europe and North America (Turtle Island).

Nature's Way

WEBBED FEET PLANTED on the Antarctic ice, a father bends down to tend his son. High in the canopies of the Amazon, nestlings raise their beaks to join the family chorus. Under the heat of the African sun, trunks of mother and aunts reach out to help the newborn stand. Below the sparkle of Atlantic waves, a baby Whale glides alongside his mother. Large or small, land-born or water-born, they are immersed in love. Their hearts beat with the same song that has been passed down generation after generation, lessons from the mother of them all, Nature. These melodies are faint in our human lives today. Heavy from forgetfulness, hearts and minds have grown weary and brittle. How do we recover this reverential song of wellness? When we relearn, rejoice, and rejoin Nature's way.

In the dazzle of Nature's extraordinary diversity, it's easy to overlook how similar we are. Even though humans and other Animals look different on the outside, inside—beneath the fur, fins, feathers, scales, and skin—we are very much alike, including our brains. Animals ranging from the giant Sperm Whale and the tuxedoed Penguins to the ancient African Elephant and the astonishing Octopus share with humans brain structures and processes that give us capacities for consciousness, thinking, feeling, loving, and dreaming.[1] We also share a common system for raising our young: the *evolved nest*.[2]

Evolved nests are developmental systems tailored to nurture psychological, social, and physical needs in a species-unique manner.[3] "Nests" don't always look like the cupped constructions of twigs and branches that many Birds make. The African Elephant evolved nest is a social and ecological environment centered around the natal family—mothers, aunts, cousins, sisters, and brothers—who form a nucleus of care. The same goes for Sperm Whales. Their evolved nests are shaped by the folds of ocean currents and a matrilineal family that nurtures young Whales' minds and bodies in the ways of their watery home.

Every species' nest has been perfected through evolution to optimize health and well-being, starting from conception through adulthood. Each is a tried-and-true system validated over millions of years. The more an Animal and their young mesh with the natural surroundings, the better chance they have to thrive. *The same goes for humans.* We and our children do best in conditions like those in which we evolved as a species.

Today's culture of cars, manufactured houses, and technology in which most children are immersed, however, is a far cry from our evolutionary roots. As Jean Liedloff discovered, the gap between how our ancestors lived and how we live today has generated issues and symptoms in our youth and society that are absent in cultures that retain humanity's natural heritage. The poor mental and physical states of industrialized humans might be widespread, but they are in no way "normal" relative to our Nature-based human ancestry.[4]

Jean Liedloff was a fashionable socialite living in the rarefied circles of New York and Paris of the 1950s until one day, on impulse, she joined an expedition to the jungles of Venezuela in search of diamonds. It was a decision that took an unexpected twist, transforming her very core, and leading her to write the landmark book *The Continuum Concept: In Search of Happiness Lost*.[5]

During multiple visits over two and a half years, Liedloff lived among the Amazonian Ye'kuana, who took in this stranger from a strange land to partake in their everyday lives. At first, Liedloff was both enthralled and appalled—enthralled by Nature's beauty and appalled by village life. With disbelief, she observed the cumbersome and difficult ways that the community seemed to function. She couldn't understand how women made their way down a tricky, slippery mountainside to collect water from a stream, not just once but several times a day, all the while balancing babies on their hips or backs.

In Liedloff's opinion, there must be a better way. She thought the entire enterprise was unnecessarily dangerous, tiresome, and inefficient. This was the purpose, she reasoned, of modern progress—to improve upon the way things were done in the past. More startling was the difference between her struggles fetching water, washing clothes, and cooking cassava and how the Ye'kuana women undertook the same work. They were graceful and gracious, showing pleasure and enjoyment in their work together, however difficult. Liedloff found it all perplexing. Then she had a revelation that broke through what she later realized were culturally conditioned perceptions. It opened her eyes to an entirely new view of life.

One morning, watching her European friends and Ye'kuana men dragging a heavy dugout canoe up the riverbank, Liedloff was shocked at the contrast. "Here before me were several men engaged in a single task," she reflected later. "Two, the Italians, were tense, frowning, losing their tempers at everything, and cursing nonstop." On the other hand, the Ye'kuana men "were laughing at the unwieldiness of the canoe, making a game of the battle, relaxed between pushes, laughing at their own scrapes and especially amused when the canoe, as it wobbled forward, pinned one, then another, underneath it. . . . All were doing the same work, all were experiencing the strain and pain. There was no difference in our situations except we had been conditioned by our culture to believe that such a combination of circumstances constituted an unquestionable low on the scale of well-being and were quite unaware that we had any option in the matter." The Ye'kuana men, she went on to recount, "were in a particular merry state of mind, reveling in the comradery. . . . Each forward move was for them a little victory."[6]

Liedloff had also started to notice how she had changed. Much to her surprise, she "flourished."[7] Her body became lither, her mind clearer, and her mood lighter. Life was *happier*. Relative to their North American and European counterparts, the Ye'kuana emerged as exemplars of excellent mental and physical health. They worked hard, but there was no trace of the systemic social decay that ravages modern society: illness, addictions, child abuse, domestic violence, and suicide.

Notably, the Ye'kuana lived intimately interconnected with the fabric of the natural world. Instead of trying to reshape the land to fit some abstract ideal, their lives aligned with Nature's contours and practices. Amazonian Animals, Plants, and humans thrived, water was clean and fresh, no one was homeless, and there was a deep sense of belonging.[8] Nature was not viewed as a counter-force to be reckoned with, but a river of change in which all life participated.

The Ye'kuana lived within Nature's gift economy, where food and care are shared in response to another's need rather than being withheld as a means of control.[9] Food, time, and attention were freely shared. Haunani-Kay Trask describes how a similar ethic existed in the Hawai'ian Islands (before being supplanted by the European paradigm of exchange, where giving is performed in order to receive): "Before the coming of colonization, Native society was a familial relationship organized by tribes or chiefdoms in which the necessities of life—land, water, food, collective identity and support—were available to everyone."[10]

What impressed Liedloff the most was how this philosophy carried through to childcare. Confident in children's inner guidance, the community provided support as needed, such as breastfeeding and suckling on request. Amazonian babies were loved unconditionally. Compared to what Liedloff observed in the United States and Europe, Ye'kuana babies hardly cried, and their patterns of eating and sleeping were not dictated to them. They were taken in-arms wherever everyone else went, and they were carried and cuddled in contact with their mothers, family, and other community members, with the freedom to roam and play without adult interference.

All of these observations agree with those from a long line of formalized studies of Nature-based cultures by anthropologists such as Barry Hewlett, Melvin Konner, Michael Lamb, Richard B. Lee, Margaret Mead, and Elizabeth Marshall Thomas.[11] Liedloff came to call this human-Nature spooning an example of the *ancient continuum*.[12] She maintained that to cultivate the health and well-being embodied by the Ye'kuana, and what she experienced herself, humans need to bring their lives back into alignment with Nature and the habits of our ancestors—to reorient from anthropocentrism to ecocentrism.[13] According to Tewa educator Gregory Cajete, this understanding of human nature "embraces the inherent creativity of nature as the foundation for both knowledge and action" and maintains "dynamic balance and harmony with all relationships."[14]

The ancient continuum provides a road map to heal and anneal our individual selves and our communities, which have been fractured and inflamed with alienation and intolerance. By relearning and molding our minds and relationships to fit the ways of the cosmos, we can craft wise practices and a moral path to live within Nature's capacity. As Vine Deloria Jr. (Standing Rock Sioux) observes:

> The wise person will realize his or her own limitations and act with some degree of humility until he or she has sufficient knowledge to act with confidence. Every bit of information must be related to the general framework of moral interpretation as it is personal to them and their community. No body of knowledge exists for its own sake outside the moral framework of understanding. We are, in the truest sense possible, creators or co-creators with the higher powers, and what we do has immediate importance for the rest of the universe.[15]

Liedloff's continuum concept radicalized popular Western views on culture and child-rearing. Since the 1975 publication of *The Continuum Concept*,[16] scientific studies have proliferated to validate Liedloff's personal observations on how early life experience has far-reaching impacts, not only on child health and well-being but also on that of the entire human and nonhuman world.[17]

Researchers have looked deeper, beyond behavior, into the psychology and ethics of ancient and contemporary Nature-based cultures—those that are shaped by an embodied wisdom of mutuality and respect.[18] Recalling the wayfinding of Nature-based peoples, anthropologist Wade Davis describes how "every animal and object resonates with the pulse of an ancient event, while still being dreamed into being. The world as it exists is perfect, though constantly in the process of being formed. The land is encoded with everything that has ever been, everything that ever will be, in every dimension of reality. To walk the land is to engage in a constant act of affirmation, an endless dance of creation."[19]

The point is not to portray a Rousseau-like painting of an idyllic Eden, but to underscore a vital difference between current domination-oriented human societies and those that flourished before global colonization. The reason that the Lakota Sioux, Quechua, Ye'kuana, Bears, Wolves, and Beavers have flourished for many thousands of years without destroying their habitats, as modern industrialized societies have, is because they have sought to fit in with Nature.[20] Nature-based cultures demonstrate how humans and Animals share landscapes and enhance all of Earth's life[21] by mirroring each other with similar diets, patterns of mobility, ethics, and childcare.[22] This raises the questions: Given the ancient continuum's evolutionary success, why is it largely absent in contemporary human societies? What happened?

Around ten thousand years ago, perhaps due to climate change or population pressures, human cultures in several areas shifted. Communities started to step outside their evolutionary heritage and break with Nature's gift economy. Over the course of several millennia, these few groups of humans began to enslave Plants and Animals.[23] Communities became increasingly more dependent on agriculture and less reliant on foraging.[24] Instead of regarding Animals and Plants as kin, these communities viewed and used them as commodities for human ends.[25] As concentrated settlements of these cultures developed, they required more and more land to maintain their economies. Nature-based cultures, human and nonhuman, were obliterated and entrained by an agenda of "progress."[26] This mandate has not stopped. Indigenous cultures of all species struggle to maintain the health and integrity of their communities and survive the onslaught of forced globalization.[27]

A single thought, seeded thousands of years ago, has caused a primal, life-denying wound: instead of being *part* of Nature, humans are *apart* from Nature. This one idea has fostered an illusion—a human-focused, human-constructed, human-controlled false reality—in which Nature is perceived to play a subordinate, utilitarian role. Over time, this dramatic departure from evolutionary ways expanded and exploded, pushing the planet into the Capitalocene, an era defined by massive pollution, climate crises, genocides, and ecological destruction.[28]

There has been another by-product of the move away from Nature: the ways in which humans raise children have dramatically changed. The ancient continuum—a lifestyle that cultivates a fluid and flexible way of being, one focused on dignity and relational quality,[29] on working with Nature, not against it—was abandoned. The effects of this shift away from the evolved nest are far-reaching.[30]

The first years of life lay down foundational trajectories of who and how a child will be in the future. The nature and quality of a child's early life play a key role in shaping a child's mental and physical health and how they will relate to the world.[31] A culture's ideas and values that are conveyed to a child inform the ethics and relationships that they will endorse as adults.[32] In short, how a child is treated is predictive of how they will treat the world. Biologist Humberto Maturana suggests that humans originated and evolved as *Homo sapiens-amans amans*, a species shaped by a biology of love. We all require tender, supportive care in childhood to promote our fullest cooperative capacities.[33] With the rise of anthropocentric civilization, however, two other forms of humans emerged from the violation of the biology of love: an aggressive form, *Homo sapiens-amans aggressans*, and an arrogant form, *Homo sapiens-amans arrogans*.

The result is today's dominant trauma-based culture. Instead of positive, inclusive, Nature-based ways, colonizing industrialized humans adopted what psychologists now understand to be a trauma-inducing lifestyle.[34] The normative baseline for raising children bears little to no resemblance to that of our natural, ancestral evolved nest. Rather than being integrated in all aspects of a supportive community, most children's experiences involve routine stress, isolation, and disconnection. In place of evolved nest inclusion, nurturance, and security, the unnested child experiences alienation, deprivation, and trauma, which often starts even prior to birth.[35]

Mothers and their babies have been disempowered. Medicalized birth undermines a mother's connection to and confidence in her own body.[36]

Many babies are no longer allowed to "decide their birthdays"[37] and are instead forced into the world through planned surgery, labor-inducing methods, or preterm birth that results from the intense or chronic stress many modern mothers sustain.[38] Such disruptions are carried through a mother's body to the child's.[39] Maternal and paternal stress are transmitted to the child through DNA.[40] The medicalized childbirth that proliferated in the twentieth century is now known to impair healthy child development. Practices such as mother-baby separation,[41] medically unnecessary but compelled substitution of formula for breast milk,[42] prescribed eating and sleeping schedules, and institutional care (i.e., childcare centers and preschools) are, as Jean Liedloff described, antithetical to the ancient continuum. When the evolved nest was abandoned, well-being was too.

The intergenerational support system of aunts, uncles, siblings, and grandparents, which is so formative for a child, has been torn apart across cultures over generations by slavery, industrialization, war, forced migration, and other destructive policies and agendas. Today, Western children typically live in a single-generation household without multiage companionship.[43] Instead of outdoor self-directed social play, most young children's time is spent in carriers or strollers, with a smartphone or computer, and in educational settings that restrict play and other natural patterns of expression. Aside from relationships with family Dogs, Cats, Horses, or other companion Animals whose lives, minds, and bodies have been shaped by human goals through domestication, children are not raised in sync with Nature's rhythms. Instead of feeling at home in Nature, they often reflect their parents' unfounded and exaggerated fear of the wild.[44]

In addition, children are confronted with a threatening and hostile social world. Even while experiencing elements of evolved nest nurturance, every child, no matter where they live, directly or indirectly encounters social dysfunction in peers and adults, which manifests as widespread depression, anxiety, abuse, addiction, and bullying. As physician Gabor Maté asserts, "Since we live in a society that largely denies human developmental needs— doesn't even understand them, let alone provide for them—you're going to have a lot of people affected in adverse ways. Most of the population, in fact." Denial of developmental needs significantly affects children's brains and bodies, the effects of which cascade through time into adulthood.[45] Young generations are bombarded with the legacies of their ancestors: global suffering, extinction of the wild, and threat of ecological collapse.[46]

We don't have to live this way. We don't have to subject our children to trauma-inducing practices. There is an alternative. We can embark on a wellness-informed path. We can live and thrive as other humans have who did not abandon Nature-based ways and the ancestral nest. A plethora of research ranging across neuroscience, psychology, immunology, endocrinology, anthropology, sociology, diverse health professions, and the wealth of wisdom shared by Nature-based cultures concurs.[47] Humanity and the planet can be restored "by practicing new ways of producing and caring for one another together, a praxis of redoing, rethinking, reliving our most basic relations."[48] As psychologist Alison Gopnik notes, a healthy childhood is "about providing a rich, stable, safe environment that allows many different kinds of flowers to bloom. It's about producing a robust, flexible ecosystem that lets children themselves create many varied, unpredictable kinds of adult futures."[49]

Traditional, Nature-based communities understand that children are humans in the making. For example, any aggressive actions in the toddler years are greeted with playful response, as everyone knows that young children are not yet fully empathic or aware of their actions' effects. It takes decades to grow into humanity and reach one's full, unique potential. There are critical brain developments extending well into the sixth decade of life that lend themselves to wisdom, such as synthesizing information across domains and experience.[50] Brain-body development continues to be integrated from birth through adolescence and adulthood, giving the individual a holistic sense of self-in-the-world, self-in-relationship, self-at-home-in-the-world.[51] Like the maturation of Elephants, Oaks, and Sequoias, human brains and minds take time and care.

For those with young or grown children whose upbringing has not conformed to the architecture of the evolved nest and the ancient continuum, there is no call for self-recrimination, guilt, or judgment. Even though these children may not have experienced nestedness in its fullness, families can provide the essence and principles of the evolved nest to nurture health and happiness. As Liedloff maintained, "I believe it is possible to start as we are . . . and still find a way back. . . . Even with a culture [that] developed without taking the real needs of its people into account, with an understanding of the human continuum, there is room to improve our chances and reduce our errors in every small way that presents itself from day to day."[52]

This is our core take-home message: we can infuse and transform child-rearing, family life, communities, and relationships by revitalizing Nature-based values and an ethic of oneness.

The need for restoring nest consciousness could not be greater. The stakes could not be higher. Decisions regarding whether to have children and how to raise them directly affect the fate of the planet and that of our Animal and Plant kin who are balancing on the edge of extinction. Putting the lessons of this ancient and new understanding into practice is our responsibility to present and future generations, and to those of the past who have striven to uphold Nature's ethics. As Penobscot Indigenous rights and spiritual teacher Sherri Mitchell (Weh'na Ha'mu Kwasset) asserts, "We have to stop trying to make our children fit into the world that they find themselves in, and start creating a world that fits them."[53] Nature created such a world.

Returning to nestedness is essential for the future of humanity and the planet. Unnested cultures will continue to be disordered and prone to violence, and will display a lack of empathy for others instead of the flexible other-centeredness into which we evolved.[54] This is especially so when such humans establish institutions, policies, and practices that allow them to take over the existence-scape of other species (i.e., waterways, landscape, food-source access), putting everyone—humans, Animals, Plants, and all Earthlife—at risk.

Deep, positive changes to reinstate oneness are already afoot. Human hearts are awakening to the need for a global turning, back to connection, back to partnership, back to oneness.[55] Our Animal kin who are so close to us in body and mind provide a ready guidebook for getting our species back on track to wellness in oneness. Through testimonies from Elephant, Wolf, Penguin, and other Animal lives and loves threaded with scientific insights, *The Evolved Nest* describes just how to do this—how to take the first steps along the path that restores humanity to well-being and peaceful coexistence with the rest of Nature. Let us begin this journey home together.

2

Should I Have Children?

Brown Bears

THE CHILL SURPRISED HER. Autumn's come early. Her nose lifted to catch the drift of wind. Salt—the air was salty—a sea wind. The season had definitely shifted, and winter was on its way. Returning her attention to the Pine, the Bear continued to pluck cones and swallow their fatty nuts. It wasn't time to muse about the weather. It was time to consider the children she carried within.

The turn to fall in Kamchatka is poignant. By September's end, the landscape is in retreat. Summer's flush has faded, replaced by winter's breath. Some residents have left for temperate climes; others remain, picking at the season's last fruits. Brown Bears are among those who stay, finding what they can, gleaning nuts and berries. Given enough sustenance, they can grow to five feet tall at the shoulders and weigh in at more than half a ton.[1]

But gaining this stature takes hard work. Bears are fully aware that summer's bounty may disappear at any moment, and they do not stop looking for food until they achieve the fullness needed to balance hibernation's deficit. At this point, as Charlie Russell observed, Bears ease their search and transition to the coming of winter.

Charlie's observations came from a lifetime spent with Bears. After fifty-some years living cheek by jowl with Grizzlies in his home province of Alberta, Canada, Charlie spent a decade living with their cousins, the Brown Bears of Kamchatka, Russia's stark peninsular wilderness. It was here that his journey took an unexpected turn: the rescue, rearing, and reintroduction to the wild of Brown Bear cubs.[2]

All at once, Charlie was thrust into the role of a mother Bear. She is the vital source of care that feeds the healthy growth of infants to the threshold of adulthood. Building on his deep experience with Grizzlies and living in the wild, Charlie was able to successfully function as a surrogate mother. He nurtured ten cubs whose mothers had been hunted down and killed, so they could eventually live and thrive on their own among their wild Kamchatkan kin. Charlie's experience, however, did not go unaided. He had unexpected help. Through guidance from a mother Brown Bear named Brandy, Charlie grafted into the wisdom of Brown Bear rootstock.

Brandy taught Charlie the nuanced ways of Bear ethics, values, and motherhood. Her trust and confidence in his abilities were so great that she put him in charge of her young while she was away doing other Bear business. That phase of their partnership took form one day when Brandy up and left her children in the care of their new human nanny. As Charlie pointed out, Brandy did not bother to ask if he wanted the job:

> She was in charge and never made any bones about it. Brandy was an amazing female bear and the crankiest bear I ever met. What I mean is that she was very intolerant of my stupid human mistakes and had no qualms about telling me so. She was not very tolerant of other bears either. If you heard a bear roaring in the valley, it would be Brandy. She was loudest when chasing a male, and she'd go after him for miles throughout the valley and over the mountain. I'd hear her and laugh, thinking she's after some poor soul who happened to wander into her area.[3]

In addition to mothering his own cubs, Charlie was a second mother for three sets of Brandy's. It was a relationship that lasted more than seven years.

Intimate contact with the Kamchatkan wild provided incredible insights into Brown Bear life. Charlie saw how, when the warm season begins to wind down, Bears do too. "They know exactly how much more food they need to consume before achieving the right amount of fat," he said. "The cubs were ravenous when they emerged from hibernation. But, at some point in late summer to early fall, they slowed down and became what I called 'lazy old bears.' They lost the tension that goes with an urgent need for food. When they know they have fattened up enough, bears can afford to loll around and enjoy the remaining warmth of the year."[4] Similar to their traditional human neighbors, the Itelmens, Kamchatka's Brown Bears live with Nature's pace.

Fat or slim, Bears possess powerful arms and unretractable six-inch claws. To view these claws as weapons alone, however, is a mistake. While they can serve Bears in this capacity, claws have many roles and are wielded with delicate care. Charlie describes the finesse with which his cubs used their paws and claws when harvesting Pine nuts:

> They'd pick up a pinecone and carefully lay it on the back of their hand where it forms a hollow. Then, one by one, they'd bite and separate the scales and nuts in their mouth. When one side was done, they'd switch over to the other hand and do the same thing. The cone was rotated, back and forth between paws, with a steady stream of its scales pouring out from the cub's mouth. After four or five bites, the cubs would drop the empty core, reach up and grab another cone to start the process over, just like a conveyor belt.[5]

A mother Bear uses her clawed hands for all manner of things including digging roots, catching Salmon, and making a winter den where her babies will be born and overwinter. While human children are born throughout the year, baby Bears are birthed during a single season. Brown Bears hibernate for up to seven months until spring breaks, when they can emerge from their winter retreat. At that moment, Bears join everyone else in a common, pressing mission: find food and start packing in calories. Bear hands instantly transform into skilled implements for fishing and harvesting nuts and fruits.

Every year, migrating Salmon populate the inland waters of Kamchatka. Salmon have a double life: they are anadromous, living part of their lives in the ocean and the other part in fresh water. On average, ocean waters are three times as concentrated with ions (salts) as a Salmon's interior. In fresh water, the opposite is true. To accommodate this radical change in chemistry, the Fish have evolved an ingenious method that pumps salts in and out of their bodies to maintain internal chemical balance, a process called *osmoregulation*.[6]

Salmon life begins in fresh water. A few months after they are born, young Salmon called *alevin* travel downstream to the open ocean, where they do three things: drink a lot of water, decrease urine production, and start osmoregulating pumps in their gill cells. After a few years, the process reverses when Salmon return to spawn in natal waters. Their exteriors also change, morphing from an ocean-blue complexion to crimson as internal carotenoids move into their skin.[7]

The journey home is challenging. After navigating a network of ever-smaller waterways—sometimes as long as a thousand miles (1,600 kilometers)—Salmon bodies are spent by the time they reach their spawning grounds. When a female Salmon arrives and finds the right spot, she uses her tail to build one or several nests, called *redds* (the word's origin is credited to the Gaelic, meaning "to clean and clear an area"). When construction is completed, she lays her eggs in the nest, and a waiting male fertilizes them. The mother then covers the eggs with gravel. Her task accomplished, she remains, vigilantly guarding her precious brood until she dies, which can be less than a scant ten days later, two months short of the birthing of her young.

Meanwhile, on land, Bears wait impatiently for the annual event. They line lakes and streams, pacing up and down riverbanks and shorelines in hungry anticipation. After months without food or water, Bears are depleted. Their bodies crave the rich protein, fat, and nutrients that Salmon bodies provide. As Salmon die, Bears revive, and so the cycle goes.

Often, Fish and berries aren't enough. Brown Bears also need Kamchatka's white pearls, Pine nuts, to create a blanket of honeycombed fat encircling their midriff. This layer of adipose tissue provides crucial insulation and slow-burning calories that sustain a Bear through hibernation.[8] Mother Bears need even more. Not only do they have to maintain good health and strength to survive until and into spring; they also have to have enough stores to provide nutritious milk for their cubs.

Infant Animals require resources appropriate to their species-specific needs as they approach and complete sensitive periods of development. *Altricial* species—those that depend on intensive postnatal care, such as Bears and humans—must have sufficient internal and external resources for both mother and children. An infant's health directly relates to their mother's health. If a Bear mother receives proper nutrition, experiences low to negligible psychological and physiological stress, and has not experienced trauma, such as the violent orphaning that Charlie Russell's rescued cubs endured, a mother can usually provide well for her child before and after birth. Primates are no different.

While Brown Bear mothers are designed to care for their cubs on their own, humans evolved to be cooperative child-raisers.[9] The core structure of humanity's ancestral evolved nest is a family and community who give a mother physical and emotional support to create a space of nurturance—a biology of love.[10] Unlike other Primates, however, who travel using long arms in conjunction with legs, humans are bipedal. Evolutionary shifts in posture and motion have led to other changes in our species.[11]

As a result of walking on two limbs instead of four, humans evolved smaller pelvises, and at the same time, they evolved bigger heads with larger brains.[12] Among hominids, human baby brains and bodies are the most developmentally plastic and have the greatest and longest-term needs.[13] Human brains are three times larger than would be expected in another primate of the same size. In anticipation of extensive postnatal growth in brain volume, the human cranium does not seal completely for about eighteen months. Because a human mother's narrow pelvis forces a baby to exit her womb when the fetus is highly immature compared to other Mammals,[14] the human brain is the least developed Primate brain at birth, and it needs long-term nested care.

Neural tissue requires a lot of energy to grow and maintain itself, so having a large head and brain is an expensive adaptation. Almost 60 percent of a human infant's energy intake goes to growing the brain.[15] Seventy-five percent of our brain size develops after birth, co-constructed through baby-carer partnerships. If most of our brain growth is influenced by what we experience, then it matters what that experience is. Basic brain and body systems and their circuitry are established by the care and environment in which a baby grows. From the brain stem to the limbic system to the neocortex, the infant's brain organizes around social experience.[16] These features are reflected in the design of the human evolved nest.

The human evolved nest comprising family and community creates a web of nurturance. Parents and other carers serve as external regulators— sources of comfort and care—who assist infants in developing their internal capacities, including such crucial neurobiological systems as the immune, neuroendocrine, and stress response systems. With this external scaffolding of nested care, body and brain systems are immersed in a bath of supportive biochemistry, ensuring that neurobiological systems form optimally. Biological anthropologist Ashley Montagu describes this essential external womb, an *exterogestation*, as a postnatal "womb with a view."[17]

Every child is a self-organizing, dynamic system who increasingly interacts with and depends on an expanding, supportive environment.[18] These interactions shape the extent of an infant's mental and emotional complexity and body-mind integration. Bodies are implicit memory banks, imprinting perceptions of the world—whether those experiences feel loving and sensitive or frightening and insensitive—that seed the mind-self foundation. *Companionship care*—loving envelopment in the evolved nest of human and nonhuman relations—builds a child's self-confidence, resilience, and ability to regain internal balance after experiencing change or stress. The appropriately nurtured child-turned-adult learns how to maintain healthful balance and respond effectively to their experiences.

In the case of humans and other Mammals, because mothers have evolved to carry the embryo to term and provide nurturance through breast milk, they generally form the fulcrum of the community's nested organization of care. Human maternal health and a mother's ability to provide committed care for her young are strongly influenced by the communal support they receive.[19] Our species has evolved to need a great deal of community support to raise a child, each of whom requires upward of thirteen million calories to reach maturity.

A mother communicates to her baby behaviorally, verbally, and nonverbally. Her states of mental, emotional, and physical health transmit to her infant through her actions, which are informed by culturally imbued values shaped during her early life experience. Genes, however, are inert without experience. What the baby experiences in the environment influences which genes are strongly or weakly expressed.[20] Experience turns genes on or off during sensitive periods, a process referred to as *epigenetics*. Interactions between genes and timed experience play a significant role in child development.

Care quality, which includes a carer's attitudes, feelings, and psychological states, is more than skin deep. It directly translates to a baby's body and brain and sets them on a given postnatal path. Mammalian breastfeeding, for example, is a formative regulatory mechanism that shapes budding minds and brains.[21] When a newborn is allowed to crawl up their mother's belly to massage and suck a nipple to start the flow of milk, they start on a path of positive self-confidence and trust. Suckling comfort, colostrum, and breast milk are fundamental elements of interpersonal development. In cases of adoption or other circumstances when breast milk is not available, an infant can experience the essential physical and emotional connection that breastfeeding embodies when provision of formula is combined with skin-to-skin contact.

As soon as a human or Bear baby is born, mother and child form a synchronized dyad whose interactions of feeding and nuzzling seamlessly shift from synchrony *(attunement)* and dyssynchrony (brief *out-of-attunement*). By experiencing dyssynchrony—as when, for example, a mother moves and milk flow stops—followed by rapid restoration of synchronic attunement— as when the baby finds the nipple again and milk flow resumes—an infant learns that when environmental change takes place, they have the power to restore connection. Over time, babies learn how to resynchronize diverse social interactions after synchrony is lost, thereby expanding their response "vocabulary." These minute experiences set the stage for establishing the foundation for social self-efficacy, the belief in oneself and the understanding that one can function in the social world securely and successfully.[22]

In this relational dance, babies follow the lead of their carers through the "communicative musicality" of body-to-body signaling.[23] As their physical skills grow, infants acquire new methods of interaction. They learn subtle nonverbal signaling and how to recognize the diverse workings of social relations—things like starting and stopping conversations, reading and understanding facial expressions, and expressing affection.[24]

Early relational processes also affect how an individual develops a sense of self-with-others, the sense of who-I-am that is defined by the more-than-one. We may perceive ourselves as individuals, but every individual is formed through relationships. I am because we are.[25] Social experiences begin in the womb and carry through birth and beyond.[26] An infant's myriad internal psychosomatic networks, which range from cellular biochemical reactions to scheduled neuronal network formation, anticipate external networks of communal care and develop in coordination with the multiplicity of their surroundings. Through living with others, an infant's *core self* begins to gel with the awareness of self as a feeling body, first in relationship with the mother and gradually with the ever-expanding world of family, community, and Nature.

Key to being part of this world outside the womb is the development of three basic systems. The first system focuses on the state of the body, through *proprioception* and *interoception*. Proprioception gives us an internal sense of our body in the world—how our movements and our bodies are in relationship with the environment. Interoception gives us the sense of what is going on inside our body. Similar to our senses—smell, touch, taste, sight, hearing, balance—proprioception and interoception are forms of communication. Proprioception helps keep us in contact and harmony with our environment, and interoception helps keep us in contact and harmony inside our body. Together, they monitor and coordinate with a shifting environment the overall state of the body, physiological processes, and felt emotions of well-being.[27]

The second system is *exteroception* or *pragmatic intelligence*. This faculty integrates awareness and information about specific situations, objects, and future events and our aesthetic response to them. The third system, *alteroception*, is concerned with coordinating body-to-body connection and emotional sympathy with others. It is integral to capacities for empathy.

Alteroceptive exchanges between a mother and baby finely tune interoceptive integration. Through touch, movement, and breastfeeding, the infant's immature nervous system and rapidly growing body are sated, and they settle. Body-to-body contact fosters healthy sleep cycles, arousal, and exploration levels.[28] Even precocial Animals, such as Chickens, Geese, and Turkeys, who are able to forage on their own almost immediately after hatching, still need the nurturance, protection, and love of their mother and siblings. Chicks will sleep under their mother's wings and bodies at night for heat and protection; at the same time, they are receiving essential social and emotional "nutrients" that touch and cuddling provide. Indeed, the terms "precocial" and "altricial" are now appreciated as opposite ends of a continuum, the "precocial-altricial spectrum," along which various species may share traits of both developmental classification extrema.[29]

Touch and caresses increase levels of oxytocin—the "love" hormone that typically makes us feel "cuddly"—and establish baselines of this neuromodulator for lifelong production in a child.[30] While oxytocin helps facilitate a sense of connection and empathy with others, it also counteracts stress effects by decreasing blood pressure and reducing activity of the autonomic nervous system's sympathetic branch (flight/fight).[31]

To healthfully coordinate and integrate proprioception, interoception, exteroception, and alteroception, infant brains need nurturing care to self-organize. Companionship care provided by the evolved nest within a complex natural world ensures that these capacities form harmoniously from birth. As nested children expand their capacities and relationships, they increase social skills and empathy because they have been treated with empathy.[32] When a baby receives affection and responsiveness early on, their social brain is primed to care for others in return. A baby reflects back what they have experienced. Brown Bears are no different; their infants also need and flourish with somatic love and nurturance.

During their journey from loins to independent life, young Bears rely on their mother for everything. In utero, the female Bear's blood and body provide nourishment for her growing babies. As soon as the one to four Bear babies are born, weighing less than a kilogram, they crawl to their mother's nipples and begin to nurse. Den time is spent touching, nursing, nestling, and playing together. In spring, when the family leaves the den, nested care continues under the watchful eye of mother Bear. After two or even three years of constant companionship, including seven-month spells in the hibernation den together, the cubs wean and strike off on their own to eventually start the next generation of Brown Bears and repeat what they learned from their mother.[33]

Mother Bear wears many hats. She is protector, resource, and teacher. Although Bears are born with a genetic library of inborn knowledge, there is a lot that a mother's children must learn and experience if they are to thrive in the wild. Living in the wilderness takes more than inheritance. It demands careful observation, vast social and ecological knowledge, and experience. As Charlie Russell discovered, skill levels vary across individuals and families, and using them well takes practice. Not all Brown Bears, for example, are born expert fishermen.[34] Interspersed between play and forays of exploration, young Bears watch what their mother does and how she does it, be it fishing, snuffling for roots, artfully collecting Pine nuts, or, critically, exercising the ethics of Brown Bear society.

While female Bears may parent on their own, they are partnered at every step with mother Nature. Every aspect of a Bear is shaped in relationship with Nature's grain. This refined union of self with surroundings has been passed through innumerable generations over millions of years. To optimize their children's security and wellness, mothers-to-be must be aware of external states as well as their own internal states. In parallel to Salmon who use osmoregulation to retain inner balance amid changing environments, Bears maintain coherence between their bodies and the environment by using accurate knowledge of self and Nature reality.

Nature reality is the unspoken web of ethics and principles by which all Animals and Plants live.[35] It is a sense of self born from and in relationship, resonant with what was referred to by Buddhist teacher Thich Nhat Hanh as "interbeing"[36] and by German philosopher Martin Buber as the nexus of "I-Thou" encounters.[37] This interdependence and vibrant betweenness of wild existence is part of Nature's coherence and beauty. Nature reality is reflected in Justo Oxa Díaz's description of Quechuan relational living: "The community, the *ayllu*, is not only a territory where a group of people live; it is more than that. It is a dynamic space where the whole community of beings that exist in the world lives; this includes humans, plants, animals, the mountains, the rivers, the rain, etc. All are related like a family. It is important to remember that this place [the community] is not where we are from, it is who we are. For example, I am not from Huantura, I am Huantura."[38] Wholeness is the essence of our ancestral evolved nest and those of other Animals. We are placed in, and our ethics emerge from, that space.[39] This exquisite sensitivity to perceiving oneself as fully part of Nature is woven into every aspect of life, including the time leading up to pregnancy and birth.

Male and female Brown Bears begin courting in early summer, after enough food and warmth have revived their bodies and minds. Generally, they do not mate until they are around five years old. By this time, Brown Bears are grown and sufficiently seasoned in the wisdom of the wild to take on the responsibility of a family. Unless a female is without children or her cubs are ready to wean, she will not mate. If she is solo, without children in tow, a female Brown Bear tends to wait to find a suitable male. If the pair "clicks," they partner, and encased in the safety and warmth of the winter den crafted by their mother, a handful of hairless, blind baby Bears are born—but not always. While they may be fertilized, Bear eggs do not implant with conception.[40] In fact, in humans, up to half of all embryos never implant after conception.[41]

Animals have evolved innumerable ways to adapt to changing and challenging environmental conditions. Birds like Canada Geese migrate when cool weather begins and food becomes scarce. Others stay put. Some, such as Black-Tailed Deer, can eke out a living despite the cold. Others yet, like Brown Bears, enter a period of dormancy, a sleepy state of lowered metabolism, heart, and breath rates.[42]

Biologists generally group dormancy methods into four main categories: *hibernation, estivation, brumation,* and *diapause.*[43] Bears and many other endothermic (or internally heat-generating) Animals hibernate in winter. Estivation is a kind of hibernation that does not occur in cold weather but rather when conditions become too dry and hot. Ground Squirrels do this in the summer. Brumation is Reptile hibernation designed for the needs and physiology of ectothermic (cold-blooded) Animals. All three strategies are ways to stay in alignment with the environment by adjusting habits or physiology to shelter and conserve energy. A fourth physiological technique, embryonic diapause, is specifically aimed to optimize successful reproduction.[44] Mother Bears accomplish this by delaying implantation, pausing before fertilized eggs implant into their uteri.

While denning, mother Bears stop eating, drinking, urinating, and defecating. They rely on stored fat to provide the necessary energy to survive and, if pregnant, nourish their cubs. This is another example illustrating why the relationship between a mother's condition and her circumstances and environment is so important. It determines whether she gives birth and if her children will live through hibernation and beyond. Bears in peak condition, for example, seem to den early on, when winter begins to descend. They can afford to leave off finding food and start the process of making a family because they have enough inner resources to sustain their cubs through hibernation and in the first days after emerging in spring. This gives their children an edge because, relative to cubs born to less fit and less fat mothers, they have had more food and time to develop faster and more fully.[45] Young Bear growth and fat storage characteristics are cross-generational, influenced both by their mother's body condition before birth as well as their own postnatal nutrition.[46]

Processes such as delayed implantation are usually regarded as automatic, not involving active participation.[47] Deeper reflection, however, suggests that while implantation mechanisms may be hardwired, the decision to implant is mindful of present and future conditions. Evolution created the pause between fertilization and implantation for a reason. All Animals express mindfulness and psychobiological self-regulation, the awareness of and ability to respond appropriately to environmental cues.[48] Mindfulness—awareness of self and environment—is vital and integral to being one with Nature. Consciously or unconsciously, at the cusp of implantation, female Bears seem to hold the mirror of self-scrutiny close and ask: *Am I ready to care for my babies?*

This is not a strange concept for human cultures that, similar to Bears and other Animals, live as part of Nature's skin. The *now* is connected to the following seven generations.[49] Charlie Russell noticed this invisible connection and profound understanding with his Bears in Kamchatka. He was continually amazed to discover how they were able to see and anticipate things in ways so much more subtle than what modern humans consider possible.[50] The decision to be a mother is one such example.

Mothering is a matter of more than just what the female does; it also matters who and where she is—her state of mind and body, and her past, present, and future circumstances. A potential mother-to-be must feel confident that she can build a solid, safe space to den her children. A Bear must also assess whether her body has accumulated sufficient resources to supply her cubs with milk through hibernation, all while maintaining her own fitness and readiness to provide optimal care needed after hibernation. Outside the den, a mother's energies will be doubly taxed. It isn't easy to secure food while at the same time keeping a wary eye out for danger and tending to her children's education.

Until Nature releases summer's riches, the few islands of green peeking out from melting snow service the entire neighborhood. Everyone is depleted from winter's deprivation and eager to pull from Nature's flesh. Poor berry crops and scarce Salmon runs intensify competition, and while the force and determination of a mother Brown Bear are not to be taken lightly, she is at a disadvantage with vulnerable young in her charge. A mother may be physically and mentally fit, but the environment may not be adequate. Climate change, scarcity of food, conflict, and overpopulation may tilt the scale against pregnancy. On top of all this are the dangers and pressures of human disturbances and hunting, which can prematurely drive a female Bear out of her den and cause the loss of her fetuses.[51]

In keeping with Nature's gift economy and ethic of mutualism,[52] Bears and Nature-based humans keep close track of what is happening in their homelands to determine when it is necessary to refrain from any given action, whether it is sexual activity, egg implantation, exiting from hibernation, or other decisions. By refraining from pregnancy and birth until conditions are sufficient to meet the huge investment that having babies requires, Wildlife stay in tune with the rest of Nature. Maintaining communication and alignment with the environment is central to evolution's plan.

While some assert that Bears are the only Mammals who can and do delay egg implantation, gestation, and birth, similar strategies have been identified in many more Mammalian species.[53] Adaptive mechanisms that evolved to match a mother's and child's needs to resource conditions, such as nonimplantation or spontaneous abortion, are also found in humans and other Primates. Baboons, for example, who are able to conceive year-round, show a marked peak in births at the "ecologically most optimal time."[54] By being sensitive to environmental changes such as harsh weather, food shortages, and demanding social dynamics and conditions, a mother increases the chances of her and her offspring's survival. All these factors deeply influence her babies' health and how well they will be able to integrate with their community and the world at large. They are yet another way Nature guides and partners with the various members of her ecohome.[55]

Deciding whether to have a child is a time for naked self-honesty and a stark assessment of reality. The correct answer to the question *Am I ready to care for my babies?* may not be what a potential mother or other parent/carer anticipates or desires. The biological momentum to pull ancestral heritage into the future is potent, and the yearning for the love, joy, and intimacy of family is strong. Yet her babies' very lives depend on the mother's ability to care well for them and maneuver outer social and ecological worlds successfully.

If the results of the mother's evaluations of self and environment do not align, she risks her life and that of her offspring, and hence her lineage. If she has misjudged her capacity or that of the environment, the babies will fail to thrive. As witnessed today writ large, society spirals into poor mental and physical health if care and concern for one another are not reciprocated and ecological well-being is disregarded.[56]

Unnested care—the absence of an evolved nest—often leaves a baby fearful, uncertain, and vulnerable in a threatening world. Baby learns to feel that she is bad and may never feel truly secure. She does not see her environment, others, and Nature as welcoming and joyful, but rather as potential agents of harm and hurt, undeserving of her care and concern. Charlie Russell saw these consequences play out in Bears. Orphaned baby Bears, abused and traumatized, their nests shattered by their mother's death with the blast of a hunter's gun, similarly suffer. Bear and human brains, minds, and psyches did not evolve in anticipation of the violence and trauma intrinsic to the dominant human culture.[57]

All organisms have evolved to align with the environments in which they are born and live. Animals and our Nature-based ancestors enjoyed the bounty of a nested world for millions of years because the nested world is a relational world of reciprocity, fullness, and respect. It takes years of intimate, caring companionship in community and Nature to build well-functioning physical and emotional support that nourishes a baby's body and spirit. It is only recently in human history that our species has created environments that are antithetical to those in which our species evolved. Instead of the ancestral nest, the majority of humans today follow a specific human-constructed world that is out of step with Nature. The difference between living in our natural ancestral environments and the largely human-constructed world of the present has generated widespread physical and psychological ill health affecting our species and the planet as a whole. Without the resources that our ancestral continuum and evolved nest provide, a child's ability to thrive is challenged.

Self, inner and outer circumstances, and other unanticipated factors affect how babies will grow and whether they will be able to flourish in the world into which they are born. Taken together, these factors underscore the weighty responsibility that starting a family entails. In the words of Rae Maté, "We all need to realize that entering a pregnancy should be like entering a shrine, a sacred place and time: a baby is being built. . . . Society needs to protect pregnant women because everybody is creating this child. It takes a world to make a baby."[58] It is this realization that may give a female Bear pause. Without the foundations to provide resources of an evolved nest and a social and ecological world that can support the health of mind and body, a child's future is precarious.

3

Mutual Accompaniment

African Elephants

THE CLOUDLESS, AIRLESS sky almost swallows the land. As she raises her trunk to taste the weather, the mother's face suddenly stills. A rolling lurch pulls her attention inward. The moment has come. Huge wrinkled gray shoulders lean in. Red dust billows and pillows as other mothers trace a circle around the laboring mother. Blood stains her legs. She sways, and the miracle begins—the slippery sliding of an infant pushing his way out from her womb into the space below, a patch of Earth amid churning feet. Like so many tentacles, trunks wind their way, touching and caressing the newborn as his trunk wriggles free from the amniotic sac and he takes his first breath of Africa. One mind, one body, is pulled into the constellation of many. A baby Elephant is born.

Thousands of miles from Brown Bear homes, far from Kamchatka's biting cold and knife-sharp skies, African Bush and Forest Elephants are raising babies as they have done for millions of years. Despite differences in physical appearance and distance, Bears and Elephants share nesting values and principles. Species may differ on the outside, but inside, they travel similar terrain.

Wildlife nests coevolved with Earth's diversity of landscapes and climates, as did those of Nature-based humans. Brown Bears fashion dens from saplings and snow. The Algonquin Peoples of northeastern North America used bark, branches, and wood to keep their families safe and warm.[1] Caribou journey hundreds of miles between summer and winter homes. The Northern Piikani Blackfoot (Aapátohsipikáni) adapted to seasonal change by moving to warmer climates, pulling their tepees and belongings on wooden-poled travois. In the tropical geographies of the South Sea islands and the Kenyan savanna, little to no shelter is needed. Samoans build thatched *fales* with open walls and hang coconut blinds when storms blow through. African Elephants follow ancient migration paths leading to water and food during drought, spray water and dust over their skin to block the sun's powerful rays, and use their bodies to shield and shade their young.[2]

None of these evolutionary adaptations are combative strategies; quite the opposite. They are means to stay in alignment with Nature's rhythms. Charlie Russell spoke about Alberta's snow and ice as he might describe a neighbor. He regarded the natural world as his family and community: "People talk about how peaceful they feel being in nature. I think what they're feeling is the harmony which comes with mutual respect. If you play by nature's rules, you begin to fit in and that creates a feeling of mutual belonging. This kind of respect brings a quiet peace. Bears respond to this. They are naturally respectful. . . . Natives generally lived like the bears and other animals because their reality and truth fit in with nature."[3] Fitting in was one of Charlie's core principles for living congruently and respectfully with Nature's ways, and it explains why Animals and humans were able to flourish together for as long as they did.

Just as species coevolve with their environments, so do their nests. Evolved nest designs are the fruit of millions of years of refinement, with the overarching goal of keeping a baby in harmony with their surround-ings. From conception onward, our ancestors' babies were nourished by the ecosystem in which they were conceived. The oneness of the ancient continuum was embodied. Their breath, mother's milk, and bedding all smelled and drew from the Plants and land in which they were born and where they would live their Earthbound lives. Before the baby was born, he was already a child of the land; native stream waters ran through his body as it took form inside his mother. It is only recently in human history that some of our species split from Nature's ways and kinship, which as a result has forced nearly all species to struggle to survive, including the Elephant. Despite their mild herbivory and gentle natures, they, too, have suffered.

Before European colonization, African Elephants lived in all but the northern deserts of a continent that spans seventy-two degrees of latitude, a distance greater than any other continent on Earth.[4] Today, the lives and lands of Elephants are rent and wounded. Young Elephants are born into a brutal world. Millions of Elephants have died by hunters' guns. Millions of mothers have watched their children being slaughtered, and millions of children have watched their families killed or abducted and sold to zoos.[5] Nonetheless, their moral resilience continues to reach into the future, driven by the generative engine of their evolved nest.

If a mother Brown Bear is the North Star for her young, then the natal family is the constellation for infant Elephants. It is a dense network of mothers, allomothers (older females), and younger members of various ages, all of whom are guided by the wisdom of a Matriarch. As they traverse traditional migration routes, the family travels as one, almost amoeboid in their coordinated movements. Individual families are further embedded in a multilayered complex of social and ecological relationships that extend deep into space and time.[6]

At every moment during her pregnancy and throughout her entire life, a mother Elephant is accompanied by others. Accompaniment is more than physical presence—or rather, physical presence is more than what meets the modern human eye. Accompaniment describes the commitment of one to support and journey with another, to put oneself in the space of mutual need and vulnerability with someone else.[7] The depth of this concept is found in its etymological origins. The linguistic roots of accompaniment relate to the Spanish *compañero*, "friend," which is derived from the Latin *ad cum panis*, "to break bread." In today's urbanized world of fast food, the ceremony and significance of sharing sustenance in a leisurely manner with others has lost much of its meaning. "Breaking bread"—preparing and eating food together, practically and symbolically—means participating together in life and all its vicissitudes. Liberation psychologist and activist Mary Watkins reflects on this sense of wholeness, which integrates the social, ecological, and psychological: "Psychosocial well-being is not independent of ecological or environmental well-being. Ecopsychosocial accompaniment requires radical availability, steadfast witnessing, self-reflexivity, attunement to others' needs and desires, and committed response-ability."[8] Embraced by this philosophy, when an Elephant baby is born their transition from womb to Earth is unbroken. They enter the world welcomed, soothed, and safe through accompaniment by the entire group, much like human children are in humanity's ancestral context.[9]

Elephant bodies and minds have evolved to be shaped postnatally after spending twenty-two months—almost two years—in utero, more than twice as long as humans' nine months. During the first months of life outside the womb, infant Elephants depend solely on their mothers' milk. Even when they begin to venture out to eat other food, they continue to nurse. It is not unusual for babies to suckle until they are four or so years old. While young Elephants are capable of eating on their own at three years of age, they do so in the company of their family. Infants spend much of their proximal time with members of the family other than their mother. Often there is communal suckling amid the flowing dance of touch, play, and assurance.

The Elephants' close social network makes certain that a baby will experience the uninterrupted security and love needed for healthy infant body-brain development. The intimate exchanges and nursing that a baby experiences ensures healthy development of internal systems such as the immunological, endocrinal, psychosocial, and nervous system.[10] This is particularly important for the brain's right hemisphere, which grows more rapidly in the early years.[11]

The brain's left hemisphere is typically involved with focused, logical, and analytical thinking and is wired within itself. The brain's right hemisphere is generally concerned with social connection, unboundedness, creativity, and emotions and is interconnected with the rest of the brain.[12] An integrated brain that utilizes and optimizes the totality of neural capacities relies primarily on the wisdom of the right brain.[13] In a sense, the right hemisphere provides the context in which the left hemisphere functions, particularly with respect to lifelong socioemotional intelligence.[14] The right half of the brain grows more rapidly in early life likely due to its importance for the development of critical neuronal pathways and patterns of affect through an ecosocial "tuning," and its governance of psychological and physiological regulation (e.g., breathing and heart rate). Rapid brain growth is one of evolution's clever ways to help a baby adapt to their new environment.

The galloping growth of the postnatal brain requires nested care to keep up with time-sensitive periods in brain-body development. Greater social connection and embeddedness optimize children's ability to grow and thrive successfully in the community where they will spend their lives. If carers are unresponsive or neglectful, neural growth factors critical for baby brain development can diminish, which with age may lead to compromised memory and cognitive deficits.[15] In contrast, intimate, responsive care correlates with improved cognitive development.[16] It is easy to appreciate why nested companionship care is common and crucial to Bears, Elephants, and other Animals whose children's very survival depends on highly refined cognitive, emotional, and physiological functioning.

Similar to Elephants, our ancestral companionship care was also communal. Communal care is more than a matter of "many hands make light work." It draws from a deep ancestral bench of values, lessons, and experiences that have accumulated across millions of years. Among many present-day nomadic foragers, communal care extends not only to the nuclear family but often beyond, to nonhumans.[17] In Nature-inclusive cultures of mutual care, relationships are fluid, porous, and reflective of a gift economy, giving without expectation of reciprocation.[18] At the level of the individual, the way in which ecocultures are maintained and communicated over time is through what we might call "enactivist care": embodied sensorimotor knowledge that begins with connection between carer and child through proprioceptive, interoceptive, and alteroceptive coordination. An enactivist carer simultaneously holds the child's perspective and that of the broader environment.

Enactivist care is anticipatory and cognizant of Nature's dynamics and changes. Similar to Brown Bear mothers, a ready Elephant or human carer is able to detect and respond appropriately to nuanced social and ecological patterns. A baby's developing, sensing, relational self is enveloped by those around her. In this way, children remain in a connected oneness with the rhythms of mother, family, community, and the natural world. Relational knowledge brings the inner and outer worlds into harmony and enhances a child's intuition about how to respond well in a variety of future situations. Mothers who are naturally in tune or who have learned these rhythms from elders, for example, know not to overwhelm or confuse their babies.[19] Confronted simultaneously with two novelties, such as a new routine and a new food, a human baby may become stressed and dislike the food because it becomes associated with difficult change.

A mother's intuition can be nurtured by seasoned elders involved in maternal support and childcare. Elder mentorship was how our human ancestral context functioned. Mourning Dove (Humishuma, pen name of Christine Quintasket [Okanagan Salish and Colville]) of the northwest coast of North America[20] speaks of her people's attitude toward children and the role of elders:

> Indian people loved their children above all else, for they were the hope of the future and justification for the trials and tribulations of their parents. They guaranteed the perpetuation of the family and continued the upholding of its honor. They were a special gift from the Creator and the promise of a bright and happy future. They were the focus for much of our time and attention, but they particularly spent time with their grandparents, as these had both the most free time to devote to their care and wisdom to pass on to the next generation. Their parents were in the prime of life and were often too busy working and scouting up food to give them the full attention they deserved. Our most important sense of self and continuity, therefore, came from the very old, who were so kind, gentle, considerate, and wise with us, particularly as children.[21]

Elders are considered the wisdom keepers of the culture—repositories of cumulative understanding, ceremonies, and practices of respect and responsibility toward the Earth. Strongly bonded to the young, elders provide perspectives and patience that teach, guide, and empower the young on their path to adulthood.[22] Orphaned Elephants at the Sheldrick Wildlife Trust outside Nairobi, Kenya,[23] provide spectacular examples of how communal values and care ethics can be successfully conveyed, even by "replacement" elders.

Dame Daphne Sheldrick founded the sanctuary in 1977 to care for the increasing numbers of injured Wildlife, and in particular, orphaned infant Elephants. As a result of poaching, hunting, human attacks, and land appropriation, many Elephants lose their mothers and families. Orphans are rescued and brought to the Trust's healing compound to recover and, with time, rejoin their wild community. Most arrive severely dehydrated and undernourished, but all are traumatized. Without the Sheldrick Trust's knowledgeable, supportive care, the infants would perish. Since its inception, the sanctuary has rescued and saved hundreds of infant Elephants who have gone on to join their wild community and bear babies of their own. By emulating Elephant accompaniment, human carers not only save lives but also help replenish and revitalize Elephant civilization.

Elephants at the Sheldrick Trust live in an integrated human and Elephant natal family. Babies are never alone, even sleeping nights with a human carer ("keeper"), arms and trunks entwined. During the day, accompanied by human carers and other orphans, the young Elephants play together and take walks to explore adjacent forests. The human-Elephant natal family nurtures and mentors the growing infants much as their families of origin would.

The sanctuary's success can be credited to Dame Daphne, who, as a fourth-generation Kenyan, spent decades watching, listening, and acquiring Elephant elder knowledge and cultural understanding. She used her insights to recreate the experience of the wild Elephant evolved nest, even inventing a coconut-based formula similar enough to an Elephant mother's milk to meet the basic needs of orphaned infants. Daphne and seasoned carers serve as bridging, replacement elders, who act in the absence of a mother to calm infant distress and soothe away despair through accompaniment.

Nonetheless, some of the most important lessons were learned the hard way, as is often the case. For example, early in the Sheldrick Trust's existence, a little Elephant arrived in need of care. She was so newly born that she was "still covered in the soft fuzz of elephant infancy, her tiny trunk tinged with pink, toenails of pale yellow—soft and brand new."[24] Aisha, as she was called, had been rescued after falling down a well. The fragile infant pulled through with round-the-clock care and attention. Gradually, the tiny frame filled out and the bond between Elephant baby and human mother deepened. One day while out on a walk, they encountered some German tourists. Startled, the infant Elephant stopped, and "her soft pink ears stood out like round dinner plates from her tiny face as she gave a mock-charge that ended with a squeak, an early attempt at a trumpet."[25] The tourists laughed and called out, *"Schmetterling,"* German for "butterfly." From that day on, Aisha was called by the diminutive name Schmetty.

When Daphne was satisfied that the young Elephant's health was sufficiently stable, she decided she could leave Schmetty with a babysitter in order to attend her daughter's wedding. However, much to her distress, Daphne was informed while she was away that Schmetty was failing to thrive. The moment she returned home, Daphne ran to Schmetty's side: "As she struggled to get up to greet me, she collapsed in my arms. Cuddling her close, I wept tears of grief, for I knew her life was ebbing away. With her head cradled in my lap, she managed one last loud cry that ended in a sigh and then her body went limp."[26]

Daphne realized that Schmetty had believed that she had lost her mother—again. In that moment, she decided that no rescued orphans would be cared for by a single person. They would emulate Elephant communal care, what Elephant families do in the wild, to build in resilience and multiplicity: "During the orphans' nursery period, the keepers, sufficient in number to represent the orphans' lost family herd, are in physical contact with the babies twenty-four hours a day."[27]

Nested care involves extensive whole-body learning within the particular ecological context in which a community lives. The orphans' outings at the Sheldrick Trust provide opportunities to find out which Plants and roots are edible, who lives in the neighborhood, and where to find thorny bushes and Trees to brush their skin. Finally, when they are old enough, Elephant infants graduate from the nursery and join an older group whose members are eventually reintroduced into wild herds. Later, when they have joined the broader setting of wild society, the young Elephants learn how to negotiate the vagaries of weather—floods, drought, and resultant food shortages—and possible attacks from Lions. Whether the repatriated Elephants are genetically related to the wild herd or not, the community absorbs the newcomer.

Bonds grow deep in this gifting culture. When one of their members has been injured by a poisoned spear, a gunshot, or another harming agent, Elephants travel to their human family for aid. Former orphans, reintroduced and living wild, often return with their families years later to visit the Sheldrick Trust, new babies in tow. Sometimes the newborn is a grandchild of a former orphan.

It is vital to appreciate that the sanctuary's work entails more than saving lives. The process of rescuing and resuscitating infant Elephants involves nurturing Elephant ethics and values by reconstructing the Elephant evolved nest through cross-species companionship care. Every interaction reflects companionship care, and every revitalized orphan embodies this ethos, even in infancy, as two infant Elephants at the Sheldrick Trust demonstrate.

Out on one of their daily outings accompanied by human allomothers, two-year-old Naleku and three-year-old Kindani started to argue about who would become the new Matriarch to lead the family on these excursions.[28] In the middle of Naleku and Kindani's negotiations, a third infant, delicate one-year-old Kerrio, was accidentally knocked to the ground by a two-year-old, Mukutan. Instantly, Naleku and Kindani stopped their debating and ran to help Mukutan raise Kerrio back on her feet. This simple scene, which took no more than a few minutes, shows that even though they have individual bodies, the Elephant relational sense of self eschews any ego and overrides individualism. Differences are superseded by a commitment to group well-being and a sense of at-one-ness. The Sheldrick Trust's healing companionship care can prevent orphaned Elephants' innate ethic of accompaniment from being quenched by trauma.

The potency of companionship care is reflected elsewhere among Elephants in captivity. An Asian Elephant named Pocha was sent from Germany to an Argentinian zoo in 1968.[29] She was mated and gave birth to her daughter, Guillermina, who would spend much of her life in the depths of a concrete trench with her mother. In 2022, when Pocha was fifty-five years old and Guillermina was twenty-two, they were released to a sanctuary, where Guillermina touched soil and Grass for the first time. Despite the deprivation to which she had been subjected, Guillermina is full of joy, laughter, and a sense of infectious humor.

Psychiatrist Henry Krystal, a survivor of German concentration camps, might have noted a parallel between Guillermina and former camp prisoners. After working for many years with other survivors, Dr. Krystal noted that if an individual had been raised in a loving, caring family, then even when confronted with overwhelming trauma, they had a much greater likelihood of restoring their capacity for healing and love after release.[30] Perhaps, somehow, Pocha was able to pass on to her daughter the love she had received from her mother.[31] Tragically, however, the torture and deprivation of zoos is too much for most Elephants and other Animals. Many die young, while others age and perish, decrepit and withered inside and out.[32] Even companionship care cannot always counteract the magnitude of human miscare and violence.

An infant Elephant's ethical inoculation comes from immersion in communal values. This includes acquiring competency in customs and dialects that weave through the greater Elephant society. Deep learning comes from experience and watching their elders. While the Matriarch is the main repository of ancient wisdom, other family members must amass enough of her experience to be able to take her place in case of her injury or death. Elephants must become experts in their habitat and culture, including childcare.

From firsthand observation and their own natal experience, every Elephant—male and female—is instilled with the art of childcare. Young males (commonly referred to as bulls) are also infused with their culture's ethic of care. Unlike their female counterparts who remain with the natal family, bulls leave somewhere between nine and twelve years of age. Not infrequently, they are reluctant to leave, but eventually they do part from mother and family to continue Elephant life in the companionship of older, mature bulls. At about thirty years of age, bulls enter *musth*, the hormonal period marking the onset of sexual maturity, and begin to court. Meanwhile, they maintain strong emotional bonds with other males who mentor— not dominate—them. Similar patterns of maturation are found in human Nature-based societies, but thoughtful companionship care and lifelong learning from wise elders have become rare in the dominant human culture.

When fragments of humanity broke from Nature ten millennia ago, these practices atrophied. Social cohesion among families and communities began to disintegrate, eventually leading to the dissonance and alienation so widespread today. Instead of the reciprocal, egalitarian, and care-based ethics that characterize Elephants and other undamaged Nature-based cultures, the dominant human society promotes individualism over community, competition instead of cooperation, and relational detachment instead of connection—all of which are contrary to Nature's predominant ethics and processes.[33] Among humans, respect for mothering, inclusion of women in decision-making, nurturing, and gender diversity found in matriarchal, or matrilineal, societies[34] were replaced with the hierarchies in patriarchal societies and the enslavement and muting of Plants, Animals, land, water, elders, women, and Nature-based human communities.[35]

Intensified colonization, capitalist globalization, forced migration, genocide, and industrialization-driven agendas tore traditional communities from their ancestral homelands.[36] Those leading a nomadic, subsistence life were forced to abandon it, breaking generations-old circles of communion.[37] Postnatal care fell further away from the nestedness of community and Nature, leaving children bereft, their vital needs unattended. Indigenous children were taken from their families and communities and sent to boarding schools across Canada and the United States as a way to deal with the "Indian problem."[38] Destruction of community relationships and social structures decimated ancestral knowledge, purposefully, through the removal of Indigenous children.[39]

Within settler-colonized societies, many modern mothers lack prior experience in caring for babies, and many have no connection with elder maternal wisdom concerning infant needs.[40] Even though neuroscience has increasingly demonstrated the importance of nested care, cultural momentum continues to push practices and beliefs in the opposite direction.[41] As a result, a baby's essential needs are often ignored.[42]

The term "need" is appropriate. A baby's cry, for instance, expresses an unmet and unfilled need, and a signal of nonconsent. Needs that repeatedly go unmet undermine a child's sense of security in the new, unfamiliar world outside the womb. What may appear to be a minor discomfort to an adult may be devastating for a baby who is completely helpless to address her distress without the aid of a carer. Daphne and the Sheldrick Trust's carer/keepers are fully aware of this.[43]

Olmeg was a baby male Elephant who was "orphaned when he was just 2 weeks old, when his family stampeded under a hail of poachers' bullets. It is not known how many elephants were killed or wounded on the day that Olmeg was left an orphan."[44] Although Daphne designed a formula to substitute for Elephant mother's milk, some orphans refuse to nurse from the large-nippled bottles. Olmeg was one. He was tiny, only a month old, weak and debilitated by severe diarrhea, when he arrived at the Trust.

Olmeg's situation was extremely dire. It was imperative for him to get sustenance. Yet, despite his severe condition, he would not take the milk that was offered. Then Daphne had an idea. Seeing how he kept walking over to a small tent that had been set up in the garden, she decided to try to offer him milk there. When she did, much to her great relief and joy, Olmeg began to suckle. The tent reminded him of his mother. Later, when another infant showed a similar reluctance to nurse, the carers, inspired by Olmeg and the tent, hung a large gray wool blanket on a laundry line with clothespins. From behind the blanket, Daphne stuck a nippled milk bottle out from beneath while another carer coaxed the infant over. Within moments, the baby began to suck from the bottle. Baby Elephants instinctively push up to their mother's gray rough-skinned body as they search for and find her nipple to nurse.[45] The tent and blanket setups provided a semblance of their mothers and support for the infants' trunks. Baby Elephants usually have their trunks supported while they nurse, especially those who are so young. The alternative support system offered an adequate substitute for what their mother's body would have naturally provided.

We have forgotten many similar details that make up the human evolved nest. Gabor Maté describes our modern culture as traumatogenic, the product of successive, unhealed, unresolved traumas filling individuals with discord, fear, and disconnection: "The greatest damage done [to children] by neglect, trauma or emotional loss is not the immediate pain they inflict but the long-term distortions they induce in the way a developing child will continue to interpret the world and her situation in it."[46] Early toxic stress is the first step on a trauma-inducing pathway. It can lead to disconnection, ill-being, loss of heart, and destructive lifeways across generations.[47] Studies of epigenetic inheritance show how children are affected by their parents' exposure to traumas that occurred before their birth, including those that occurred prior to the children's conception.[48]

The fracturing of Nature-based life and the substitution of contemporary medicalized practices for natural ways pervade almost all aspects of infant development in Westernized societies.[49] In contrast to gentle birthing in community, few human births today occur in Nature or are even accompanied by supportive family. Only recently have supportive friends and family been allowed to accompany a mother during labor and witness birth, which decreases labor time and perinatal complications.[50] In many hospital settings, babies emerge from the womb into a clinical world, dopey from drugs administered to the mother for her labor, blinded by the glare of artificial lights, and exposed to other noxious experiences that are harmful to growing brains and bodies.[51] Women's bodies are frequently anesthetized and subjected to induced labor, ignoring variations in gestation that naturally differ for lengths of up to fifty-five days.[52] A baby's first connection with the world outside the womb is usually plastic-gloved hands, stinging eye medication, and lung suctioning. Medical personnel typically take infants from their mothers to be weighed and examined. These practices have been associated with maternal postpartum depression.[53]

What happens on the outside—who and what infants experience—also happens on the inside to brain, body, and mind. Being born with a highly malleable brain means that an infant is extremely sensitive and receptive to experience, whether the encounter promotes health or ill-being. If they are met with responsive affection and attention appropriate to their needs, infants grow up with a positive sense of self, good physical health, and well-being. On the other hand, if children experience a lack of emotional and physical support and care, they are susceptible to depression, a lack of confidence, ill health, and interpersonal challenges as youngsters and later in life. An understanding of the evolved nest starkly shows how radically different the experiences of most human babies are today relative to the heritage and environment in which our species developed. These differences are found at multiple levels.

Although humans evolved to raise children together—grandmothers, fathers, kin and nonkin, and other mothers supporting mothers[54]—our modern, individualistic society tends to forget that mothers require community support. During pregnancy, mothers frequently experience depression that is associated with stress hormones and that can contribute to preterm labor and epigenetic changes in the baby's capacity to control stress effects.[55] For the mother, stress effects include disorganized sleep, decreased responsiveness to stimulation, and lack of bonding with the infant.[56] When a mother becomes less responsive, it can directly affect development of the baby's brain and multiple additional physiological systems.[57] Children with depressed mothers, for example, often exhibit chronically high or chronically low levels of cortisol, an important steroid hormone generated in the adrenal glands that is responsible for regulating a broad range of processes, including metabolism and the immune response.[58] Those raised in urban poverty, whose families typically experience deprivation, insecurity, and high levels of stress or trauma, frequently show sustained low cortisol and poor immunity.[59]

When stressed or traumatized, a mother or other carer can become out of step, or *asynchronous*, with her baby's natural positive emotions.[60] Babies interpret a routine lack of positive *synchrony* as a lack of love because their sense of reality and self are informed by the microenvironment they experience.[61] For an infant, a lack of love and lack of accompaniment signal rejection. We understand this unconsciously as adults. If, for instance, our partner says and does loving things, like bringing us a special present or giving us a hug and kiss, we can usually sense if they are sincere—whether the overtures are made in deep attunement and positive synchrony or are simply empty gestures. Babies who never learn the intersubjective "dance" of attunement can grow up without an understanding of what love is and what it really feels like. Humberto Maturana contends that we evolved to be dependent on loving relationships throughout life as part of human *neoteny* (the carrying forward of characteristics associated with the young into adulthood): "Physiologically we are social love-dependent animals, so much so that we become ill and our social life at all ages is disrupted, when we are deprived of love."[62]

Caring for an infant is similar to building a house. Nonresponsive or inconsistent care in early life is like having an unskilled builder who constructs crooked frames, off-kilter joists, and a poorly attached roof. All of these misalignments undermine the strength and integrity of the whole house, or, in the case of a child, the strength and integrity of their inner physiological and psychological resources that are intended to serve a lifetime. The foundations will not hold when stressors overwhelm a nonresilient system. This is where and how communal support can be so critical. As the Elephants at the Sheldrick Trust illustrate, therapeutic interventions that restore communal care and carer-child synchrony help heal a traumatic breach.[63] The absence of this kind of care can lead to very different outcomes.

In the 1980s, in anticipation of the dismantling of South Africa's repressive system of apartheid, parks and other ecotourist businesses began massive importation of "Big Five" Wildlife (Elephants, Leopards, Lions, African Buffalo, and Rhinoceroses). Most of these species had been extirpated by trophy hunting and poaching. The purpose of the importation was to refill parks and private reserves with charismatic Wildlife, which would, in turn, fill human coffers with ecotourist revenues. The enterprise, however, took an unexpected turn.[64]

A decade or so later, park biologists started finding the dead bodies of White and Black Rhinoceroses, both of whom are endangered. As the years progressed, the Rhinoceros fatalities exceeded more than one hundred. Ordinarily, park personnel would assume that poachers had killed the Rhinoceroses, whose horns are valued for traditional Asian medicine; but the horns were untouched and intact. After a few chance encounters, including photos taken by a passing tourist, the source of the violence was discovered.

The killers were teenaged male Elephants. Not only were young male Elephants killing Rhinoceroses; in some cases the young male Elephants were observed sexually assaulting them. Scientists were baffled. Such behavior on the part of Elephants at the parks was unprecedented; these giant gray herbivores are renowned and revered for their pacific natures and inclusive ways. It took a careful reconstruction of the young males' biographies to solve the perplexing, disturbing puzzle.

At the time of the mass importation, there were no practical means to transport someone as large as an adult Elephant. This limitation led to the capture of small infant Elephants whose transport by truck was more feasible. Elephant families were slaughtered by gun-bearing helicopters, and any surviving infants were corralled and tethered to their mothers' bodies. Following these terrifying experiences and witnessing the bloody deaths of their mothers and families, the one- and two-year-old Elephants sustained further severe traumas: premature weaning, shattering of the natal family, and translocation to an unknown ecology. Instead of four years of continued breastfed nursing and extended nested care beyond weaning, the infants were abandoned to survive on their own with no elder Elephants present to help heal and make sense of the senseless.

Although females suffered severe trauma and had none of the nested care and education they needed from their mothers and allomothers, males suffered their own deficit on top of the trauma. They never had relationships with older, experienced males, a process that traditionally continues companionship care through mentoring. These experiences occurred during critical periods of brain development. When the Rhinoceroses attacks began, the young bulls had prematurely entered musth. Instead of entering musth in their thirties, the traumatized young Elephants began musth at least fifteen or twenty years sooner than is normal. The abnormal onset of musth indicates trauma-induced neurobiological dysregulation underlying the young males' pattern of aggression, confusion, and disorientation.[65]

The impacts of human violence on the Elephants have not stopped.[66] Trauma, past and present, changes minds, bodies, and cultures. Infanticide, intraspecific violence, and killing—all signs of an epidemic of PTSD that was never observed in Elephants prior to European occupation—are now rampant. Today, female Elephants kill each other and each other's children, and at times, even their own. In one park, 90 percent of male Elephant deaths are caused by another male—another phenomenon unprecedented prior to European colonization.[67]

The stories of male Elephant trauma eerily echo those of human infants and young men, who also require extensive developmental support to reach healthy maturity.[68] Trauma transmits through time, across generations, and across space, through interpersonal relationships and culture, disconnecting us from our place in family and community and on Earth. But trauma is not our heritage. We evolved accompanied, like our Animal kin, by Nature's warm embrace. It is no exaggeration to say that by returning to our practices of villaging, with wise elders guiding the young with interpersonal relationships aligned with Nature, we can revitalize human health and well-being. The evolved human way follows Nature's way, with ongoing practices that support the wellness of all our kin, balancing and harmonizing our relationship with Earth.

4

Breastfeeding

Sperm Whales

A PERFORATION OF TURBULENCE interrupts the otherwise tranquil blue sea. The anomalous patch is caused by boxlike faces cutting in and out of the water. Amid the froth, a pale floating line appears: the umbilical cord of a newborn Sperm Whale. The mother gently lifts her baby's body to the water's surface for his first breath of air. She then slowly guides the baby to meet each member in the circle of family. In an exquisite coordinated gesture, the infant finds his mother's nipple, fits his mouth, and begins to nurse.

Far off the Spanish and African coasts lies a remarkable archipelago, a group of islands called the Azores. On the surface, they are no more remarkable than any other distant isle, but something about them pulls the eye, like a magnet, to venture beyond the cover of ocean glass to the depths below. It is here, where sunlight grows dim and dark replaces dazzle, that you find the ancient birthing waters of giant Whales.

These waters are a meeting place of many kinds. The islands are located along a triple tectonic junction where three plates come together: the North American, African, and Eurasian. Millions of years ago, ascending molten mantle plumes pushed through the poorly stitched tectonic seam to form a beaded string of volcanic isles as the triple junction migrated north.[1] Around this seismic diverging convergence is another intersection, the nexus of cold and warm ocean currents that cultivates a superrich chain of food for marine life, including the Sperm Whale.

Sperm Whales belong to the order *Cetacea*. The name comes from the Greek word for "huge fish," and indeed they are. Males reach eighty feet (twenty-four meters) in length and weigh in at one hundred thousand pounds (45,359 kilograms), and the relatively smaller females can reach an eye-opening forty-five feet (almost fourteen meters) and thirty thousand pounds (13,607 kilograms). Along with Dolphins, Porpoises, and Orcas, Sperm Whales belong to the suborder *Odontoceti*, toothed Whales. In contrast to their food-sifting cousins, Blue Whales, Sperm Whales and the other odontocetes are armed with an effective set of conical teeth and a sophisticated sonar system, enabling them to pursue, catch, and chomp their food.

Each day, adult Sperm Whales consume nearly a ton of Squids, Octopuses, and Sharks, a quantity comparable to the weight of their own newborns. To catch their food, Sperm Whales can dive as deep as 1.9 miles (three kilometers) and hold their breath for up to two hours. They have the largest brain of any Animal on the planet.[2] Their very big brains, combined with a cranial "melon" (or "junk") composed largely of fat and connective tissue, give rise to the Sperm Whales' distinctive box-shaped head.[3]

In terms of social and ecological habits, Sperm Whales and Elephants have much in common, exhibiting a "colossal convergence."[4] The organizing nucleus of both Elephant and Sperm Whale societies is the natal family, a group of closely connected, related adult females and variously gendered youngsters who travel, eat, and rest in contact with other families.[5] Although they are Mammals, Sperm Whales have some precocial traits; for example, newborn Sperm Whales can swim up to hundreds of miles on their own power during their first week of life.[6] Nonetheless, they are also altricial. Much of Sperm Whale culture revolves around the birthing and care of babies. Like the allocare culture of the Efé in the Ituri Rainforest of the Democratic Republic of the Congo,[7] and nomadic foraging peoples in general,[8] Sperm Whales are immersed in the accompaniment of many.

They spend the majority of their time together, in intimate contact. Every day, often in the afternoon, Sperm Whales stop their diving activities for about six hours and gather together in tight, slow-moving clusters at the surface.[9] "During these times," according to researchers Linda Weilgart, Hal Whitehead, and Katy Payne, "the whales often touch and move about one another, sometimes caressing each another with their flippers and jaws."[10] Critically, these activities are carefully designed to maintain infant care continuity. When, for example, the family is out on expeditions to find Octopus and Squid, adult and juvenile Whales "stagger" dives so that younger Whales who are not yet able to make the forty-plus-minute foraging dives are always accompanied.[11] Allomothers help nurse and tend to baby when biological mothers are gathering food, engaged in other activities, or too ill to nurse. According to Hal Whitehead, who has studied Sperm Whales for decades, compared to other species there is "a big difference in the degree of allonursing in sperm whales. The infant sperm whale typically suckles off a number of females."[12] Sperm Whales are "a kind of poster child for allosuckling" because half of all calves observed suckle from "at least 1-2 non-mothers."[13] Similar to the weaning of our human ancestors, Sperm Whale weaning takes place after four years of age or when the first adult molar appears.[14]

At some point, when internal clocks begin to quicken, young male Whales leave the matrilineal family to swim forth and explore wild waters where they join southerly "bachelor" groups.[15] Although they roam quite widely to the edges of the ice,[16] and distances between individuals are significant compared with the spatially tightly knit natal family, male Sperm Whales form deep, long-term relationships with each other.[17] Their keen click communication system, which allows them to hear one another at distances of up to six miles (almost ten kilometers), maintains connection in the absence of sight.[18] At any sign of threat or distress, such as danger from Orcas or human hunters, Sperm Whales respond at high speed. In preparation for and during an attack, they may form a "marguerite," a circle of protection, where the Whales face inward like petals on a daisy.[19] If one of their family is injured, others remain, often with fatal consequences.[20]

Sperm Whales remind us that differences in outward appearances can belie internal psychological and physiological commonalities. We share much more with this immense, sensitive being than our physiognomy suggests. For one, humans and Sperm Whales possess the innate response, predating the Dinosaurs, to be close to a maternal physical form. Like Salmon drawn to natal streams, we return to source, often the arms and breasts that first gave us life. This ancestral pull can show up at any and all points in life, particularly when a profound vulnerability reminiscent of being a newborn is experienced. As a seasoned Elephant sanctuary worker commented: "In all my rescue work, I have only known a handful of times when an Animal in need does not gladly warm to being held, their head resting on my chest. Even someone as large as a Horse or Elephant instinctively yearns for the reassurance of being held to a mother's breast. I have experienced the same thing with gravely wounded humans, many close to death, who finally relax and rest when their head and shoulders are held in the protection and love they received as a baby."[21]

Nursing is an extension of life in the womb. Before birth, the embryo is an integral unit enmeshed inside his mother, completely engulfed with love and buffered from external stressors. Until newborn Mammals emerge from their mothers' wombs, they are sustained by uninterrupted nourishment transfused into their bodies through the mother-child interface organ, the placenta. The placenta delivers nutrients and oxygen to the embryo from the mother's bloodstream and, in reverse, removes wastes via the umbilical cord.

Inside mother, the baby knows no danger. At birth, however, everything changes. From a realm of safety and nurturance, the baby is pushed into an unknown void outside. In response to the abrupt shift from unity to separation, there is an immediate effort to restore union. Infant-initiated connection and nursing are among the first gestures of agency in a newborn. Under natural conditions, mothers instinctively move to protect and feed their young, and babies seek that same connection, as part of the continuing maternal body-to-body biochemical signaling that supports healthy development during early life years.

The first food for Mammalian young is the gift of milk. Breastfeeding is an intricate, interactive process of "need-receive" communications between a mother and her baby. In a universal gesture, Animal young sidle up to mother and, by pressing their heads against her body, tell her, "Mother, I want some milk—*now*." In naturalistic human births at full term, where there is no or minimal involvement from institutionalized procedures, a human baby instinctively moves to reach mother's breast, pushing and pulling himself along in search of reconnection by crawling up to find and massage a nipple. After a few moments of licking the nipple, the child actively milks the breast, drawing in the areola and the nipple to the back of his mouth.

Milk and its delivery are seamlessly coupled. As we saw at the Sheldrick Trust, in most cases Elephant orphans are instinctively drawn to the triad of carer, nipple-bottle of constructed formula, and blanket that must serve as a makeshift, make-do substitute for an Elephant mother. As Daphne Sheldrick describes it, "Each elephant hones in on its particular spot, knowing exactly which bottle is his or hers. Some hold the bottle themselves, curling their trunk around it and tipping it up until it is drained, downing the contents greedily before waiting for the keeper to hand them another."[22] Reunion after birthing separation among Sperm Whales is also, as D. H. Lawrence writes, immediate and love-infused, in which "enormous mother whales lie dreaming suckling their whale-tender young and dreaming with strange whale eyes wide open in the waters of the beginning and the end."[23]

Evolution has matched breast, body, and milk to fit every variation of the species' theme. The coevolved milk-mammary-mouth architecture is a beautiful, efficient nursing system designed to optimize baby-mother connection. Unlike human nipples, however, those of mother Sperm Whales do not protrude, and in lieu of arms, baby Whales are held in the fluid embrace of the sea, mother's touch, and family. To nurse, an infant Whale presses up and nudges his mother's body. Stimulated by her baby's communiqué, a mother Sperm Whale's nipples emerge from mammary slits. At the same time, the infant rolls his tongue into a *U* shape so that it wraps perfectly around the nipple. Mother's nipple muscles relax, milk begins to flow, and the baby suck-les.[24] This time-tested fit allows baby to take in thick, nutritious milk without it being seriously diluted or dispersed. Mother's milk is not to be wasted.

Lactation—the making and provisioning of secretions for young Animals—is an ancient phenomenon that has been a part of Nature for more than three hundred million years.[25] Each species has evolved its own milk recipe with varying amounts of fats, sugars, and proteins that, detail by detail, mirror the ecology of the world in which the baby will grow, mature, and participate. Infants separated from mother for hours or days at a time—like Lions and Wolves, who use protein as an energy source—tend to receive thick, protein-rich milk, while those in continuous contact with their mothers—like Red Kangaroos and Bears—tend to receive less concen-trated nutrients.[26] Primates, who grow slowly and stay with their mothers for extended periods of time and feed frequently, have lactose-rich milk. Human milk, with 3–5 percent fat,[27] and that of Black Rhinoceroses are on the thin side relative to other species, such as the Sperm Whale, at 35–50 percent.[28] Sperm Whales have evolved to thrive on a milk diet higher in carbohydrates and lower in fat content than, for example, Harbor Seals. Young Seals nurse for six weeks on a fat-saturated milk (60 percent)[29] before they wean and can begin catching and eating Fish on their own.[30] The length of time spent breastfeeding in the human species lineage has increased as evolution has progressed. Our *Homo* ancestors, for example, breastfed for years longer than our extinct relations *Australopithecus africanus* and *Paran-thropus robustus*, who weaned after a few months.[31]

If Daphne Sheldrick's coconut-based formula had not matched Elephant milk closely enough, it would not have been possible for her and the other carers to save as many rescued infant Elephants as they have. Still, even a carefully prepared formula cannot come close to the real thing. A formula can serve in emergency situations to bridge a baby from certain death to resuscitation, but it lacks the vital ingredients of a species-typical breast milk that includes, for example, appropriate proportions of amino acids and bacteria for the developmental stage and state of the child. Modern breast milk replacements have typically lacked many key ingredients that breast milk provides.[32]

Mammal milk is filled with species-designed enzymes, hormones, and immunoglobulins that promote the health and development of an infant's brain and other body systems.[33] Breast milk builds the immune system, which for humans takes five or six years to reach adult levels.[34] Its content is 80 percent alive,[35] containing digestive enzymes and other factors that feed the gut's microbiome to build the immune system and foster healthy digestion.[36] Colostrum, a mother's first milk, and breast milk are particularly important early on because infants do not have the enzymes to properly digest anything else until several months after birth.[37]

Importantly, breast milk amino acids can cross the blood-brain barrier, and in so doing they create a "brain bath" of hormones needed for neuroendocrine and neurotransmitter system development.[38] In the first year of life, the human brain doubles in size with the expectation of receiving human breast milk loaded with the right proportions of oligosaccharides, enzymes, and amino acids. Major advances in the field of glycomics have allowed increasing insight into breast milk composition. One finding shows that human milk appears to have more soluble oligosaccharides of greater complexity than any other Animal milk.[39] An infant who is fed formula misses out on these healthy brain- and body-building ingredients that contribute so significantly to short- and long-term health.[40] Through breastfeeding, epigenetic effects take place that decrease the child's stress reactivity.[41]

Adiponectin, for example, which is available in breast milk but not in formula, affects how the body processes sugars and fatty substances in the blood, and is associated with lower levels of obesity.[42] Breast milk fats and cholesterol co-occur with specific enzymes, such as lipase, that break down fats and carry vitamins and minerals that are more readily absorbed than those included in formulas. While formula manufacturers continue to add certain ingredients to their products in attempts to match breast milk, these formulae are not derived from human sources; nor are they systematically monitored for safety and effectiveness.[43] Mothers' milk, however, is not just about basic nutrition; there are more dimensions to nursing and milk that reveal the intricacy of evolution's design.

Mother's milk is minutely tailored and individualized to meet a baby's specific developmental arc and environmental setting at the moment of need. This precision is essential. With signals from the baby's saliva, for example, the mother's breasts change milk composition, thereby increasing fat content during periods of growth spurts or creating antibodies to guard against infectious agents.[44] Not only does the breast produce different milks depending on the biological sex of the baby;[45] breast milk composition also varies throughout the day, such as in the case of tryptophan levels.[46]

Tryptophan is an amino acid linked to the sleep-wake cycle and is a precursor to serotonin, an ancient molecule common to vertebrates and invertebrates that is associated with learning speed[47] and self-regulation, like food intake. Serotonin is released via the brain stem with a key form (5-HT) that resides primarily in the gut, where it is modulated by the microbiome that breast milk populates and feeds, as part of the gut-brain axis.[48] In early life, tryptophan ingestion leads to more serotonin receptor development.[49] At night, breast milk contains more tryptophan and amino acids that promote serotonin synthesis.[50] Only recently have infant formulas started to include tryptophan.

When we start to map the "rhythms" of various vitamins, hormones, and other breast milk ingredients, it is astounding to discover the intricate timetable that mother's milk composition follows. Mother's milk directly from the breast is synchronous with the circadian cycle, which enables baby to recognize night and day and behave accordingly.[51] Cortisol, a mobilizing hormone, is almost three times higher in morning milk than in evening milk. On the other hand, levels of melatonin, a hormone secreted by the pineal gland at night that aids sleep and digestion, are negligible in mother's milk during the day but increase as night unfolds. Night milk also contains higher levels of certain DNA building blocks that help promote healthy sleep. Day milk, however, has more activity-promoting amino acids. Iron contained in milk peaks at around noon, and vitamin E peaks in the evening. Minerals such as magnesium, zinc, potassium, and sodium are all highest in the morning. Key antibodies and white blood cells that fortify the immune system are also much higher during the day.

All these differences reflect the tight coupling between parent, baby, and Nature. The synesthesia that a child experiences when breastfeeding—smell, touch, taste, sight, balance—merges with their relational connection to their first "other," the mother. This experience promotes a sense of unity and oneness in multiplicity.[52] Perinatal neuroscientist Nils Bergman, cofounder of the Kangaroo Mother Care movement, describes it this way: "Breastfeeding is a behaviour which shapes and sculpts the brain and that brain shaping stays for life. Skin-to-skin contact is what the newborn requires in order for the brain to be shaped in the best possible way, and breastfeeding in the fullest sense is not about eating, but about brain growth, and the development of good relationships."[53]

Many other aspects of breastfeeding dynamics directly relate to brain development. Human newborn brains start out at no more than 25 percent of adult brain volume, and they more than double in volume in the first year.[54] Over one million neuronal connections per second grow during that time period, requiring a constant intake of calories to build a healthy brain and body.[55] To accomplish this, Nature has created a number of strategies in addition to milk composition specificity.

During suckling, for example, the human tongue, lower lip, mandible, and hyoid bone coordinate together as an "oral motor organ." Nursing promotes proper facial, jaw, and tooth morphology, unlike bottle-feeding, which can impair such morphology and lead to sleep and orthodontic issues in later life.[56] While nursing and cuddling, baby and mother bodies spontaneously move and mold together, their heartbeats coming into synchronous rhythm. Breastfeeding promotes proper motor development, better sleeping patterns, psychosocial development, and other critical areas of early infant development.[57]

Human babies are born with a subcortical brain that operates automatically, but postnatal care is needed to expand and refine cortical control. Because babies don't breathe in the womb, newborns must learn to shift from their inborn subcortical system to an externally learned cortical control. Some babies do not achieve this milestone, which, if not practiced and mastered, increases the chance of death.[58] Breastfeeding offers a holistic way for babies to learn to cortically control the flexibility of using the nose or mouth for breathing. This helps a baby learn how to alternate from using the mouth to the nose as needed in a given situation. Breastfeeding on request provides the necessary scaffolding to learn to live (breathe) outside the womb. This technique is best facilitated by what biological anthropologist James McKenna calls "breastsleeping": breastfeeding while safely sharing a bed.[59] Through the mechanisms of breastfeeding alongside the mother's body rhythms, the human infant learns to breathe, and breathe deeply. It's a brand-new skill acquired after spending nine months as a fetus receiving oxygen through the red blood cells of the liver. While bottle-feeding delays this development,[60] babies who are not breastfed can receive similar scaffolding through extensive carrying, holding,[61] and safe co-sleeping.[62]

Breastfeeding matters for mothers, too, with long-term health benefits such as decreased risk of cardiovascular disease,[63] diabetes,[64] and stroke,[65] and less cognitive decline.[66] It also has immediate beneficial effects. Just after birth, when a newborn licks their mother's nipple, oxytocin is released into mother's bloodstream, causing the uterus to contract and expel the placenta, decreasing the chance of hemorrhage.[67] Whether she is a Sperm Whale, Bear, or human, a mother's prolactin and oxytocin prepare and stimulate her breasts to let down milk, simultaneously providing oxytocin to the infant. Suckling also increases prolactin. Facilitated by estrogen, prolactin increases with maternal caregiving behavior.[68] Sensory input from baby activates specific regions in the brain that contribute to and play important roles in maternal behavior.[69] Women who breastfeed tend to display more sensitivity to their children over the following ten years.[70]

In many ways, it is more accurate to think of breastfeeding as full-body nourishment. Not only are the milk, function, and shape of a mother's breast designed for her baby; her breast is part of a partnered constellation of mother-baby mind and body. When we look at artwork from around the world depicting mothers and babies, in most cases the mother will be holding her baby to the left and face-to-face, in what is called a *left-cradling bias.* This is no random choice; in fact, left-cradling bias is positively related to maternal empathy and inversely related to depression.[71] When a mother left-cradles, her left eye's visual field and that of the baby are directed toward each other. While activities such as foraging correspond to the brain's left hemisphere, left-cradling positioning of mother and baby allows for visual information to be readily processed by the brain's *right* hemisphere, where most social and emotional learning occurs. Body motion, posture, and geometry affect brain function and development, which in turn affects psychological and emotional states.

Left-cradling is reflective of lateralization, the preferential choice of position for diverse activities experienced and expressed in both vertebrates and invertebrates. Bird infants recognize kin and nonkin through the right brain hemisphere; Coho Salmon, a favorite summer meal of Grizzly Bears, prefer to watch their fellow species-mates with their left eyes. Frog tadpoles do so as well, a choice that positively influences their growth and development.[72]

Left-sided bias in mother-infant interactions is also found in Whales.[73] Belugas, Orcas, and Humpback Whales prefer to travel and nurse on the right side of their mothers, and they reverse to her left side in the presence of a threat, such as a boat.[74] While left-cradling has not been observed among Sperm Whales, "there is a left-side bias in peduncle diving, which is related to nursing," probably because, it is speculated, their blowhole position is to the left of center.[75]

In Nature-based human societies, it is common for carers to use all manner of slings, baskets, pouches, and movement to hold their baby while carrying out a task smoothly and safely. Baby is part of it all.[76] Often, carers wear loose or thin clothing that maintains physical intimacy and skin-to-skin connection.[77] This coupled closeness satisfies a baby's need to be sensed and optimizes the opportunity to breastfeed at will, as well as mother's ability to respond. As soon as she hears or senses her baby lip-smacking, fist-sucking, or rooting to nurse, mother offers her breast. Even older children are carried in ways that allow the mother to work and the child to retain easy access to a breast for suckling.[78] In some societies, if mother is busy, a grandmother, another female, or even the father will offer a breast for suckling comfort.

Baby-initiated feeding has nearly vanished in modern human societies, causing a deep and growing concern for health professionals. In modern industrialized nations today, breastfeeding only takes place for a brief time, or not at all.[79] The World Health Organization (WHO), for instance, maintains that "over 820,000 children's lives could be saved every year among children under 5 years, if all children 0–23 months were optimally breastfed."[80] A special panel of scientists convened by preeminent medical journal

The Lancet concluded that "children who are breastfed have lower infectious morbidity and mortality, fewer dental malocclusions and increased intelligence, which persists until later in life. There is also growing evidence that breastfeeding protects against overweight and diabetes. . . . Breastfeeding also brings benefits to women, including prevention of breast cancer and birth spacing, as well as likely reductions in diabetes and ovarian cancer."[81] (Notably, most comparisons are made for three months of feeding practices, not the fuller length of time for which our species evolved.)[82]

As a global effort to promote breastfeeding, in 1991 the WHO and UNICEF launched the Baby-Friendly Hospital Initiative.[83] In 2011, the US surgeon general mobilized hospitals to become more "baby friendly" in light of the fact that only 4 percent of US hospitals and birthing units were rated as baby friendly.[84] Baby-friendly practices include immediately allowing mother and child to practice skin-to-skin contact after birth, avoiding certain common practices like giving newborns sugar water (to quiet them) or giving them formula for no medical reason, and making sure medical personnel know how to support breastfeeding. However, in 2022 less than 30 percent of US hospitals were baby friendly.[85]

The movement to promote breastfeeding has been thwarted by pervasive formula marketing designed to "free up" nursing parents, and by the widespread offerings of free formula samples in hospitals and clinics. The WHO created the *International Code of Marketing of Breast-Milk Substitutes* (i.e., the "Code") as a way to control advertising for formula that often touted formula feeding as the scientific way to feed infants.[86] Although the Code was aimed at practices in *all* countries, its focus was diverted away from practices in high-income countries, and greater attention was paid to lower-income countries. Since then, the World Trade Organization has undermined countries' ability to enforce the Code.[87] With an ongoing lack of education about the vital importance of breastfeeding for long-term health combined with the presence of aggressive marketing,[88] formulas continue to be considered a sufficient replacement for breastfeeding under normal circumstances, rather than being limited to use in emergencies.[89] In the United States, exclusive breastfeeding rates fall to 25 percent after six months, and only 34 percent of babies are still breastfed at one year.[90] Parental leave after a new baby is born facilitates breastfeeding, as does the ability to take baby to work, but both options are lacking for most US mothers.[91] In some communities, milk banks[92] or wet nurses[93] are available so that breast milk can be provided to infants whose mothers cannot breastfeed.

The practice of breastfeeding is also hampered by numerous misunderstandings and misperceptions. For instance, there is a common belief that a baby can't be hungry less than an hour after feeding. Actually, in our ancestral context, young babies fed on average three times an hour. Baby brains are growing millions of synapses a second, and they need the fuel. The young human stomach is tiny, and human milk is thin. Another common belief is that you can overfeed a breastfeeding baby. This is also untrue. Unlike bottle-fed babies who can hardly control the amount of liquid pouring down their throats, breastfeeding babies have control over how much they eat and will not overeat. Feeding a baby not when they are hungry but according to a schedule is a dangerous practice that has led to many infant deaths.[94] Putting baby on a schedule to match the needs of an adult world does not follow Nature's rhythms.

Scheduled feedings fail to keep in tune with the baby's metabolism and often make them feel starved, stressed, and that the world is a place of scarcity. A baby's growing intuition of how to be in the world, as well as their know-how for getting what they need at the right time—whether it be affection, hormones, lactose, or antibodies to fight a local infection—is disrupted. Anthropologist Ashley Montagu explains how scheduled feedings are detrimental to babies: "They deprive the infant of the feeling that it was his own signals that resulted in the satisfaction of his hunger. Disregard of his signals discourages, and he tends to lose the impulse to develop the mental and emotional techniques for handling the environment, and thus for the adequate development of self and personality."[95] Baby-initiated breastfeeding is vital for optimal psychosocial development, self-confidence, and motivation.

Restricting feeding time also affects milk content. The milk at the front of the breast, the first to come out when the baby suckles, is like an appetizer—tantalizing, but lacking the punch of calories and nutrients of the "hind" milk, the flow of milk that follows. As a consequence, restricting the amount of time a baby is allowed to suckle on each breast restricts the baby's access to the richer hind milk. The breasts misinterpret what is going on—they receive the signal that less milk should be prepared—so natural milk composition and flow are disrupted. Nursing a baby from two breasts is like feeding them "two servings of soup and no main course," according to developmental psychologist Penelope Leach.[96] If milk accumulates in the breast and the breast is not emptied, that inhibits the production of more milk, which can happen if an infant favors one breast over another.[97] Milk buildup in a breast can lead to mastitis, an inflammation of milk ducts.[98]

When feedings are controlled and limited, a baby may fail to take in enough calories, and the breasts will decrease their supply. This deficit is particularly acute during growth spurts. Milk mistiming can cause a cascade of problems. If mothers do not understand the importance of baby-initiated feeding and its frequency, they may feel like they don't have enough milk or that something is "wrong" with the baby or the milk itself. When a baby's desire for frequent feeding is misinterpreted as a mother's inability to provide sufficient milk, the mother may feel inadequate or think she needs to supplement with formula. Decreased natural milk supply confuses and confounds the baby's natural nutritional rhythms. Digestive difficulties may develop and precipitate further dissonance, such as the decoupling of weaning and maturing systems that otherwise cultivate a baby's deep sense of living in an "expectable environment" where needs are met without significant delay.

With regard to learning natural mother-baby breastfeeding, it is crucial not to approach it like a schoolroom lesson. If it is a lesson, then it is a lesson more akin to learning a dance of relaxation in repose. When the baby feels mother relax, the baby will follow suit. With this attitude, a mother will be able to pick up on details that need attention. If a baby struggles to breastfeed, the cause may derive from a tongue or lip tie and may thus require remedying. A newborn may be too lethargic to breastfeed and may need special assistance if drugs were used during labor, because a baby's organs are not sufficiently developed to eliminate toxins for several weeks. Epidurals (pain medications for the mother during labor) can impede breastfeeding initiation and length.[99]

Although breastfeeding is adaptive, there has been a significant loss of breastfeeding wisdom. The absence of mothers who model breastfeeding to the young at home and in public to demonstrate its normalcy has created a gap in breastfeeding knowledge. Breastfeeding parents and babies often require practice and guidance provided by experienced mothers, elders, or other mothering accompaniers. The journey to breastfeeding is one of mutual benefit for baby and mother that must be supported by the community. Communal companionship care helps fill any gaps a mother may not be able to address.

Mother's milk is just one way that companionship care of the evolved nest brings a baby's entire system in harmony with Nature and optimizes health and well-being. When a baby can suckle at will, the baby's communications and needs can be immediately "heard" and responded to. A mother's responsive feedback fosters a baby's first sense of self-efficacy, an understanding that they can have an effect in the world. The coupling of a baby's and mother's rhythms through breastfeeding bridges the temporary gap created in the shift from womb to world, and connectivity is maintained. At the moment suckling begins, the baby experiences being part of Nature's cycles and the ethos of kinship with all. In the Andean Quechuan understanding of life, a baby becomes, as anthropologist Christine Greenway puts it, part of a "cosmology in which bodies and spirits are intertwined with mountains and stars in webs of reciprocal duties."[100]

5

Sharing Care

Emperor Penguins

WHOOSH, *WHOOSH* . . . whoosh, *whoosh* . . . whoosh, *whoosh* . . . *this was his world, his entire being. Then, suddenly, there was an abrupt change. Instead of being the sound, he became witness to the sound—the sound of his mother's heartbeat. He felt a strange sensation, a feeling of falling away from the whoosh, whoosh. There were whispers of voices, movement, and a more distant, different whoosh, whoosh began, fainter, with a slightly faster pace. This was his father. The egg had left his mother to live in the enfoldment of his father's feathered warmth. The egg was home; a different home, but home.*

As the Earth's northern pole tilts toward the sun, Russian Brown Bear bodies begin to quicken. It is time to leave the hibernation nest and reenter the world beyond. As they push through spring's melting snow, other communities, those to the far south, are pulling into warmth. Antarctic waters have returned to "fast ice"—sea ice that "fastens" to the land. While Antarctica enjoys its temporarily expanded land base, Emperor Penguins begin to gather. Every fall, thousands of these flightless Birds gather in the ceremony of making a family.

Their pilgrimage is extraordinary. Standing four feet tall, flippers at their sides, Emperor Penguins march up to sixty miles (almost one hundred kilometers) over the ice to rendezvous where Penguins have gathered for generations. At times, their purposeful stride shifts to tobogganing as they drop to the ice and, propelled by flippers and legs, continue their journey. It is an ardent and arduous trek.

When they finally arrive at the communal space, new couples meet, and partnered pairs renew their vows. March and April is courtship time, called *pariad*. Air and ice resonate with songs, calls, and elaborate dances of flashing black, white, and yellow plumage. Facing one another, the pair makes a deep bow proclaiming love, commitment, and intention. After making or renewing their vows, relationships are cemented with consummation, and about a month later, the female Penguin lays a single beautiful egg.[1] But much happens well before that event. Just as their parents journeyed over ice, incipient Penguins make an equally demanding voyage before entering the open world—one that starts inside their mothers.

When a female's follicle reaches maturity, it is released down her reproductive tract. The ovum is mostly yolk, the rich foodstuff that will sustain the embryo until hatching. After Penguin lovemaking, the soon-to-be father's sperm swims up the tract in search of the egg. When sperm and ovum make contact, respective gene halves join, and a new Penguin is conceived.

Contracting muscles of the mother Penguin's reproductive tract move the fertilized egg along. Spiral ridges rotate the egg to create an evenly coated cover of albumin. As the spinning egg floats on its way, spiderweb strands of albumin bind the delicate egg with protective membranes. This clear, sticky substance hydrates the egg, provides it with protein, and shields it against infection. However, at this point the process of egg-making is far from complete. The embryo still needs a shell.

Over the preceding months, mother Penguin has stored extra calcium in her bone cavities, which is now carried to the soft egg to surround it. Bit by bit, calcium precipitates and grows into a fully formed shell. As a final sealing touch, a layer of waterproof cuticle is laid down. The eggshell, however, is not completely sealed off. It contains thousands of pores that allow the embryo to breathe, taking in oxygen and exhaling carbon dioxide and water.[2] Finally, the embryo in his world-of-his-own egg is ready to step off the internal reproductive conveyor belt. The embryo will continue to grow for a total of approximately sixty days.

When the momentous day arrives, the egg emerges. This is no time to dawdle. Antarctic temperatures plummet as low as –40°F (–40°C), and wind speeds have been recorded reaching 199 miles per hour (327 km/hr). The lowest recorded temperature on the planet was measured in the Antarctic at –129°F (–89°C). The egg is well protected, but it cannot withstand this cold.[3] Emperor Penguins are the only species to birth in the Antarctic winter, but they have evolved nest practices that outwit these extremes and nurture their young in safety.[4]

Adélie Penguins and Gentoo Penguins build more classical nests fashioned from stones and Grass. In contrast, Emperor Penguins come with their own built-in nests. As soon as the egg emerges from the mother Penguin, it slides off her feet and onto those of the receiving father, who brings the egg into a feathered den just above his feet. The brood pouch, or skinfold, has feathers in front and highly vascularized skin in back.[5] Nestled next to the father Penguin's bare skin, the beautiful white-gray egg is kept at a perfect incubating temperature between 98.6°F and 100.4°F (37°C and 38°C).[6]

However, this initial shared event is short lived. Once the family treasure passes from one parent to the other, the mother leaves. She is depleted. Her internal resources have been directed to creating and nourishing the egg and embryo, so by mid-May new mothers depart from their nuclear family. One can imagine that departing mother Penguins have mixed feelings: on the one hand, reluctance to leave their nascent child and partner; on the other, a certain relief and eagerness for replenishment at sea. Penguin females spend the next two-plus months in the ocean recuperating. Emperor Penguins are models of self-care: caring for oneself means being able to care well for one's young.

Penguin food is largely *pelagic*, meaning it comes from the open sea, where calorie-rich Antarctic Silverfish (also known as Antarctic Herring), Lantern Fish, Krill, and Squid live. Antarctic Silverfish are members of the *Actinopterygii*, or the "ray-finned" class of Fish, that comprises more than half of all vertebrates and the majority of Fish species consumed by Emperor Penguins (89 percent).[7] Silverfish are actually pink, and at only a few inches long, they are small enough for rapid consumption. They make perfect food for hungry Penguins.

Emperor Penguins dive to great depths to retrieve their meals in a single held breath. The deepest Penguin dive recorded is 1,850 feet (564 meters),[8] and the longest recorded dive lasted 1,932 seconds, or just over thirty-two minutes.[9] André Ancel, an eminent scientist at France's Centre national de la recherche scientifique who has studied Emperor Penguins for decades, explains that the Birds use this food-diving strategy: "If a Penguin needs some stones which they use to grind up and digest food, they dive to the sea bottom. On the way to the sea surface, the water lightens to blue. Emperor Penguins see Fish and Squid as dark objects because they 'cut' the light from the sea surface, seeing the outline as such, which is why biologists refer to the outline as a 'Chinese shadow'"—named so after paper puppets used in traditional shadow plays.[10]

At the end of their sojourn, fattened and strengthened, mother Penguins retrace their steps back over the ice to rejoin their families. Mother Penguins must have a very accurate sense of time tuned to their babies because they usually arrive within a handful of days before or after the egg has hatched. Father Penguins have not been idle during their partners' absence. While mothers are revitalizing, Emperor Penguin fathers are tending to their priceless charges, each father regularly rotating his egg to make sure the embryo within is kept evenly warm.

Two months after hatching, Emperor Penguin infants have only a light covering of downy feathers, so they are quite vulnerable to the cold. They remain in their fathers' pouches where they are fed with his crop milk, an easily digested baby food of ricotta-cheese consistency made from the lining of the father Penguin's esophagus. Understandably, crop milk is high in both fat (30–36 percent) and protein (60 percent). Similar to the stimulation of human breast milk production, crop milk is produced when prolactin levels rise, which occurs during female brooding and male egg incubation.[11]

There is still much more to the Emperor Penguin evolved nest. Although Penguins' fat and thick feathers—which provide 85 percent of their total insulation[12]—may provide critical protection, they are not sufficient. To compensate for the cold during the father Penguin's two months of solitary parenting, which intensifies as winter deepens, father Penguins coordinate with each other in collective allocare.[13] Fathers gather to form huddles of varying sizes and densities depending on the weather.[14] Huddles act as a social thermoregulation mechanism that helps conserve and regulate heat. Every so often, groups coalesce or break up in response to wind conditions, solar radiation intensity, and ambient temperature. Although environmental temperatures are frigid, heat generated by the collection of Penguin bodies can raise temperatures within the huddle to 100°F (38°C). Huddle reorganization serves to cool off those who are getting overheated and warm those who are getting too cold.[15] Penguin huddle dynamics is a beautiful example of how individuals cooperate and coordinate within a larger community to provide seamless social and ecological connection and security for their children.[16]

By the time female Penguins return and meet their new chicks, father Penguins have fasted for four months and have lost almost half their weight. The colony atmosphere is taut with expectation and anxiety. Tragically, not every chick will have survived, but when reunion occurs, there is much to celebrate. Connecting, however, is not always easy to accomplish. Penguin colonies can number in the thousands.[17] To make their way through the melée, each couple uses their own distinctive call, which their chick learns on the spot. In contrast to other Penguins, who hold their beaks high with outstretched necks, Emperor Penguin heads and beaks arc downward to make their calls.[18] Somehow, despite the chaos of the crowd, this posture transmits calls and brings the various threesomes together. Penguins are very mindful of others' needs. To avoid any "cross-chat" that might hamper another's ability to find their family, they observe the "courtesy rule."[19] If a Penguin sees that their neighbor is about to call out to their mate, the Penguin politely waits until the "line" is free. Dolphin mothers conform to a similar conversational rule. Two weeks before and after birth, each mother provides a signature whistle that baby is expected to and does learn. Other members of the pod refrain from whistling their own names during this period to avoid confusing the young.[20]

After reunion, mother Penguins take over infant care. It is now the fathers' turn to replenish. Although fathers are in great need of food, some show hesitation to hand their babies over to the mothers.[21] Eventually, after dragging their feet a bit, male Penguins do what their spouses have done: begin the pack ice journey to the ocean, where they will dive into the waters to enjoy marine repasts. When a compressed month of eating is completed, father Penguins return.

At the point when baby Penguins have gained enough weight and feathers, the community transforms into a crèche where young Penguins engage with others of their own age. During this period, parents take alternating trips to the ocean to maintain health. Any feeding gaps are bridged by allo-parenting.[22] By the end of November, when it is summer in the Antarctic, the babies molt, replacing fluff with shiny waterproofing feathers. The young Birds, however, remain very dependent on their parents until late December or early January, when they become big and strong enough to make the seaward trek together with the rest of the Penguin community.

As joyful and adventuresome as the march to water is, young Penguins are on a steep learning curve. It is a long journey from life inside an egg to being a full-fledged adult Penguin. During the trip and at the ocean, the young continue their socioemotional and physical lessons. Not only must they learn how to find and catch Fish, Squid, and Krill; they are also acquiring details about their homeplace and society. Maturation involves more than passing physiological milestones and accumulating knowledge. Sensory phenomena, whether it is internally or externally derived, must be processed and understood in the context of self and society. A "mature" Penguin is mature in more than years. They are the process and product of their experience, ancestors, and environment. Maintaining congruence in time (lineage) and space (social and ecological environs) is integral to evolved nesting. While their evolved nest design differs from those of other species, Penguin care reflects the principles, practices, and patterns of nurturance embraced by Nature-based humans and nonhumans around the world, many elements of which were brought to the fore in modern society through the work of John Bowlby.

Bowlby was an English clinical psychologist born in 1907. His work—resonant with the work of others such as New York psychologist William Goldfarb,[23] Bellevue Hospital pediatrician Harry Bakwin,[24] and Viennese psychoanalyst René Spitz (responsible for identifying and documenting *hospitalism*, the wasting away and deaths of formerly healthy children in hospital care)[25]—would significantly influence Western human developmental sciences for years to come. Bowlby sought a new theory to explain the effects of maternal deprivation, the foundation of which would lead to what he called *attachment theory*.[26]

Prior to Bowlby and similar thinkers, such as Pierre Janet and Mary Ainsworth, the reigning theories of child development were psychoanalysis and behaviorism. According to the proponents of these two schools of thought, children needed nothing more than good physical nourishment and shelter. In contrast, Bowlby made visible what had been overlooked: how early relationships shape developmental health and mental well-being.[27] He drew attention to the critical role of early-life relationships beyond food and protection.[28]

Attachment is considered key in setting an infant onto a specific path of social development that persists through the entire trajectory of life experience.[29] In this framing, carer-child relationships extend beyond an elemental carer behavior control system, *proximity* or *protective caregiving*, in which parents maintain proximity through retrieval during immaturity, to include a *safety caregiving* system[30] that orients the carer to the needs of the child.[31] Through processes of *attachment* to the carer, an infant internalizes their social experiences, creating an internal working model of social relations—that is, embodied social conceptualizations that are applied ever after.[32] Caregiving and attachment systems are evolutionary prepared mechanisms that recruit the child and carer into a maturational process of socialization and building trust.[33] The evolved nest deepens and expands upon this idea by emphasizing *companionship attachment*[34] as a Nature-based environment that fosters holistic child development through spontaneous, attentive interactions with human and nonhuman relations, enabling full membership in the Earth community.

Bowlby's insights into child raising implicitly interfaced with social and cultural patterns. He was enlisted by the World Health Organization to address children who had been separated from their families in the wake of World War II. His interest in maternal separation had first arisen during his work with maladjusted children. The English psychologist found that even well-fed institutionalized children fared poorly relative to their counterparts who lived with their families. Despite receiving proper shelter and nourishment, institutionalized children exhibited profound depression, anxiety, and unstable personalities. With prolonged separation and repeated loss of replacement mother figures, children were prone to becoming self-centered, materialistic, and socially detached.[35]

Bowlby was sympathetic to their plight because of his own childhood experiences. Although he came from a wealthy family and was afforded plenty of food and comfortable shelter, Bowlby rarely saw his parents. He spent an hour or so with his mother each day, and he only saw his father a few times a year—they left his care largely to nannies. In instances such as Bowlby's, nannies or childminders are often the only possible source of emotional nurturance and dependable love that a child receives. In this capacity, a childminder can save a child from complete unmooring. But at the same time, as Bowlby experienced himself, these relationships can be quite fragile and significantly destabilizing to a tender young psyche. For example, a nanny with whom Bowlby formed a deep attachment left when he was four. As many scholars have noted,[36] human nannies and childcare centers may end up functioning, intentionally or not, as a culture of cruelty, because they are bound to prioritize what a parent or institution wants over the natural needs of a child. Even if they seek to provide attentive care for their charges, childminders such as Bowlby's nannies can be vulnerable to their employers' whims and values.

At seven, Bowlby experienced yet another relational rupture when he was sent to a British boarding school,[37] which he later described as "the time-honoured barbarism required to produce English gentlemen."[38] Since Bowlby's time, others have recognized associated and resultant symptoms now referred to as "boarding school syndrome."[39] Indeed, boarding schools and other institutions were deliberately designed by colonizers to control children and impose outside values and standards—with disastrous consequences.

Countless Indigenous people have been subjected to forced Western-style physically and psychologically abusive education and economic systems that have destroyed entire families, communities, and cultures, thus tearing apart the delicate web of ancient wisdom traditions. Commenting on the results of this education-driven culturicide, anthropologist Wade Davis identifies two great myths that have obfuscated the reality of imposed education:

> We promote Western education around the world as if landing in a void, as if people around the world did not educate their children. Well, of course they did, in complex, sophisticated ways, whether it was 2,500 years of empirical observations as to the nature of the mind in Tibetan Buddhism, the nocturnal studies of the elder brother who literally believed that their prayers maintain the cosmic balance of the world, in textile traditions of Peru and throughout the South Pacific. The other great myth is that somehow education lifts people out of poverty. I have never in all my time in traditional cultures seen the wretchedness that one encounters around the periphery of almost any city in the so-called third world. In the end we have to ask ourselves: What is this thing of Western education?[40]

When the critical psychophysiological bridge from the inner world of the womb to social support and meaning-making communal processes collapses, a child is subjected to damaging relational rupture and, as happened to Schmetty, the young Elephant, a broken heart. However, early trauma can be mitigated in many cases if, as the orphaned Elephant infants at the Sheldrick Trust illustrate, evolved nest practices and experiences are reinstated and embedded in a community of holistic life values and supportive culture.

The difference between the children whom Bowlby met and the orphans rescued by the Sheldrick Trust is that the Elephants are provided with a caregiving experience that emulates their natural, natal family evolved nest. The work at the Trust is regarded as reparative, furnishing the orphans with a protofamily as a replacement for the family who was taken away, and treating the infant's inner and outer wounds of trauma. The Sheldrick Trust serves as a healing bridge to traditional Elephant culture and the Elephant evolved nest. Not only do Elephant values and ethics imbue orphan care, but their Elephant carers never leave. Only when infant Elephants are mature enough to move from the nursery to an intermediate space and then eventually join a wild herd does separation occur. This transition is in keeping with natural processes and structures of Elephant development and society. The Sheldrick Trust has replaced human violence with a cross-species community who will always be there and available when needed. Absent reparative nest care, as was the case for the Rhinoceros-killing Elephants, a child is left wounded and unmoored.

In parallel human situations, most modern children who have experienced relational rupture via orphaning, relinquishment, family separation, neglect, or abuse (referred to as *relational trauma*) do not receive reparative care. Unlike healthy Elephant society and the reparative society crafted by the Sheldrick Trust, industrialized human culture generally lacks the wherewithal, will, or holistic orientation to child raising that could otherwise fill in and stabilize change, as occurs in Nature-based societies. In lieu of holistic support of body-mind-spirit,[41] modern-day educational facilities tend to emphasize detachment and disconnection through a focus on intellectual knowledge.[42]

The modern, conventional emphasis on obedience, reading, and "factual" knowledge derails holistic development.[43] Forcing young children into school-like learning, which usually entails a focus on alphabets, numbers, and reading, pushes the child away from the right hemisphere and into left hemisphere functioning too soon, which undermines the development of Earthcentric practical intelligence and a holistic receptive intelligence.[44] Tyson Yunkaporta, of Australian Indigenous heritage, identifies these holistic ways of Indigenous thinking that are often missing in unnested individuals and cultures: kinship-mind (relationally connected mind), story-mind (a method for remembering ancient knowledge), dreaming-mind (using metaphors to link abstraction with concrete experience), ancestor-mind (deep engagement in timeless reality), and pattern-mind (perception of the meaning of systems of patterns).[45]

The Western emphasis on factual knowledge, in contrast to embodied know-how, leads dominant-culture achievers to think they know the answers to life based solely on abstract models[46] or lab experiments.[47] Too often, modern schooling teaches cleverness, cunningness, and habits of drawing conclusions without relying on experience. Alternatively, "knowledge in the traditional world is not a dead collection of facts. It is alive, has spirit, and dwells in specific, sacred spaces and places. Traditional knowledge comes about through watching and listening, not in the passive way that westernized schools demand, but through direct experience of songs and ceremonies, through the activities of daily life, from trees and animals, and in dreams and visions."[48]

Decontextualized, abstract theorizing ends up substituting for real-life understanding, and this has led to a great deal of damage around the world by "experts" with the simultaneous devaluing of those who do not conform to collective (dominant culture) standards.[49] Dismissive of other modes of knowledge, through detached understanding of what is good, Western education has undermined the well-being of Animals, Plants, and the planet and their ability to maintain their respective evolved nests.

Bringing the formative nature of relational bonding and responsive care into the forefront of Western science was revolutionary. Unlike the progression of most modern science after World War II, Bowlby's theories looked beyond the bounds of conventional academic disciplines. He drew from diverse fields of study, integrating ethology, biology, and psychology, and he enjoyed lively exchanges with leading scientists of the time, such as Konrad Lorenz, Niko Tinbergen, and Julian Huxley. Indeed, Bowlby's now-famous trilogy that lays out the architecture of attachment theory and relational trauma calls upon Animal kin for illustration of its principles.[50]

Konrad Lorenz's work with goslings had a particularly significant influence on Bowlby's theory of human attachment. Bowlby was struck by Lorenz's description of how newly hatched Geese immediately attached to him, a human, and they remained so, even after they later encountered their biological mother. Lorenz and his goslings vividly demonstrated how an infant attaches to the physical presence of their carer,[51] which, in humans, occurs over the first year of life as part of a biosocial tuning to the lifeways of the family and culture.[52]

Bowlby's work also stresses the importance of appreciating ancestral heritage and its embeddedness in Nature, which he called the *environment of evolutionary adaptedness*, the context for a species' evolutionary development. Not only do humans share with other Animals a common brain and comparable cognitive and socioaffective capacities;[53] in addition, our evolved nests derive from common principles. We all evolved from common ancestry. We are all kin, so it is no wonder that we also share our evolutionary roots of childcare. By linking nonhuman and human attachment patterns and values, Bowlby brought nonhuman and human development under a single conceptual umbrella.

Because attachment theory and its studies originated in the modern European and North American cultural and Mammalian contexts, it has conventionally revolved around the mother-infant dyad. As a result, attachment researchers have generally emphasized maternal sensitivity as the mechanism for healthy attachment, taking the norm to be a stay-at-home mother. However, innumerable cross-cultural studies of humans and nonhumans, including those described here, reveal that attachment encompasses a variety of relationships and multiplicities.[54]

For instance, although a primary carer is not always female, in the case of Mammals it usually is. Mammal infants are naturally born with a "set-goal" to stay close to mother. They live inside their mother for months; then, when they emerge into the outside world, their first experience is their mother. Emperor Penguins contradict this model. A baby Penguin is formed and lives as an egg inside their mother, and they experience her inside the egg. But their first socioemotional experience outside the egg is their crop-milk-providing father. Furthermore, attachment is not necessarily limited to a single primary carer but can be multiple.[55] A baby Emperor Penguin is initially tended to by their father, then by their mother, followed by both parents and the communal crèche. Moreover, attachment bonds can expand beyond the species to all of Nature.[56]

At the core of these various examples of healthy attachment is the idea of a *secure base*. Attentive care provides this foundation of safety from which the baby learns about the world into which they have been born. From this intersubjective space of security, an infant feels free to explore physically, emotionally, and mentally. This permits a child to openly explore and develop relational experiences that create a kind of subconscious how-to guide for social interactions elaborated upon throughout their life.

Although Bowlby and his followers emphasized that to develop secure attachment babies should experience *contingent communication*—coordinating with an adult who responds to their overt signals in timely and effective ways—most cultures *anticipate* the needs of a baby and meet those needs to prevent any distress.[57] A child's internal milieu is brought back into balance or *homeostasis*, which, with learning flexibility and adaptation to change, reflects *allostasis*.[58] Learning to balance emotions and establish a healthy internal baseline are major partnered tasks that create a generative space for infant growth. A carer's ability to tune into a child's emotional state shapes the infant's sense of body-mind resonance that cultivates internal and interpersonal coherence. Over multiple experiences of being comforted, the child learns how to co-regulate with their carer and find balance with others in diverse situations. The process of co-regulation is evolutionarily designed to provide an infant with appropriate support for optimal development.[59]

Internally, processes that establish emotional allostasis involve developing links between subcortical brain structures and cortical structures. Our brains, and those of Bears, Penguins, and other Animals, evolved to be the social organ of the body, whose job is to regulate internal states of being while simultaneously adjusting to external changes. At birth, an infant brain has a proliferation of neurons but very few interconnections among them. Carer-infant interactions contribute to connections initially forged.[60]

The kind, number, and locations of these interconnections shape a child's psychophysiological circuitry during sensitive periods that influence how they will perceive, process, and interact with the world through adulthood. A child's immaturity and plasticity at birth require comparably refined carer responsiveness in order to shape well-functioning neuronal connections. The evolved nest provides the appropriate nurturance needed to grow healthy brain connections and body systems. Bowlby and psychiatrist Sigmund Freud were among the few Western scientists to predict what neuroscience has now confirmed: early relational experiences are drivers of core infant brain and neuropsychological body capacities, inclusive of other Animals.

Whether a Parrot, Beaver, Elephant, or human, a baby perceives mother's (and/or father's) facial and body expressions and mirrors them back. The parent-offspring relationship is the first medium through which "inside-outside" calibration occurs. "Outside" interactions (carer-infant exchange) are mirrored on the "inside" (in the brain and gut). Balanced, responsive connection with the baby, body-to-body co-regulation,[61] establishes *limbic regulation* (or psychobiological attunement).[62] Psychologist Allan Schore, hailed as the "American Bowlby," describes it this way: "Secure attachment thus depends on the mother's psychobiological attunement not with the infant's cognition or behavior, but rather with the infant's dynamic alterations of autonomic arousal, the energetic dimension of the child's affective state. To enter into this rapid communication, the mother must resonate with the dynamic crescendos and decrescendos of the infant's bodily-based internal states of peripheral autonomic nervous system (ANS) arousal and central nervous system (CNS) arousal."[63] The carer-baby co-regulation dialogue is a duet, with the carer initially taking the lead.

Whole-body, autonomic, unconscious baby-carer co-regulation is fundamental to healthy brain and body development. The body and the brain work as one through the *gut-brain axis,* the communication superhighway between the CNS and the gastrointestinal system, the seat of immunity, governed by the vagus nerve (also known as the X, or tenth, cranial nerve).[64] Children grow health through co-regulation.[65] They learn who and how to be from embodied experiences with others. Even before cognitive development, infants—including newborns—are prepared for body-to-body communication.[66]

After nine months of gestational synchrony, within moments after birth, human mothers and babies shift into an interactional synchrony of sound and movement.[67] Babies move with rhythm and expression, communicative musicality, in nonverbal conversation with their carer.[68] Embryos of diverse species are able to detect this "music"—sounds and vibrations from their parents, their siblings, and the broader environment in which they will live—well before birth.[69]

Prenatal communiqués play a vital role by helping shape an embryo's developmental trajectory. Communiqués from outside the womb or egg are anticipatory, alerting the embryo to social and environmental conditions. Red-Eyed Tree Frog embryos discern the difference between the benevolence of the wind and the potential danger of a preying Snake or Wasp. Incubating Zebra Finch parents use "heatcalls" to tell their offspring-in-egg about higher-than-normal temperatures that influence how the baby Finch will develop in optimal readiness for the present environment. We see a version of this environmental adaptation in the case of human babies. Relative to human embryos who are stimulated primarily by their mothers' heartbeats and voices, those who are exposed only or mainly to hospital noise develop smaller auditory cortices.[70]

Successful attunement is significantly affected by the physical and mental wellness of the carer, as the Emperor Penguins' parental egg-infant tag-team strategy illustrates. The father looks after the egg while mother Penguin recharges in the ocean. When she returns, father Penguin takes his turn to recharge. In this way, high-quality health is maintained for egg-infant care. Emperor Penguins could have evolved a different care strategy, such as having the parents both leave for the ocean with the egg; but, given the harsh conditions, this type of care would have introduced a significant vulnerability. The tag-team nest model evolved for a reason. The unbroken, paired care and presence by mother and father smoothly midwife the egg-encased baby's transition from mother's womb to feathered cavity nest. This attentive protection and nourishment ensure that parents and children retain oneness with their ecology. Engrained generation after generation and further developed by personal experience, parents pass down how and what they have experienced to their children by the shaping of neurobiology. This ensures evolved nest integrity over time.

What all this shows is that a brain develops or exists not in isolation but rather according to an *interpersonal neurobiology*, coordinated brains and nervous systems. In this way, carer responses create embodied patterns and schemas of how the world works in the mind-brain of the child. Relational processes synchronize the infant's right brain to the mother's right brain. It is thought that this is why left-cradling is so prevalent.[71] Early on in life, the right hemisphere governs the functioning of the vagus nerve that inner-vates all major body systems. Carer presence and comfort shape how well the vagus functions, either fostering healthy functioning or, if there is early-life neglect or adversity, leaving it underdeveloped. Physiologically, the responsive carer comforts the child's distressed, immature reflexive systems, teaching these systems how to calm themselves.[72]

When the critical psychophysiological bridge from the inner world of the womb to social support outside collapses, a child may experience a damaging relational rupture. In reaction to nonresponsive care, the baby may shut down expression of emotion, making them appear to be fine when cortisol readings would indicate they are not.[73] The absence of responsive reassurance sets up a biochemistry of fear that can lead to anxiety disor-ders in later life. If a baby is left to cry for a length of time, baby's brain is flooded with high levels of toxic stress hormones that eventually kill neu-ronal connections.[74] Pain circuits become activated, and the baby's endog-enous (internal) opioids, which promote feelings of well-being, diminish.[75] Ongoing experiences of grief from physical or emotional isolation also tend to set up conditions for chronic mood disorders. When a baby experiences long or frequent periods of stress, they become prone to clinical depression or anxiety in adulthood.[76]

Unrelieved distress influences the genetic expression of a key neu-rotransmitter, gamma-aminobutyric acid (GABA), which leads to anxiety and depression disorders and addictions.[77] Repeated states of fear and anx-iety become traits that are expressed as oversensitivity, hyperreactivity, and predispositions for depression, anxiety, a host of physical health issues, accelerated aging and mortality, or violence.[78] In short, routine nonrespon-sive caregiving leads to limitations in brain and body organization.

Responsive care, on the other hand, cultivates good *vagal tone* (activation of the myelinated vagus in the parasympathetic system), which is critical for digestive, cardiac, respiratory, immune, and emotional health. When carers show consistent, affectionate care, children develop systems that respond to the pleasure of relationships, releasing endogenous opioids, and that are capable of responding to stressors.[79] Allan Schore describes this unfold-ing: "Regulated and synchronized affective interactions with a familiar, predictable primary caregiver create not only a sense of safety but also a positively charged curiosity, wonder, and surprise that fuels the burgeoning self's exploration of novel socioemotional and physical environments. This ability is a marker of adaptive infant mental health."[80]

According to attachment theory grounded in modern Western contexts, differences in child-to-carer relationships can be categorized as different "attachment styles." A child deprived of consistent care from a responsive carer, for instance, develops an *insecure attachment.* Insecurely attached children are likely to mature into adults who, if left unhealed, are unable to connect in deep and perceptive ways, even with their own children. The child's systems, which cannot regulate on their own, do not receive the appropriate co-regulation that responsive care provides. A lack of carer synchronization leads to toxic psychological and physiological stress.

An infant's stress response can be described in three stages: *alarm resistance, mobilization,* and *exhaustion.*[81] When a baby expresses discomfort through movement, utterances, and/or gestures, they are signaling that their well-being is being challenged. Responsive caregivers move at once to reestablish contentment and security. If signals are ignored or are not attended to in a timely manner, the baby moves into a state of *alarm resistance.* It is a sign of deeper fear and a louder, more insistent plea for help. A baby has no other recourse. The child requires external help to restore a feeling of security and biochemical and psychological well-being.

In the second stage, when external help has still failed to arrive, the child shifts to an extreme state of *mobilization.* The child screams in an overwhelming sense of helplessness and desperation. Without carer intervention, the infant moves into the third stage, *exhaustion,* sometimes referred to as *despair.* It is an experience of desperation and the effort to survive. The infant withdraws into a catatonic state, the oldest vagal system state, which has evolved to protect life through *passive avoidance.* The exhaustion stage is usually less physiological than psychological, but its effects are just as pernicious. A drop in the body's natural calming neuroendocrinal opioid activity is triggered, causing a feeling of panic. Many adult panic disorders are linked to such early, extensive bouts of separation anxiety.[82] Even a single experience can have an extremely negative effect on the child's brain and body, depending on the timing, intensity, and duration of distress.[83]

We can also look at the attachment system in terms of love and threats.[84] When a threat is perceived, a securely attached child responds by trying to get close to the carer to restore a sense of safety and calm. A secure child develops a repertoire of effective responses that clearly communicate needs and express socially in-tune emotions appropriately. As secure children grow, they learn to seek comfort from a variety of sources and find ways to maintain a sense of safety. They can socially connect with others when faced with some kind of threat, such as an accident, a natural disaster, or social aggression.[85] According to attachment theory, those who develop an insecure attachment style experience a completely different social terrain. These infants have learned that social interaction is dangerous ground. There is mistrust in self and in others. The world becomes filled with shadows, and there is a need for self-protection from threats of pain and uncertainty.

Unfortunately, because of modern humanity's departures from responsive care, insecure attachment has become culturally normative in some Western societies.[86] Many collectively accepted parenting practices such as separating babies from parents, day or night, promote infant panic and grief, and frequently lead to perennial anxiety and depression.[87] For example, while sleep training is regarded as helpful to parents, it can be severely detrimental to an infant because it can push them into a physiological stress response path of alarm resistance, mobilization, and exhaustion.[88] Inconsistent and unreliable care disrupts a baby's systemic development, including the circuitry of emotion and self-regulation. A baby's homeostasis settles around dysregulated behavior such as emotional tantrums, numbness, or habitual emotional shutdown in an effort to feel safer. As the child matures, they become less and less capable of rebalancing when thrown off-balance. Epigenetic changes occur, tending to make the individual more dispositionally anxious.[89] As exhibited by the institutionalized children whom Bowlby and others observed, when denied essential nurturing and steady care, young children fail to thrive, showing developmental delays, social apathy, and a lack of an emotional "thereness."[90]

Insecure attachment styles tend to make the individual less socially flexible and more self-focused, indicating an internal deficit of security and a neurobiological imbalance. Children who develop an insecure attachment generally adapt in three main psychological ways to cope with care deficits: *feeling (emoting) but not dealing, dealing but not feeling,* and *neither feeling nor dealing.*[91] Dealing but not feeling minimizes emotion and emphasizes thinking *(avoidant attachment),* whereas feeling but not dealing maximizes emotion and minimizes thinking *(ambivalent attachment).* In the case of abuse, a child's emotional or cognitive development may reflect what is referred to as a *disorganized attachment* pattern (neither feeling nor dealing).

Avoidant attachment is a relational style in which the child seeks to maintain equilibrium without assistance from the carer. Children often develop this coping style when they have been left unattended, crying to the point of exhaustion. Eventually, they learn to dissociate from their body and psychologically turn away from others and the world. The child learns to dismiss and detach from their feelings, which often express as unrecognized somatic symptoms. In social interactions, they exhibit indifference and show little to no emotion. Because they were ignored and their needs were left unmet as an infant, these individuals learn to distrust their own feelings and those of the carer. As an adult, they tend to rely on cognition, seeking refuge in intellectualizing experiences and holding others at arm's length.[92] In instances when the carer is withdrawn, the child may take up "compulsive caregiving," where the child inhibits their true feelings and takes on a false positive affect. Those who are reared with hostile and demanding carers may become "compulsive compliance" carers who are quick to comply with any perceived desire. In all of these cases, a child inhibits any personal preferences in order to accommodate what they sense is demanded of them.

Adult avoidant attachment is referred to as "dismissive behavior." Intimacy is uncomfortable, and relationships are perceived as troublesome, frustrating, and unreliable. Instead of experiencing the joys of close, intimate relationships, which nurture and enhance a positive sense of self, the avoidant personality rationalizes distancing from others and denying needs for relational or emotional intimacy, practicing "defensive self-enhancement."

Although individuals with an avoidant attachment style may be regarded as highly functional, fully capable of doing basic tasks in life—work, socializing, and so on—they have limited access to their emotions. Despite underlying insecurity, anxiety, or distress, they may deny their need for nurturance and often portray themselves as rational, logical, emotionally strong, and in control. Showing weakness is perceived as too risky. In the absence of responsive care, the baby was left completely vulnerable; so as an adult, when they are stressed, instead of seeking intimacy and nurturance they tend to become irritable and short-tempered.[93]

Ambivalent or anxious attachment style—feeling but not dealing—develops when the carer is inattentive and inconsistent. Because the carer's words often do not match their actions, there is no predictable connection between what is said and what is enacted or expressed emotionally. The child perceives an intrinsic disconnect and contradiction with their carer. Words are not trustworthy; nor are reasoning and logic. Instead, the child learns to use emotion to get their needs met. They learn that exhibiting high-intensity emotions leads to the most favorable outcomes.

The third major relational pattern stemming from insecure attachment, neither feeling nor dealing, is referred to as "disorganized attachment." These patterns are most common in abused and extremely neglected children who are frequently left alone. They have no one to show them tender care or any other sort of care. They must fend for themselves. They may live in fear of their carers. These infants seek out their carers when they feel alarmed, but when the carer is threatening, the infant is caught in a paradox of contradiction, desiring comfort and connection yet fearful of danger.

These four attachment styles—secure, avoidant, anxious, and disorganized attachment—are useful as pointers for understanding how experiences in infancy can become relational traits carried forward into adulthood.[94] Yet attachment theory is only one of a host of descriptors of children's experiences and outcomes, including various forms of conditioning, social and cultural learning, imitation and collaboration, and narrative construction.[95] Children grow into their cultures through multiple processes and experiences. The evolved nest's companionship care widens the scope of care beyond a responsive, attachment-building relationship with one carer. It is essential to be grounded in accompaniment by and with Nature and to experience a welcoming community for carer and child, a life infused with positive touch and play.

Free Play

Beavers

AFTER A FEW weeks of living in the lodge's embrace, three young Beavers are ready for the plunge. Attended by their parents and older siblings, they dive through the lodge entrance that leads from the inner sanctum to the watery world outside. One young Beaver hesitates, unsure, less confident than his siblings. His family urges him on. This reassurance is just what is needed, for within a few moments, he dives down and out. Before long, all three babies are slapping and splashing without knowing how or why, just that it feels good. Siblings and parents circle near, watchful. Keeping an eye on their young and looking out for a Wolf or Coyote at the same time requires attentive presence. It's easy to lose track of danger in the midst of the children's first day of outside play. The furred water babies, chasing, diving, watching, and wondering at the fantastic new world, laugh with joy in the way only Beavers can.

Play is pervasive in Nature[1] and is found across Animal phyla.[2] Young Wild-life lives are filled with social play as part of their self-development and self-organization. Ethologist Gordon Burghardt, who has studied species as diverse as Crocodiles, Snakes, and Bears, describes play as something that is initiated under stress-free conditions. It is voluntary, functionally incomplete, extensively modifiable by the players, and iterative, but not stereotypic (referring to repeated gestures and actions that emerge from and are related to stress and discomfort).[3]

Self-directed free play is spontaneous and pleasurable, with rough-and-tumble activities including climbing, wrestling, and chase involving the entire body-mind complex. It is imaginative and invented on the fly, and it does not include organized sport or children's activities that adults direct. Play occurs when the person is relaxed, promoting a sense of belonging and a feeling that all is right in the world.[4] Free, self-directed play is also fundamental to growth. All Animals play when they feel safe and well.[5] When play is absent in a young Animal's life, it signals illness, fear, anger, or other states that keep the individual disconnected from the rest of life.[6] Play is one way for the young to learn how to be a member of their species.[7]

Recently, scientists have started to pay more attention to play and how it influences brain development. Self-directed play has epigenetic effects, affecting expression of more than 1,200 genes.[8] It activates both subcortical and neocortical areas that are responsible for diverse cognitive processes and spatial reasoning.[9] Social and self-directed play and exploration prompt secretion of brain-derived neurotrophic factor (BDNF), which is vital for neuronal growth and maintenance.[10] Dopamine, the energizing hormone indicating positive anticipation and prosocial enhancement, is also secreted during play.

Effects of play extend to other aspects of life and living. Social free play cultivates empathy and increases sensitivity and perceptions of emotions in others.[11] This affords opportunities to balance autonomy and social engagement. By developing appropriate patterns of self-regulation—emotionally, psychologically, and physiologically—a growing child becomes increasingly well-tuned to their community, culture, and overall environment. Better tuning leads to better functioning, better social skills and understanding, and better ways of navigating the environment in which they live. Self-initiated free play with others is integral to humanity's evolved nest heritage.[12]

Industrialized human societies, however, have turned away from play to a work-dominated culture, encouraging even its very young to labor instead of play. As our Animal kin demonstrate, however, play and work are intertwined. Although Wildlife must work very hard to make a living, play is central to their lives, in the young and the old—even among those regarded as exemplar workers. A good example is the Beaver. Perhaps above all species, other than the "busy Bee" or the Ant, Beavers are considered to be the most work-oriented species. "Hardworking" and "tireless" are almost synonymous with Beaver life and culture.

The planet's second-largest rodent (South America's Capybara is the biggest) has played an amazing, positive, and essential role in cocreating healthy lands and water.[13] The plentitude of Beavers in Canada and the United States, before their mass eradication, had an enormous effect on stream morphology and aquatic processes. Beavers sculpted both large and small rivers throughout Turtle Island (North America) into a complex mosaic of pools and networks of anastomosing channels. North America was no untouched garden when colonizers arrived. Its beauty and peaceful coherence reflected the prosocial relationships that Indigenous humans and Wildlife cultivated with the rest of Nature.[14] Beavers are just one of Nature's cadre of artists whose hands—and, in this case, teeth—have been instrumental in constructing the awesome landscapes that first greeted European eyes.

At the center of Beaver culture is a dynamic compound co-constructed with Nature and perfected over millions of years. The central purpose of this complex, made of branches, water, leaves, and mud, is to ensure the safety and well-being of Beaver communities. This physical nest comprises four main parts: the lodge, a pond, canals, and the iconic dam.

The dam is a cornerstone in the architectural Beaver complex. Dam construction reduces streamflow and creates a pond where Beavers build their lodges. To an untrained eye, a Beaver dam may appear to be just a random pile of wood and earth, but it is far more than that. Taking advantage of natural riverine bends, benches, and banks, dams take form bit by bit as Beavers bulldoze sediment and rock to form a ridge or build on one already in existence.[15] Expertly cut branches, saplings, leaves, woody debris, and more mud are added for fortification. Sapling stems are fashioned into points by the Beaver's iron-fortified yellow-orange teeth and deft five-fingered hands. These wooded buttresses are carefully oriented and pushed into mud on the downstream side to anchor the construction.

Beavers are amazing architects. The number, size, and type of dams in a colony vary with climate, stream dynamics, vegetation, and other factors. They are built to optimally conform to Nature's contours. Sometimes, in mountainous regions where streams are narrow, Beavers' successive dams are built in a staircase fashion;[16] in other locales, "wings" and secondary dams are added and attached to the main structure to help with any overflow.[17] Working with, not against, Nature's grain is both more successful and more efficient.

Like any good engineer, Beavers maintain an attentive eye on dam integrity.[18] Using their famous patterned and powerful tails as a rudder and webbed back legs to paddle, male and female Beavers patrol the length of the dam top to bottom, searching for and repairing any damage. Stream levels and patterns can shift radically with drought or floods and threaten pond and lodge strength and durability.

Safety is foremost. A strong dam is a crucial line of defense; it must be able to weather the elements during seasonal cycles and maintain sufficient pond depth throughout the year. The pond is not just a pretty fixture in the Beaver nest complex; it plays a core strategic role. Ponds extend protection from carnivores, such as Wolves, when Beavers are conducting their activities. The dam-pond-canal-lodge architecture allows Beavers to leave and return, from home to work, while retaining a relatively unbroken protective cover.

Pools have to be deep enough to cover the lodge entrance. These underwater doorways open into the pond below the surface, which reduces risk from attack by making it possible for Beavers to come and go protected by the cover of water. To deepen a pond and increase its efficacy, river bottom sediment is often excavated upstream. Some lodges have more than one entrance. This provides response flexibility in the case of an attack or other emergency. Beavers also dig interconnected canals—safeguarding under-water roads—that extend outside the pond to trails and slides leading to areas of forage.

Beavers are premier planners. They love contingency plans such as food caches.[19] During winter in frigid locales, caches are sources of nourishment when streams freeze. The family pulls together large branches and small Trees to make a raft under which gathered foodstuffs are placed. Over time, raft limbs become sodden and then sink, pushing the food down to the stream bottom, where it lies until needed. Leafy Willow branches are added near plunge holes as handy snacks.

While Beavers also make burrows in riverbanks, all the effort that goes into dam and canal construction and maintenance is directed toward secur-ing a safe home for the family. The dam-made pond and canals are func-tional mechanisms that make the heart of Beaver family and culture—the lodge—possible. A Beaver lodge may be built in open water or can extend out from a pond or riverbank. As with other aspects of Beaver life, there are as many variations on the theme as there are Beavers.

To create the lodge, Beavers artfully pile sticks and branches high enough to peak well above waterline, keeping in mind that the height of water will vary with the seasons. To increase structural coherence, pro-tective capacity, and insulation, Beavers paste on river bottom sediments, always being mindful to retain sufficient porosity to permit free flow of air within the lodge's inner quarters. Vents keep the lodge interior dry and supplied with fresh air. When water levels begin to drop, Beavers fortify the dam to keep the door covered and to maintain plenty of pond water for safe underwater travel.

Beavers are good citizens in the community. Beaver construction accom-modates others in the neighborhood as well as their own families. Ponds are a rich habitat for diverse Fish and other aquatic fauna and flora, and the associated lodge can provide a handy and safe location for Bird nests, such as those of Canada Geese. When a pond drains, either after its resi-dents have left or because of a shift in climate, nutrient-rich meadows and wetlands provide homes and resources for Frogs and diverse Insects, not to mention innumerable other organisms.[20]

Woven into this carefully designed architecture is the web of Beaver familial and friend relationships that turn the Beaver complex into a living, breathing, loving community. Similar to the cultures of Elephants and Sperm Whales, Beaver culture is nucleated by the family unit. Beavers live, work, and play in community. At any one time, a lodge is occupied by an extended family: usually an adult pair, young Beavers less than a year old, Beavers aged one to two years, and on occasion, Beavers older than two years. In large lodges, there may be more than one family group.[21]

Beavers openly show emotions—kissing and expressing deep love for their lifelong partner—and a commitment to care for their families and other nonpredatorial neighbors.[22] After Beavers find and fall in love with their lifelong partner, and the female becomes pregnant, she will give birth to several babies after three months. Birthing is an event anticipated by the entire family. While lodge maintenance is ongoing, several days before the birth the lodge interior is readied by plastering it with mud, gnawing down protruding branch ends, and covering the nest floor with soft edible Grass or wood chips. Father Beaver and yearlings, while periodically leaving to retrieve food and supplies, spend extensive time in the lodge with the pregnant mother.

There are layers of evolutionary underpinnings that contribute to how and who a Beaver becomes. As Mammals, Beaver infants are dependent on mother's milk and require extensive periods of companionship care. Similar to many Bird species,[23] Beavers lie somewhere along a developmental continuum, having both precocial and altricial traits. Baby Beavers, for instance, are born with open eyes, can eat solid food in a few days, and are, while a bit awkward, ambulatory. Young Beavers nurse and remain in the lodge for four to five weeks before emerging into the watery part of their world.[24]

Every species has evolved its unique nest—processes and structures that provide their babies with a microenvironment perfectly suited for optimal growth and health—and the Beaver is no exception. The physical Beaver nest is exquisitely tailored to meet the baby's internal and external needs, as well as to provide companionship care for baby Beavers. The lodge provides what all young require and what is essential to early care: warmth;

food; responsive, loving relationships; safety; and more—in essence, companionship care.

Similar to infant Brown Bears born in the den, time spent in the Beaver lodge is an intense period of development and learning for young Beavers. They learn verbal and body language, social mores, how to groom, and *emotional* and *social intelligence*—abilities to regulate their feelings and interactions with others appropriately. They stay in proximity with parents and siblings in the intimate quarters of the lodge, which provides the first stage of evolved Beaver nesting. If a baby somehow falls into a plunge hole, a babysitter is always at hand to scoop him out and back into warmth and safety. Infant Beavers can swim, but they are too immature and buoyant, lacking the fur's waterproofing oil that develops later and protects them from cold water. When an adult's or adolescent's babysitting shift is completed, the babysitter remains until their replacement arrives. Infant Beavers not only learn from their parents but also learn from their one- and two-year-old siblings. This is another example of communal care that provides well-rounded sources of information and affect. Just like human children in evolved nest conditions, Beavers learn by observing and then pitching in, growing into community membership.[25]

The next stage is a journey to water life, where young Beavers learn how to stay submerged and begin to get acquainted with the pond habitat. When they do take to the water, youngsters are always accompanied by family members as they explore and hone their swimming, foraging, and perceptual skills. At two years of age, the young Beavers begin to expand the family business: dam and lodge building.

While much of the Beavers' family focus is on the care of the young, there are many tasks to accomplish. The family is kept busy "washing" Grass bedding or adding wood chips to the lodge floor. This entails scraping it out from the lodge floor, soaking it in water until it is clean, and returning it inside.[26] In addition, family members bring back nutritious food, fortify the dam, and last but not least, spend time socializing, grooming, snuggling, and playing. A lot of learning occurs through play, both the self-directed variety and that conducted with other members of the group. Play engages the young in Beaver ethics and manners, which cultivate inner and social trust. Naturalist Enos Mills, founder of Rocky Mountain National Park, provides a snapshot of young Beaver play:

> Beavers have great fun while growing up. . . . They nose and push each other about, ofttimes tumbling one another into the water. In the water they send a thousand merry ripples to the shore, as they race, wrestle, and dive in the pond. They play on the house, in the pond, and in the sunshine and shadows of the trees along the shore. . . . Beavers grow up with the many-sided wild, playing amid the brilliant flowers and great boulders, in the piles of driftwood and among the fallen logs on the forest's mysterious edge. They learn to swim and slide, to dive quickly and deeply from sight, to sleep, and to rest moveless in the sunshine; ever listening to the strong, harmonious stir of wind and water, living with the stars in the sky and the stars in the pond; beginning serious life when brilliant clouds of color enrich autumn's hills; helping to harvest the trees that wear the robes of gold, while the birds go by for the southland in the reflective autumn days.

Perhaps intending to underscore his own appreciation of play and leisure and remind other humans about the nature of a good, nested life, Mills goes on to add: "Justly renowned for his industry, the beaver is a master of the fine art of rest."[27]

Today's human world has lost this culture of spontaneous play and a sense of its importance. Much of today's industrialized, technology-centered human culture remains dominated by a work ethic. Everyday life and social interactions are pressured by career demands, for both economic and cultural reasons. Unlike traditional, Nature-based communities where play, Nature, family, and daily tasks are integrated, the rearing and care of children are "managed," rather than *nurtured,* in order to fit around work schedules.[28] Children's time and activities are increasingly structured and intensified via schoolbook learning, with the result that playtime is diminished.

Free play has been marginalized in comparison to activities and goals designed to teach people how to "get ahead" in life. Similar to the commons, spontaneous play is frequently cordoned off and limited to certain spaces and circumstances such as "play time," theater, formalized dance, jokes, or other collectively accepted exchanges. In a work-obsessed society, play is often ridiculed unless one is in a creative field or situation. Play is fragile; the flow of its intrinsic creativity can quickly shut down if there is associated pain, threat, or anger. In a highly stressed or traumatized population, play and playfulness of spirit can be easily quenched.

Although modern human society typically contrasts play with work, play is not the opposite of work. Extensive observations of foraging societies around the world demonstrate that creativity and "fun" are, as Jean Liedloff perceived during her sojourn with the Ye'kuana, blended with work in everyday activities.[29] This universalism suggests that play is not just for kids, not just important in early life, but something that benefits everyone *throughout life.*

Neurobiologically, play is one of the best ways to grow the brain's right hemisphere, even in adulthood.[30] Social free play keeps one in the present moment, growing systems governed by the right hemisphere, which include self-regulation of various kinds and intersubjective responsiveness (emotional presence with others).[31] Children who do not play enough are more likely to be aggressive.[32] Similarly, adults who did not play often as children show high levels of aggression.[33] Undercare in early life (lack of evolved nest components) is usually associated with an inability to regulate intense emotion,[34] in part because nested care modulates neurohormones that are associated with the capacity to control thoughts, feelings, and actions at multiple levels, psychologically and physiologically (e.g., autonomic, neuroendocrine).[35]

Synchronization with caregivers and others, which play requires, helps a child organize self-regulatory capacities.[36] All self-regulation systems are beneficially affected by play, such as impulse control, delay of gratification,[37] and emotion regulation.[38] Self-directed play strengthens neural networks in the prefrontal cortex, the part of the brain that is involved in regulating emotions and in directing executive functions such as solving problems and making decisions.[39] Play facilitates the growth of an adaptive physiology—the ability to adjust to the situation at hand, such as increasing heart rate under challenge or decreasing heart rate when in a relaxing situation—as part of a healthy personhood.[40]

There are other ways that play acts to enhance a child's health.[41] Full-body self-initiated play fosters self-discovery through the development of self-manifesting-in-the-world through proprioception and exteroception. Young humans and Animals discover how their bodies work and how to use them, and in response, their motions and gestures provide feedback to their brains. While observational learning from parents, alloparents, and other relations in the community is vital, self-directed social play is crucial for brain development because it provides opportunities to try out new ways of moving, seeing, and interacting with others within the neighborhood. These interactive experiences fortify and expand neural connections; what is experienced in the external environment translates to the interior world. Play is a somatic, formative exploration that allows a child to build know-how for getting along in the social and ecological environment in which the child is living and interacting. Exciting—and sometimes challenging—explorative experiences communicate ongoing dynamic situational information to the brain, generating new skills and refining being and meaning.

Young Beavers watch their parents cut a branch and pull it into the water, and then they imitate the moves, making the same motion in the air. When a young Beaver watches her father swim by a Lily pad, pull it off, roll the pad up, and eat it, she learns how to do this herself by grabbing the stem and pad, wrestling with it, playing with it, and biting into the leaf.[42] Over time, Lily play becomes a foraging skill. Through emulation and play, a young one fine-tunes motor skills, coordination, and overall health, integrating mind and body.

Importantly, self-directed social play fosters alteroception. It is intrinsically relational. Social play is a gentle way of cultivating patterns of cooperation (versus competition), effective communication, and conflict resolution—all skills and understandings that are essential throughout life. Playfulness contributes to social bonding and enhances a culture of peaceful cooperation. The players must cooperate or else play will stop. The goal of free play is to keep it going. Even when outside without other humans, a child never truly plays alone; the child is always interacting with their environment, the more than human. Such companionship is part of our heritage as members of the Earth community.

Before colonizers imposed their agenda of conquest, forced labor, acquisition, and division, communal life was a tapestry of storytelling, singing, sharing experiences, and playing. Play included more formalized games where competition was focused on increasing potential, not winning. Life was not seen as the poet Alfred Tennyson envisioned Nature, an existence of survival under constant threat and "red in tooth and claw." Life was cherished, richly lived, and tuned to the needs of development and thriving, and play was part of it all.

Because play requires a neutral or positive mood, joyful play can spark positive moods in others and can invite participation. All of the elements that contribute to ethical engagement—presence, reverence, synchrony, empathy, perspective taking, and play—take courage.[43] They open one up to change through full engagement with another, encouraging trust of self and others in a space of vulnerability. One's sense of self expands beyond the unit of the individual to a more porous and pluralistic sense of self. Significantly, fourth century BCE Greek philosopher Plato considered play essential for moral development; without it, he maintained, children will not grow up to be the model moral citizens of the state that they need to be.[44]

In our ancestral environment, play, like joy and love, is a multiage experience involving all generations. Because babies are ready to play from birth, a child's community of carers must be ready to play themselves in order to set in motion the beneficial effects of play. Similar to Beavers, a human baby receives diverse inputs of social interaction from siblings, cousins, nonkin of various ages, parents, aunts, uncles, and grandparents; hence, the baby receives diverse sources for brain and body development. All engage indirectly with the child through role modeling and directly through play.

The decline of Western society's engagement in play has paralleled the decline of the play-filled lives of Beavers. Dramatic increases in human populations; possessive appropriation of land and water; toxins in air, land, and water; and relentless killing and harassment have made it nearly impossible for Beavers and other Wildlife to continue their traditional ways of life. Food is scarce, water is scarce, and procurement of life's essentials is increasingly more dangerous with the proliferation of roads, houses, and human intolerance.

Beaver numbers in North America were an estimated sixty to four hundred million before European occupation of Turtle Island.[45] These aquatic artists ranged from coast to coast, from Alaska and the far north of Canada's subarctic to California and northern Mexico. Similar to their cousin, the European Beaver, who was also nearly hunted to extinction,[46] North American Beaver populations were decimated for their fur and meat, then later because they were regarded as impediments to human progress.[47] After the demand for fur decreased at the start of the twentieth century and Beavers started to recover from centuries of slaughter, their persecution continued. Instead of being pursued for their pelts, Beavers were trapped and killed as pests.[48]

Together, private landowners and government agencies almost eradicated the species across the land. Beavers were shot and killed for doing what they do to make a living and care for their young: gnawing down Trees, flooding fields when building their dams, and interrupting unyielding human control of land and water. In one bizarre instance, the Idaho Fish and Game Commission trapped Beavers live, boxed them up, and dropped them by parachute into the Frank Church-River of No Return Wilderness Area.[49] Only very recently have scientists begun to appreciate that Beavers are highly intelligent, discerning architects of ecosystem health. Beavers are not the problem; rather, Bavarian biologist Gerhard Schwab asserts that the problem is "the overuse of landscape by man."[50]

The settler-colonizer attitude toward Beavers and other Wildlife radically contrasts with that of Native Peoples, as described by Chief Luther Standing Bear (Teton Sioux):

> From Wakan Tanka, the Great Spirit, there came a great unifying life force that flowed in and through all things—the flowers of the plains, blowing winds, rocks, trees, birds, animals—and was the same force that had been breathed into the first man. Thus all things were kindred, and were brought together by the same Great Mystery. Kinship with all creatures of the earth, sky, and water was a real and active principle. In the animal and bird world there existed a brotherly feeling that kept the Lakota safe among them. And so close did some of the Lakotas come to their feathered and furred friends that in true

brotherhood they spoke a common tongue. The animals had rights—
the right of man's protection, the right to live, the right to multiply,
the right to freedom, and the right to man's indebtedness—and in
recognition of these rights the Lakota never enslaved an animal, and
spared all life that was not needed for food and clothing.[51]

Indigenous perspectives[52] and the traditional ecological understanding of
Nature[53] account for the fact that the 80 percent of Wildlife species that
have not been driven to extinction live on the 20 percent of planetary lands
overseen by First Nation or Indigenous peoples.[54]

Western scientists are finally taking to heart what singer-songwriter Joni
Mitchell wrote: "You don't know what you've got till it's gone."[55] In the
wake of mass Wildlife and Plant genocides and attendant ecosystem collapse, modern humans are now realizing how important Beavers and all
our Animal and Plant relations are. They help us all. Play helps us all. Our
Animal kin and play are both part of our longtime heritage as a species. By
cultivating and teaching children care and respect for Animal kin, human
young can build their own understanding of the world as unprivileged
members of the natural community, and in so doing reclaim their humanity.
We must put into practice what ecophilosopher and writer Derrick Jensen
calls the time when the "beavers come home": "In the time after, the beavers
come home, bringing with them caddisflies and dragonflies, bringing with
them ponds and pools and wetlands, bringing home frogs, newts, and fish.
Beavers build and build, and restore and restore, working hard to unmake
the damage that was done, and to remake forests and rivers and streams
and marshes into what they once were, into what they need to be, into what
they will be again."[56]

7

Touch

Amazon Parrots

THEY KNEW IT was happening even before the shell was breached. They heard and felt a gentle—but urgent—rocking. Something grayish-black begins to push through: a chick. A second and third follow, and before long, there are three gaping, crying mouths reaching up to their parents' beaks. Mother and father, crossing beaks briefly, bend down to greet their children's eager faces. Father flies off, returning within minutes to offer regurgitated fruit to the newborns. Beaks almost larger than the heads that support them are open wide. Beseeching voices, mixed with joy and anxious need, pull the parents closer as they feed and touch the nest full of new chicks.

Touch is the earliest form of sensory and growth-promoting experience that teaches infants to be a member of their species, their family, and their community.[1] Even precocial species, such as Rattlesnakes, cluster together and sleep coiled upon one another, scaled bodies wrapped together.[2] This intimate contact develops a sensitivity to mother and kin smell,[3] an important sense for Snakes as well as humans and other Animals.

Physical touch assists an infant in developing self-regulation by maintaining contentment or optimal arousal for a growth-promoting biochemistry.[4] It embodies a reassuring connection, which activates calming hormones such as oxytocin.[5] Children learn how to be in the world via touch. As Gabor Maté observes, "Tactile contact is the newborn's earliest experience of the world. It is how we first receive love."[6] Even though it may vary across species, loving, responsive touch is critical for all young.

To the untrained human eye an egg may exist outside the mother, but its shell and the bodily touch of brooding serves as an extension of connection through touch. Life emerges in relationship, and when a chick is born and the shelter of the egg is lost, the connection of touch is retained. Security is immediately replaced by welcoming parental care and the physical nest. Bird nested care is designed to safeguard babies and optimize parents' ability to connect with their young through touch. Mealy Parrots, who are one of the thirty-one spectacular Amazon Parrot species,[7] are a perfect example.

Mealy, Yellow-Naped, Yellow-Headed, Blue-Fronted, and other Amazon Parrots generally measure eight to twelve inches (twenty to thirty centimeters) from beak to tail, depending on the species. They weigh ten to twenty ounces (almost three hundred to six hundred grams) on average, with mainly green plumage streaked with striking blue, red, and yellow feathers found on various parts of the body, including fluorescent pigments that absorb and reemit ultraviolet light.[8] Their beaks are large relative to the size of their bodies, and they have prehensile foot-hands that can wrest open tough nuts and grab branches with strength and efficacy. While every Amazon Parrot species is distinct and unique, their methods of childcare are similar enough to draw some commonalities.[9]

A male-female pair and their children form the Amazon Parrot's evolved nest's social nucleus. After meeting, courting, and falling in love, the pair nests. When preparing a nest, these Central American Parrots "interior decorate" ready-made cavities in the boles of tall old-growth Trees such as *Terminalia amazonia* (commonly known, depending on locale, as *roble coral, amarillón,* or *guyo*) and *Dialium guianense* (ironwood, *granadillo, tamarindo*). The mother Amazon Parrot lays two to seven eggs inside, and within a month or so, the eggs break open and enormous beaks—far out of proportion to the babies' tiny, wet bodies—poke out, mouths wide open to greet their parents and demand their first taste of food outside the shell. Both mother and father Yellow-Naped Amazon Parrots provide nourishment in the form of regurgitated seeds and fruit. Whether physically or auditorily, they are in sustained connection with their chicks to maintain synchrony.

As dawn colors the sky, Parrots waken from their treetop roosts and begin calling to each other. Flock cohesion is maintained by being in nearly constant contact with each other. Morning calls are routinely accompanied by grooming and allogrooming ceremonies, when Parrots care for their feathers and those of their loved ones. Parrot evolved nests are appropriately referred to as a "nucleus" because the family is a fractal of the greater psychosocial cloud of the flock. Within each nest, Parrots preen each other with the meticulousness of a fine jeweler and the tenderness of a lover, spending hours touching and exchanging murmurs of affection.

All Animals groom, and their reasons are similar. In Birds, preening keeps their feathers—up to twenty-five thousand per Bird, on average—clean and neat. *Clean* means free of bacteria, dust, and other particulate matter that might cause infection. *Neat* means every feather, from the large wing feather to the tiniest innermost fluff, must be clean and in place for effective, safe function. Like airplanes whose mechanics are in disrepair, a Parrot with wet or disarrayed feathers will have impaired flight. Feathers also keep a Bird's body dry. Even though they live in the tropics, Amazon Parrot feathers help the Bird adjust to changes in humidity and temperature.

Grooming also activates protective substances. Birds and Beavers have essential oils that grooming plumbs and spreads throughout their bodies. For Beavers, such oils keep them dry and fortify their fur's ability to keep them warm. Emperor Penguins possess a uropygial gland near the base of the tail that produces a waxy substance that keeps feathers flexible and waterproof. Parrots lack these glands, and instead they have specialized feathers that disintegrate into "powder down," a dust that looks like dandruff.

Aside from physical practicalities, grooming and allogrooming are means for communication and connection. Language and grooming are the audible and tactile webbing that connects everyone. Parrot preening and allopreening ceremonies are particularly important in the morning, during daytime rest periods, and before nightfall. These are check-in points to see how each other is doing physically and emotionally, and to make sure everyone made it through the night and back home after day is done. Allopreening is not limited to life partners. It includes other flock members and begins before birth. By definition, touch starts with conception. Babies take form inside in their mothers, in connection, in contact. An embryo's mind and body draw from maternal embodiment and first know their mothers through feel and touch.

When they are born, human infants experience a radical change in feeling and touch with vaginal birth, beginning what Ashley Montagu refers to as "the tactile stage." Mammalian infants experience the contracting uterus, pressure from the pelvic bones that jump-starts the child's body systems. This is especially critical for human babies, since their mothers do not lick them—unlike other Mammal mothers and their babies. Human babies who experience surgical birth by cesarean section miss the vaginal welcome, but they can benefit immensely from postnatal massage as a way to mimic natural birthing.[10] Nursing, holding, and caressing during the first two years of life reflect the whole-body holding environment of exterogestation. At birth, the skin learns adaptive responses to a felt environment that includes "air movements, gases, particles, parasites, viruses, bacteria, changes in pressure, temperature, humidity, light, radiation, and much else."[11] A carer's touch is one way in which a child learns how to adjust to ongoing changes without excessive stress. Developmental psychologist Erik Erikson described touch as critical in humans' first two years of life, when children build their sense of trust—or, conversely, without responsive care, distrust. Full companionship care includes trust in Nature, specifically the local ecological environment, as essential to the circle of trust.

Young Animals expect to be cherished by their parents. Needs are to be noticed and met without much signaling by the offspring required, much like the Japanese notion of *amae* or friendship.[12] In *amae*, the needs of another are picked up subliminally and met without the need for vocalized language. This concept is similar to how pediatrician and therapist D. W. Winnicott described mothers who spend the early weeks of their child's life in an infant-preoccupied state *(primary maternal preoccupation)*. This preoccupation allows the mother to know and anticipate the infant's needs without the infant needing to signal, a communication capacity that the infant will not develop until later.[13]

Skin-to-skin contact facilitates "motherliness" and "total relatedness," which infants require for healthy development.[14] After the embodied synchrony experienced during pregnancy, mothers move into interactional synchrony with their newborns using multiple sensory and cognitive channels, the most basic of which is touch. In the first hours after birth, contact has long-lasting effects on the infant's self-regulation and maternal-child relational co-regulation.[15]

The mother-child dyad is symbiotic. Physical connection with baby is just as vital for the mother as it is for the infant. Body-to-body contact immediately after birth helps a mother's body contract the uterus, expel the placenta, and prevent hemorrhage.[16] Human mothers also need supportive care that allows for greater touch and bonding with baby. Family members, doulas, birth coaches, and other community members help in this process by providing the mother with a period of "lying in" that allows her to heal and the mother-child dyad to focus on bonding and relating.[17]

Touch involves more than these intimate exchanges. It pervades and relates to all our senses. While those of us living in the anthropocentric world of mind and objectification might overlook it, we are immersed in a world of touch. Even in modern society, touch is always with us. Clothes, wind, humidity, and whatever we encounter involve some form of contact.[18] Touch even infuses our language. We describe others as "in touch" or "out of touch," "abrasive" or "soft." Someone who is unyielding is described as "hard," and a friendly, loving person is "warm." Interactions between individuals are variously "smooth" or "rough," depending on the quality of exchange. These are all metaphors based in the physical sensations of touch.[19]

Critically, unlike Nature-based cultures, settler-colonizer culture all too often seeks to block direct contact with Nature except as a consumer completing a bucket list. Indeed, most of Western "civilization"—housing, clothes, technology, cars, and so on—is driven by the desire and effort to distance humans from direct contact with Nature. Chief Luther Standing Bear (Teton Sioux) describes how touching, being in constant contact with the Earth, was so important for the Lakota people:

> The Lakota was a true naturalist—a lover of Nature. He loved the earth and all things of the earth, and the attachment grew with age. The old people came literally to love the soil and they sat or reclined on the ground with a feeling of being close to a mothering power. It was good for the skin to touch the earth, and the old people liked to remove their moccasins and walk with bare feet on the sacred earth. Their tipis were built upon the earth and their altars were made of earth. The birds that flew in the air came to rest upon the earth, and it was the final abiding place of all things that lived and grew. The soil was soothing, strengthening, cleansing, and healing. This is why the old Indian still sits upon the earth instead of propping himself up and away from its lifegiving forces. For him, to sit or lie upon the ground is to be able to think more deeply and to feel more keenly; he can see more clearly into the mysteries of life and come closer in kinship to other lives about him.[20]

The centrality of touch shows that we are more than our brains or minds; we are embodied. We build understanding of the world through our bodies. Our bodies are in constant connection with our surroundings, sensing rhythms, smells, tastes, movement, pitch, and timbre. The infant at the breast, in the carer's arms—or, in the case of aquatics, in the carer's wake—has a synesthetic experience of smell, taste, sound, touch, and loving affirmation. Breastfeeding facilitates the child's sense of being cherished by mother (and perhaps others). Physician Margaret Ribble notes that as the result of being "mothered," a child learns to combine and coordinate suckling with full sensory intake—looking, listening, smelling, and grasping—establishing their first complex behavior.[21]

With or without breastfeeding, young Mammals need extensive, firm carrying, rocking, and skin-to-skin contact for a well-developing body and brain.[22] Ribble notes that "those who are not held in the arms sufficiently, particularly if they are bottle-fed babies, in addition to breathing disturbances often develop gastrointestinal disorders. They become air-swallowers and develop what is popularly known as colic."[23] Babies who experience extensive positive touch and have their needs met, including being carried more, generally have less colic,[24] a condition that is uncharacteristic of human ancestry.[25] That all-important nerve, the vagus, which innervates all major body systems, is shaped by early-life touch.[26] Over time, even touch as expressed through a carer's voice will affect a child's vagus nerve regulation.[27]

Physical experience translates to and conveys emotional experience. What we feel in our bodies imbues our perceptions. Touch is the physical medium for staying connected in the material and emotional world. Whether furred, feathered, scaled, or unadorned, skin is a social organ. Skin is "the oldest and most sensitive of our organs, our first medium of communication, and our most efficient protector."[28] Just as the infant's digestive system needs assistance in establishing probiotic bacteria and proper functioning, which is facilitated by ingestion of breast milk, a carer's touch and affectively attuned responsiveness supports the brain and body systems in developing emotion regulation, including building systems formative to secure attachment.[29]

Received as vibration, texture, temperature, or pressure, touch begins even before a chick hatches or an infant Mammal is born. Prenatally, the womb, whether eggshell or placenta, provides a constant sensation of being touched and held. Postnatally, babies expect similar levels of feeling from the external world. For altricial species, this means from mother, other primary carers, or community members. Among nomadic foragers, children are touched nearly constantly in early life, being carried and held during naps, first by mother and then half the time by other adults and community members.[30] Precocial Birds who are born more or less ready to go out into the unknown on their own are also "prepped" to do so; they are epigenetically "tuned" while encased in their shells. Hatching Parrot chicks hear and are welcomed by the familiar rhythm of their mother's body and voice. "Rhythm" reminds us that touch is not static.

All Animals are sense-makers, building understandings, an Umwelt, through movement.[31] Animals are meant to move,[32] which means that species such as humans, who have a limited ability to move as babies, need a carer's help to gain the *somatosensory* experience of moving with and against gravity. Infants expect to be held and rocked, facilitating breathing and digestion.[33] As a child matures, self-generated movement, which includes play as well as touch, improves nervous system function because it promotes the ability to make predictions and decisions in active, goal-directed movements that fit the environment.[34] Modern-day human living, however, has become increasingly sedentary and restricted.

While mandatory car seats, strollers, and carriers may have their place in work-dominated, industrialized, anthropocentric environments, extended periods of inhibited movement and limited carer touch are a radical departure from evolved nest design. One study found that strollers that have a child facing forward are linked to developmental delays.[35] Other human cultures consider many practices in the United States, such as isolating children in their own beds and rooms, to be cruel.[36] Isolation during night hours is an extremely unusual practice in human history that limits touch and breastfeeding. That practice alone, and its enforcement in early life, can be enough to push children into an emotional or moral detachment that is unseen in cultures that do not separate and isolate young children. Notably, dominant-culture humans are the only humans who intentionally separate mother and child after birth for extended periods of time, despite infant distress.

On the other hand, infants who receive more maternal touch are found to cry less and to have better sleep and behavior organization, heart rate regulation, socioemotional development, and quality attachment.[37] At the same time, their mothers experience *less* stress and depression. In addition, the pair has greater breastfeeding success and better relational quality. In his monumental book *Touching*, anthropologist Ashley Montagu observed: "When the need for touch remains unsatisfied, abnormal behavior will result." Children who are not touched enough can become fretful and anxious and sometimes develop an angry disposition. An examination of over four hundred societies found that those that breastfed for at least two and a half years and also kept their young children in arms were more peaceful; that is, they are less likely to have violent conflicts with other societies.[38]

Such positive touch facilitates effective social bonding during the critical period of life when the brain, particularly the right hemisphere, is rapidly developing.[39]

An absence of or lapses in early physical touching and rocking by a carer can undermine species-normal brain-body development. The absence of these social interactions early in life affects the amygdala, the part of the brain responsible for reactive responses.[40] An undertouched baby may develop a sense of perennial threat and fear due to the underdevelopment of systems, like the oxytocin system.[41] Touch-activated oxytocin affects development of the brain, cardiovascular system, and immune system, providing the neurohormonal substrate for all social-relational attachment.[42] Oxytocin researcher C. Sue Carter notes that "receiving love in early life can influence behavior and physiology across the lifespan."[43] Oxytocin suppression is associated with anxiety, stress, and fear, and it thereby impairs positive social interactions and the development of social bonds.[44] In contrast to children who maintained contact with their birth parents, orphaned children who did not receive personal care in the first years of life show depressed levels of oxytocin even when in physical contact with adopted parents.[45]

Carer touch, preening, grooming, eye-to-eye gaze, caressing, and body-to-body embrace are all involved with temperature regulation and a sense of well-being. A mother's body temperature, for example, will automatically rise during skin-to-skin contact with an infant whose temperature is too low. After sustained touching, a baby's temperature will return to normal.[46] Touch can play an instrumental role by lowering an infant's heart rate during a distressing experience.[47] Preening, touch, and skin-to-skin contact promote healthy infant sleep cycles, arousal, and exploration levels.[48] In contrast, separation and isolation increase dysregulation and can impair the hypothalamic-pituitary-adrenal (HPA) axis—a major neuroendocrinal chassis that helps mediate stress—for life.[49]

Touch and physical stimulation in early life also have a profound effect on lifelong immunity.[50] The quality of human caregiving in early life establishes the ratio between the two major cells of the immune system, T helper cells (cd4 surface protein) and T suppressor or cytotoxic cells (cd8 surface protein).[51] Helper T cells "help" other cells of the immune system. Cytotoxic T cells kill virally infected cells and tumors. The relationship between T cell ratios and depression (which includes diminished energy and social withdrawal) illustrates the intimate link between the immune system and psychological well-being.[52] Individuals with depression often have a decreased ratio of cortisol and epinephrine indicative of poor early care.[53] Even at the level of determining which and how certain genes will be expressed phenotypically, touch plays a crucial role.

For a long time, Western scientists asserted that individual personality and temperament, how we each react and regulate our responses and see and interact with the world around us, drew from innate propensities. In this view, a Bear looks and acts like a Bear because of the Bear's DNA and genetic heritage, and the same is true for an Amazon Parrot, Penguin, or Beaver. Together, the collection of genes makes up a given species' genome—the rule book contained in every cell for making a Bear a Bear, a human a human, and so forth. Yet in terms of who we each become, something more than passive genetics is involved.

Epigenetic changes occur by mechanisms like chemically tagging DNA—for example, adding on a methyl molecule (three hydrogen atoms and one carbon atom) through a process called *methylation,* which typically turns a gene off.[54] Through epigenetic processes an infant's brain records developmental experiences (internal triggers and signals) and environmental experiences (carer responses). There are sensitive periods for virtually permanent DNA tagging in early life, carrying a child's experience forward.[55] These "marks" can follow the child throughout life as part of their epigenome[56] (in this word, the Greek *epi-* means "on top" or "above"), which is a record of how DNA sequences are boosted or diminished based on experience.[57]

Conserved for millions of years, the evolved nest is one of our inheritances beyond genes that influence genetics.[58] The state or practices of these extragenetic elements, such as the evolved nest, culture, and ecology, interact to form the kind of person we become. The human lineage maintained the relational dynamics of mother-child love throughout the life span, like trust, tenderness, sensuality, and playfulness. Human cooperation is dependent on this biology of love,[59] which varies in its cultural manifestations. This is one way that Nature simultaneously maintains both dazzling diversity and persistent coherence through the dynamic flow of conservation and change.

During the first years of life, maternal touch influences epigenetic mechanisms that shape developing brain circuitries.[60] Maternal nurturing (responsiveness, touch, welcoming orientation) in the first months of life is associated with higher functioning of the oxytocin system more than a year later.[61] Affectionate touch is part of the "external womb" of exterogestation that is needed after uterogestation.[62] As noted, there are sensitive periods for epigenetic DNA tagging in early life, carrying forward the effects of early life adversity.[63] Environmental effects, however, are not limited to a child's direct experience. Not only do epigenetic changes occur in the womb and early in life;[64] we can inherit experience-based changes from our ancestors as an *epigenetic inheritance*.[65]

In the past, it was assumed that epigenetic changes passed onto off-spring would maintain only in the presence of the original environmental trigger and would reverse when the environmental stimulus disappeared. We now know that this assumption is incorrect. Epigenetic change can persist over multiple generations even without continued exposure to the external environmental trigger.[66] On both parental sides, epigenetic changes associated with certain physical and psychological diseases, for example, are known to persist for at least four generations.[67] Parents increase prenatal infant stress sensitivity or reactivity by transmitting their own experience of stress.[68] Repeated or chronic conditions of the mother, such as chronic hunger or social stress, can and do influence embryo development.[69] It turns out that most underlying differences in individual brain chemistry result from a combination of genetic inheritance, epigenetic inheritance from both parents and other ancestors, and epigenetic changes affecting an infant from conception on.

These discoveries reveal chilling insights into how modern humans are responsible for both the physical extinction of Wildlife and their psychological extinction, with the loss of species' internal mental, emotional, and ethical integrity through stress-induced epigenetic changes. Psychological states of trauma can become traits handed down across generations in humans and other Animals.[70] In addition to the young Elephants who killed over one hundred Rhinoceroses, other Elephants who have experienced similar trauma both in the wild and in captivity commit intraspecific violence, including infanticide.[71] Such unprecedented species-abnormal behaviors are found among other Wildlife. Deer-on-human attacks, for instance, are linked to the Deer "being overly stressed or antagonized."[72] Increasingly, Deer and other Wildlife populations are experiencing psychological trauma and stress caused by multiple factors that have intensified ever since colonization, including increased human interference, land development, and legal and illegal hunts.

One of the most striking examples of human-caused epigenetic inheritance in Wildlife is a second unprecedented change in African Elephants: the rise of tusklessness. During the 1977–1992 civil war in Mozambique, 90 percent of African Elephants in the area were slaughtered by ivory poachers. After this drastic episode, the number of females who grew tusks suddenly dropped. Researchers studying this phenomenon identified genome loci associated with Mammalian tooth development. Among humans, these genes are homologous to those associated with Elephant tusks. Analyses suggest that selective killing for tusks has resulted in epigenetic change and its phenotypic expression of tusklessness.[73]

The ability of biological systems to become modified by experience allows a species to adjust to naturally varying environments. Epigenetic change is a way for organisms to maintain healthy connection with their dynamic homes. Ideally, an organism's heritage and epigenetics work together to provide both flexibility and resilience. The social and physical contours of every evolved nest reflect the means and ends to achieve this goal successfully. When the evolved nest is lacking in some way, however, as in the case of the Elephants, health-related epigenetic factors are likely to promote poor mental and physical health. A species' changes become maladaptive, meaning that, as in the case of Elephants, adaptations to conditions radically different from those in which their nests evolved are harmful. In any species, PTSD is a natural response to unnatural conditions.

Overall, touch is how we become fully and intelligently embodied. Carer touch promotes our well-being, epigenetically protecting us and promoting our resilience.[74] Touch is a way we express our innate, underlying oneness with the world through a material medium. With loving touch, we welcome the world that welcomes us, assured of our unbroken connection with all of Nature and the cosmos.

Emotions

Octopuses

REACHING OUT a delicate tipped tentacle to the human swimming near her, she thought, "I feel, therefore I am."

One summer's day in 2012 in the heart of England, a group of eminent neuroscientists, accompanied by theoretical physicist and Nobel Prize winner Stephen Hawking, stood on the steps of Cambridge University and delivered what has come to be known as the "Cambridge Declaration of Consciousness (aka the "Cambridge Declaration").[1] It is a dense two-page document that concludes with this statement: "The weight of evidence indicates that humans are not unique in possessing the neurological substrates that generate consciousness." In short, Animals have brains with capacities comparable to our own. Other scientists, such as Erich Jarvis, a comparative neuroscientist at Rockefeller University, concur. While Tortoises, Parrots, and Elephants look and do things differently from us, they think, feel, and possess consciousness as we do.[2]

Most biomedical researchers were not shocked by the news. The Cambridge Declaration conforms to the foundations that have shaped their research practices. Scientific studies, particularly those investigating how the brain does and doesn't work, rely on cross-species commonality to draw inferences from Animal experimental subjects to humans. Bats, Cats, Mice, Monkeys, and many more species are used as surrogates to explore the workings of the human brain-mind's emotional and thought processes. We experience this relatedness in everyday living with family Dogs and Cats, as well as with other Animals.

In many ways, therefore, the Cambridge Declaration is unsurprising—except for one sentence: "Non-human animals, including all mammals and birds, and many other creatures, including octopuses, also possess these neurological substrates." *Including Octopuses.* What the scientists are saying is that, despite their common portrayal as menacing, mindless monsters of the deep, Octopuses have the wherewithal to be as aware and cognizant of their surrounds and themselves as we are—perhaps even more so.

Take Paul, for example. He was an Octopus held in captivity who was able to outcompete humans by successfully predicting the winners of all seven matches Germany played in the 2010 World Cup.[3] The seemingly endless stories of similar feats of extraordinary, almost otherworldly, mental agility and acumen have prompted some to speculate that Octopuses are not of this Earth but rather are aliens.[4]

Yet, according to evolution, they are indeed Earthlings. The Octopus we recognize today seems to have taken form around or before 164 million years ago.[5] Octopuses eventually radiated into three hundred or more different species who live scattered across the Earth's oceans in diverse habitats, from the deepest blue seas to the shallowest reef.[6] Genetically speaking, however, it has been a much longer time since humans and Octopuses last shared a common ancestor. Compared to the Cow and Dog lineages who split from humans around ninety-two million years ago,[7] our last connection to Octopuses was a lot farther back: almost six hundred million years.[8]

Although modern human beings like to think of themselves as a separate, unique species, brain capacities have been conserved across species with different evolutionary trajectories.[9] Vertebrates—backboned Animals like Parrots, Beavers, and humans—have the same basic brains attached to a spine that can do the same things. This recognition of parallel neurocapacities is a fairly recent discovery in Western science. Birds, for instance, while sharing a common ancestor with Reptiles and Mammals, went a different route and developed a different neuroanatomy (nervous system structure and organization).[10] Because of an error in nomenclature combined with a misinterpretation of Avian internal brain cell structure, it was believed that Birds and Reptiles lacked parts of the brain that we and other Mammals enjoy. Our cerebrum, which includes the neocortex, is homologous with that of Parrots and Crocodiles. Birds do have a kind of neocortex; it is just shaped differently from ours. A vast ethological inventory associated with these neural substrates shows that Ravens, Crows, Parrots, and other Bird species exhibit all manner of traits once thought uniquely human: vocal learning, complex language, episodic memory, emotional complexity, tool use, and maternal/paternal feelings and behaviors.[11] The startling statement made in the Cambridge Declaration is that, despite their radically different body and brain architecture, Octopuses also have these capacities.

Relative to body size, Octopus brains are very large. Two-thirds of their neurons, however, are located in their arms; as Natural History Museum curator Jon Ablett puts it, they function like "small brains."[12] Octopuses' arm neurons are collected into many ganglia, clusters of nerve cells that carry messages to and from the central nervous system. Each of the eight arms has its own sensors that provide an Octopus with a sense of touch, smell, and taste, and thus the ability to detect even the tiniest whiff of chemical change in the water. Not only are their arms nuanced sensors and very powerful "doers"; they also seem to participate in a kind of partnered as well as locally controlled movement and decision-making. Octopuses appear to be a perfect example of the impossibility of dividing body from mind.

But Octopuses don't fit any current understanding of intelligence or cognition. They seem to live outside usual conceptualizations.[13] Philosopher of science Peter Godfrey-Smith, who is fascinated by what Octopuses can tell us about the evolution of consciousness, compares and contrasts inverte-brate and vertebrate brains in this way: "When vertebrate brains are com-pared to octopus brains, all bets—or rather, all mappings—are off. There is no part-by-part correspondence between the parts of their brains and ours. Indeed, octopuses have not even collected the majority of their neurons inside their brains; most of the neurons are found in their arms."[14] Instead of centralized organization like vertebrate brains, Octopuses' mind power appears to be somewhat distributed, and coordinated, between their head and the rest of their eight-armed bodies.[15] An Octopus's "nervous system as a whole is a more relevant object than the brain: it's not clear where the brain itself begins and ends, and the nervous system runs all through the body."[16] Using panoramic eyes to provide information to the arms, the Octopuses' semiautonomous arms maintain to some degree a "mind of their own," and they carry out their own fine-tuned explorations. These observa-tions have led to vigorous discussions as to whether Octopuses are examples of embodied cognition,[17] which contrasts with the idea that the brain is like a computer or the sole seat of knowing.

This intriguing neural design is expressed in a variety of equally intrigu-ing capabilities. Octopuses love to play and have an incredible ability to figure things out, even when confronted with tasks and puzzles they would not find in their natural habitat. Captive-held Octopuses in laboratories and public aquaria, for example, are notorious for taking things apart, like lids from screw-top jars and parts of their holding tanks. They are perspi-cacious, accomplishing Houdini-like tricks and doing them at just the right moment when no one—no human with the potential to interfere—is look-ing. At one university laboratory aquarium, an Octopus routinely squirted water at light bulbs, which short-circuited expensive electrical systems. This happened so frequently that the institute was eventually compelled to close the exhibit and release the Octopus to the wild; they could not afford to repair the Octopus's sabotage.[18]

They also do clever things like plugging up a tank's outflow, which causes the tank to overflow and flood the room. Crab is a favorite food for Octopuses, but because of its expense, keepers and scientists often provide captive-held Octopuses with lower-grade frozen food. One Octopus was known for taking the thawed food provided by the aquarium and, as soon as the keeper passed by or left the room, flushing the distasteful morsels down the outflow pipe: out of sight, out of mind. Octopus skills of discernment also extend to making shrewd judgments about humans. Octopuses are very picky about who they like and dislike, whether the humans who keep them captive or visitors to the aquaria, and will play tricks on those who fall short of their approval. Like Elephants, Octopuses have long memories and recall who did what to them, for better or for worse.

The more we learn about Octopuses, the more fascinating they become. Differences in brain architecture is just one of their many mysteries. Octopuses have eight arms with amazing ability to move; they have hydrostatic support rather than skeletal support; they can "smell by touch" with chemoreceptors; they can rejuvenate their own brains; and they have three hearts that pump blue-green, not red, blood.[19] Oxygen-carrying copper, in lieu of iron molecules, produces the difference between Octopus and human blood color.

As if these facts were not enough, there is something else that researchers find even more intriguing: Octopus RNA editing.[20] To survive changing environments, organisms need to adapt. Adaptive evolution occurs through effective mutations, which are positively selected across multiple generations.[21] Relative to epigenetic changes, which can also be inherited, adaptation through natural selection (which involves changes in DNA sequences) is regarded as more stable.[22] Germline DNA, the blueprint instructions given to us by our ancestors, is the stronghold of genetic coding. In order for these instructions to be carried out, they are transcribed into RNA, which then translates this information into proteins—molecules responsible for performing critical intracellular tasks. DNA stores genetic data in the form of instructions; RNA passes those instructions on; and proteins follow the instructions and carry out the work. Sometimes, things get lost in translation and RNA gets "edited" before it is used to make proteins. This rapid alteration allows for changes to be made without changing the DNA instruction manual.

For most organisms, mutations occur in DNA that are then transcribed into RNA. The RNA editing process in Mammals is relatively infrequent (although researchers are discovering that it occurs more often in humans and other Animals than originally thought).[23] When it does occur, it is limited to a few, presumably relatively unimportant sites in the entire genetic scheme of things. Compared to Mammals, invertebrates appear to have much higher levels of editing and recoding.[24] RNA editing occurs in Squids, Octopuses, and Cuttlefish (but not the Nautilus) at locations that exert a tremendous effect on nervous system proteins,[25] allowing them to function at low temperatures.[26]

What this suggests is that while Mammals may largely adapt to environmental change through germline mutation[27] (changes in inherited, genetically coded DNA) across generations, along with epigenetic changes in one or more generations, the Octopus genome has remained much the same for a very long time. The Octopus's pronounced RNA editing in their nervous system suggests that it permits dynamic, real-time responses to environmental change and situations—an intrinsic flexible adaptability that does not have to tinker with the genome.[28]

RNA editing may be the key to how Octopus mental, sensory, and emotional capacities became so complex. They use processes and machinery that Mammals use differently. While Octopus DNA has remained relatively stable, RNA editing has been very busy providing Octopuses and others with increasingly complex and adaptive capacities, whether these changes have to do with responding to shifts in ocean temperature or some other experience. There are other characteristics indicating that there is much more about Octopuses' inner lives than our human philosophy can dream. In addition to body, eye, and arm movements, Octopuses express an amazing repertoire of communication, much of which may be undetectable by the human eye.

Eric Kreit is an electrical engineer who investigates ways to create intricate pixel displays. Despite the complexity that human technology is able to generate, Octopus talents remain unchallenged: "Of all of the organisms in the animal kingdom capable of colour modulation, cephalopods (squid, cuttlefish and octopus) are able to produce the widest range of colours and patterns to help them adapt to their visually diverse marine environments as well as signal and communicate with their own species and others."[29]

Skin color and texture are directed by the Octopus's nervous system, which controls tiny muscles responsible for turning on and off minuscule bags of color embedded in the skin. Chromatophores—pigment-containing cells, each one containing one specific color—are protected by the dermis (skin layer). When signaled, the neurons activate the muscles around the chromatophore, which expand or contract the color sac to turn it on or off, as the case may be. Even scientists are moved to describe Octopus coloration in poetic ways, comparing the fleeting millisecond-alternating waves of color to passing clouds: "The tremendous capacity of the chromatophore system to change its colour across space and time has allowed these animals to produce complex visual displays to conspecific and heterospecific targets, including the aptly-named 'passing cloud'."[30]

Beyond chromatophores, there are three more color elements: iridophores, leucophores, and photophores.[31] Iridophores ("bearers of the rainbow") are cells that reflect incoming light at different wavelengths and polarities (photons vibrating in one plane) and lie below the layer of chromatophores. Below them are the leucophores, directed by the chromatophores and iridophores, which become the color of the light wavelengths shined upon them. Finally, there are light-producing cells called photophores, which create light through bioluminescence and seem to function largely for communication.

Together, these remarkable mind-driven mechanics yield an incredible palette of unimaginable variety that colors the Octopus when, how, and where she wishes. Somewhat surprisingly, while they can perceive polarized light, textures, and shapes, Octopuses are color-blind, a finding that has puzzled researchers.[32] Why the fantastic ability to change colors and create stupendous displays for potential mates if the recipient is color-blind? The answer may relate somehow to the unusual U-shaped pupils that Cuttlefish have evolved and may give the invertebrate the ability to pick up and focus certain wavelengths on the retina.[33]

Generally, changes in coloration and texture are used in two ways: to blend in with the surrounding environment for protection from would-be attackers, such as Sharks (concealment), and to express and convey information (communication).[34] The fact that these changes are instigated by or managed via the nervous system means that Octopus coloration links internal information systems (emotions, feelings, and thoughts) with external information systems (communication), or language.[35] As the Cambridge Declaration maintains, "The neural substrates of emotions do not appear to be confined to cortical structures." In simpler language, this says that you don't have to have a brain with the same architecture as ours to experience the rainbow of emotions and feelings that colors our lives and experiences. Octopuses have neural substrate capacities for complex emotions.

Most scientists are slow to admit that Animals, let alone Octopuses, have emotions, despite acknowledging their neurobiological and cognitive capabilities and diverse forms of intelligence.[36] Conventionally, Octopus capacities for feelings are narrowly described according to eight criteria:

Possession of nociceptors (receptors that detect noxious stimuli— such as temperatures hot enough to burn, or a cut); possession of parts of the brain that integrate sensory information; connections between nociceptors and those integrative brain regions; responses affected by local anaesthetics or analgesics; motivational trade-offs that show a balancing of threat against opportunity for reward; flexible self-protective behaviours in response to injury and threat; associative learning that goes beyond habituation and sensitization; behaviour that shows the animal values local anaesthetics or analgesics when injured.[37]

The reluctance to admit to Cephalopod affect is reminiscent of how human babies were once regarded. Up until fairly recently, scientists and medical practitioners did not believe that human newborns felt pain like adults. It took research, such as a 2015 fMRI study, to provide hard data confirming otherwise.[38] But, as Charles Darwin observed, even without neuroscience at hand, "There is no fundamental difference between man and animals in their ability to feel pleasure and pain, or happiness and misery."[39] Western scientists have a long history of uneasiness around the subject of emotions.

Western scientists, and Enlightenment culture at large, have conventionally looked down on emotion as something superfluous, even detrimental.[40] Generally, it has been cognition that has garnered approbation, being regarded as the supreme quality, with humans at the pinnacle of competence.

In contrast, emotions were deemed primitive contaminants that marred rationality and were best kept suppressed, far and away from objective, clear thinking. Such views persist in most contemporary scientific research and scholarship as part of "objectivity."[41] Researchers are taught to block their subjective thoughts and emotions, to avoid biasing the facts. This attitude, however, is specious. We *feel* our way through the world, thinking *with* feelings, because a mind "is neither an airy spirit nor an exquisite computing device but a creaky old calculator sunk in a sticky swamp of feelings. . . . In truth, we think because we feel what we are."[42]

Although it may be possible to follow an "objective" procedure, every protocol is based in a specific worldview about what is important, as well as conscious and unconscious presuppositions. Euro-American perceptions, for example, are generally biased toward focusing on foregrounded objects rather than on a whole picture and its relationships, which is more typical of Asian cultures.[43] The "view from nowhere" that Western science employs actually represents a perspective of subject-object separation that is uncharacteristic of most thought systems.[44] Science has moved away from objectivity as indwelling, a first-person view of "feeling-with,"[45] to an externalized, third-person view of detachment.[46] Western culture has defined this view as intelligence, but it is emotionally and relationally detached and is harmful when applied in Nature, which does not match up with abstractions of a third-person view. Ironically, because neuroscience uses devastatingly cruel methods of investigation when it comes to Animals, this branch of science has been a strong contributor to changing the dominating perspective and attitudes about feelings and emotions—even in nonhumans.

Emotions are now appreciated as essential for healthy development and lifelong functioning.[47] Recognition of the importance of emotion has led to the establishment of *affective neuroscience,* the study of the neurobiological basis of emotions.[48] They play a key role in how we react, act, and make decisions. Indeed, they are core to who we are.[49] Emotions are formative to the development of an ecological sense of self and an understanding of ourselves in relation to the diverse social and physical environments in which we live. Processes of emotional development are part of becoming aware of ourselves as a bounded entity (self-coherence), how we can and do affect others by our actions (self-agency), feeling (self-affectivity), and the continuity of our personal narrative as we move through life (self-history and autobiography).[50] Feelings are not hardwired instincts but rather are developed through experience. Emotions are shaped by multiple factors: the sensations we feel in our bodies, who and what we encounter, and cultural values and norms.[51] They are sensitive players in meaning-making and helping us discern our bodies, thoughts, and feelings from those of others.

At their foundation, emotions are part of consciousness and cognition, and initiators of *conation* (the volition or will to do something). Our basic emotion systems are centrally placed in the brain to readily interact with both cognitive structures and physiological and motor outputs.[52] Prior to studies in affective neuroscience, psychological theories treated emotion and cognition as separate entities. But when we look more closely at brain structure, processes, and functions, we see that this separation is artificial.

The function of *appraisal* (how the brain cognitively assesses what is important to the self), for example, includes perception, evaluation, attention, memory, and executive functions, which involve areas throughout the brain, from the brain stem to the cerebral cortex. Emotions, which are attributed to *arousal*, including action tendencies, attention, and feelings, are generally placed in the brain stem, hypothalamic structures, and cerebellum. Appraisal is actually brought about by corticolimbic activities. Subsequently, cognitive and affective processes and functions overlap in the brain. At the neuronal level in the cortex, there is no distinction between cognition and emotion.[53] Because of the integrated nature of the brain and its operations, it is much more useful to view emotion and cognition as one functional, interdependent unit. There is no emotion without a thought, and no thought without emotion. Our actions are informed by both.[54]

Emotions are an infant's first tools. Babies are automatically geared to learn physical and emotional associations, valence, and value. Associative learning in the midbrain modifies basic functions that govern attention and alertness, thereby providing a baby with a way to learn from a given experience. Every experience involves dual coding of physical perception and emotional response—*What do I sense?* and *What is my reaction to it?* Integrated cognition and emotion are part of development for every Animal. Intelligence relies on *veridical* (coinciding with reality) cognition and well-functioning emotional systems. Early life experience influences which emotions are prioritized, which ones are more easily activated, how well they support our cooperation with others, and which actions we learn to favor.[55]

Because babies' brains are shaped by who and what they encounter, they are motivated and ready to take imaginative action when they are born. In the womb, fetuses have already begun to develop self-organizing habits and a personality in response to experiences in the womb. Under good nested care during the first year of life, an infant's amygdala begins to connect with the brain's orbitofrontal gyrus (involved in the cognitive process of decision-making) and the anterior cingulate gyrus (involved in the emotional, autonomic motor system), which builds the infant's capacity to understand and organize emotions.[56] When early experience is neglectful, abusive, or traumatic, an individual will have difficulty recognizing and interpreting emotions appropriately,[57] undermining social and moral behavior.[58] This is why healthful, species-appropriate caregiving characterizing the evolved nest is crucial.

Socioemotional development begins immediately after birth, involving the rapid growth of complex, interconnected brain and hormonal processes. We can look at these processes at three different levels.[59] *Primary-process* psychological experiences, available at birth, are basic, built-in emotions including physiological drives such as hunger, thirst, and sensory reactions to pleasure and displeasure. They seed selfhood and continue to develop further with experience. *Secondary-process* psychological experiences develop via learning within the basal ganglia, structures like those found in the body and legs of an Octopus. Early-life learning develops through a *fear* system (via the basolateral and central amygdala), *instrumental and operant conditioning,* such as the exploration system (via the nucleus accumbens), and *habit formation,* such as emotional and behavioral habits (via the dorsal striatum). Postnatal caregiving has the greatest effect here and is formative in shaping personality and preferences through effortless, nonconscious learning.

Tertiary-process psychological experiences entail more conscious cognitive processes. For this reason, they are more accessible to memory. These processes include executive functions (governed by the frontal lobe), emotional orientation and regulation (governed by the medial frontal region), and "free will," represented in higher working memory function. Early experiences with carers play a role here as well, although later life experiences can have a significant influence because executive functions take up to three decades to develop fully.[60]

While all three levels of socioemotional development are influenced by cultural patterns and values, tertiary processes draw heavily from cultural narratives to interpret our experiences. The third level guides carer behavior and thus has the potential to alter *secondary* processes in the child through carer treatment, and thereby can significantly inform the development of sociality and morality. Together, primary, secondary, and tertiary neural-emotional systems come together to create our personalities. With supportive care, they promote our well-being and provide effective solutions to basic questions of survival: *How do I stay intact? How do I get what I need? How do I keep what I need? How do I get and keep social supports?*

Through ongoing experiences of intersubjectivity—shared emotional and mental states—infants start on the pathway to socioemotional intelligence. Young children are in a receptive state during their first years, ready to embed in their personalities what they experience about self and the world, building habits by mirroring the actions of those around them. They are primed to learn how to relate well,[61] and they are wired for social interaction. Nested care is designed to respond accordingly.

Nested care teaches and tunes socioemotional systems.[62] These systems are the source of practical intelligence. When children's companions treat them receptively, these capacities develop in healthy ways through reciprocal communication. A child is immersed in a stream of emotional-cognitive exchanges that guide proper action, ways of being and behaving that are congruent with the social and natural environment in which all grow and live. Carers attune to the infant's changing expressions of energy to help ensure an optimal state of being. Another way to put it is that they tune up their baby's emotions, fluidly using multiple modes of connection, including voice, touch, and movement. In this way, playful interactions between carer and child enhance the child's physical, visceral energy. Through this process, repeated many, many times, human carers and babies build customs together, creating shared stories and games of rhythmic musicality accompanied by ever-present nonverbal expressions of intention.[63]

This period of life is a very sensitive time emotionally and neurobiologically. Babies react, for example, with "pride" when appreciation is shown of their meaningful action, and with "shame" and distress when a conversation partner is nonresponsive.[64] Something as simple as a hug, a snuggle, or an embrace—or a lack thereof—initiates short- and long-term effects in the toddler. The range of external gestures experienced by a child directly translate internally to program body and mind.

Carer-initiated neurohormonal processes facilitate the infant's capacity to develop central and peripheral response control of his emotions with his orbitofrontal cortex.[65] Repeated, positive, and synchronized caregiver-child interactions shape baby's self-regulation capacities through organizing connections among the orbitofrontal cortex, mesocortical, and mesolimbic pathways.[66] Empathy, self-regulation, eye gaze, facial expression, the experience of social pleasure, sensitivity to others, and an understanding of others are all cultivated, governed by right hemisphere development.[67] All of this is centrally involved in implicit learning and unconscious relational processes throughout life.

Consistent affectionate nested care ensures that the baby's brain and coupled cognitive and emotional development function well.[68] As we have already discussed, left-cradling is an example of how this is accomplished through mother-baby geometry, which optimizes the flow of information from the infant's left ear and eye to the mother's right hemisphere and vice versa. Signals between the dyad promote a "relational unconscious" that includes both consciousness and unconsciousness. As Allan Schore notes: "This right-lateralized emotional brain is deeply connected into the body and the autonomic nervous system (ANS). It has a different anatomy, physiology, and biochemistry than the later-forming left hemisphere. The right hemisphere processes not only emotion but, more precisely, unconscious emotion and is the locus of an implicit procedural memory system."[69] In other words, early carer-infant relationships work on the physical and psychological levels to cocreate a right-lateralized system of mind and body.

Unnested care, abuse, or neglect, on the other hand, directly interferes with right hemisphere development. Notably, core faculties governed by the right hemisphere have increasingly diminished in schoolchildren as a result of unnested care and institutional emphasis on cognitive skills. The recent parallel rise in bullying, violence, suicide, and asociality has prompted efforts to integrate social and emotional learning into school curricula.[70] This is also why early trauma, neglect, and abuse have such deep and long-lasting effects.

Responsive environments enhance our positive emotions and calm down our negative emotions, shaping a self-regulated, cooperative personality and coherent self. They set the patterns for the strength and connection of emotion systems.[71] When properly developed, emotions facilitate successful adaptation to the environment, and they generate in the child a sense of confident competence and secure attachment, thereby signaling that neurobiological structures are developing in a healthy manner.[72]

Subtle and careful reading of and responses to an infant's cues help babies refine emotional and physiological experience and increase social capacities.[73] Over time, in literate cultures perception and action uncouple and become mediated by *symbolic thought* (the use of abstract concepts through words, gestures, and numbers). Abstract ideas that emerge from lived experience retain their emotional flavoring in memory, though symbols learned in emotionally detached settings (such as classrooms) are often not retained in memory. Psychiatrist Stanley Greenspan and philosopher Stuart Shanker describe affect and emotions as "the source of symbols, the architect of intelligence, the integrator of processing capacities, and the psychological foundation of society."[74] But are these key social processes present in Octopuses?

Socially, Octopuses do not seem to show the intimacy shown by Mammals, Birds, and Reptiles. Although there is great variability among Octopus species, compared to the constant proximity of Elephants to one another, Octopuses seem much less dependent on close exchanges with fellow Cephalopods. Indeed, in some instances intraspecies relationships seem strained and fraught. But to label Octopuses as "asocial" is both anachronistic and inaccurate. As the old maxim says, "Absence of evidence is not evidence of absence." Other Animals have also been labeled asocial until it was eventually discovered that, similar to human cultures that vary hugely in their ways of interacting, Animals who do not spend a lot of time together still develop deep relationships. These relationships just work from and in different spatial and temporal frameworks.

For example, biologists used to define Pumas as the quintessential conspecific Lone Rangers who never associated with each other, save for sex. Their presumed asociality was regarded as extreme, to the point of intraspecific lethality. But when the data were examined more closely and added to observations collected from motion detector technology, researchers discovered that Pumas enjoy a rich social network, including sharing precious kills.[75]

The lesson is that each and every organism has its own social Umwelt, its own ways of interacting and forming relationships, not only with their own species but also with other Plants and Animals. The more we strip away culturally embedded projections and assumptions reified by Western science's self-proclaimed authority, the more we see and understand about our Animal kin.[76] Indeed, when Octopuses' nearly unsurpassed abilities to change body color, patterns, and texture are revisited and viewed from this perspective, we discover deep emotional and psychological waters within them—in particular, a highly refined *emotional intelligence*.

Early-life experiences are central in the development of emotional intelligence, the capacity to understand and regulate one's emotions appropriate to a situation and in socioecological interpersonal interactions. Psychologist Daniel Goleman defined emotional intelligence with four criteria: *self-awareness* (the ability to perceive what we are feeling and why), *empathy* (knowing what someone else is feeling), *self-regulation* and management (the ability to handle distressing emotions appropriately), and *comprehensive skills* that bring all of these qualities together for appropriate thought and action.[77]

Emotional intelligence is inextricably accompanied by *social intelligence*, a concept first coined by Edward Thorndike in 1920.[78] Social intelligence generally refers to the ability to understand and respond appropriately in interactions with another. In a broader, Nature-inclusive understanding, social intelligence encompasses ecological intelligence. Social and emotional intelligence work hand in hand and are cultivated in the evolved nest to optimize living well with others in sensitive and respectful ways. Octopuses seem to do this well by using their partnered head-arm brains, fantastic coloration language, and extensive RNA editing. Although young Octopuses do not receive postnatal care emblematic of altricial species, they are nonetheless raised with equal devotion.

Octopuses are *semelparous,* meaning that they lay eggs and give birth only once in their lifetimes. There is between-species variation, but generally, Octopuses find and secure a den where they lay thousands of eggs. The mother Octopus stays with her brood, protecting them and fanning them with freshly oxygenated water until they hatch, after which, similar to Salmon, she succumbs, having not eaten for the entire gestation period. Given the increasing evidence of the critical role that parent-embryo-egg communication plays,[79] it would not be surprising if we one day discover that Octopus maternal care may impart its own version of prenatal shaping.

In any case, Octopuses cultivate and make use of their keen socioemotional intelligence, which is sensitive to their own state of being as well as that of those around them, to navigate successfully in their underwater world. There is broad variation among Octopus species' personalities and cultural practices. Some are described as very curious, even gregarious, literally reaching out to meet and greet human divers and accompanying shoals of fish; others are less so.[80] Their well-known curiosity is an expression of their depth of interest in others, a social proclivity to associate with and understand their neighbors and anyone else who comes in peace without the intention of predation. While the classic Mammalian right brain seems to be absent (even though Octopuses are, like humans, bilaterally organized), Octopuses, Squids, and Cuttlefish demonstrate comparable body awareness, sense of self, social awareness, empathy, ability to interpret sociality and emotional cues, and capacities to regulate stress and mediate their behavior, all of which are integral to socioemotional intelligence.[81]

Octopuses' profound emotional intelligence is apparent when they accomplish something amazing, such as escape from captivity. One Octopus named Inky (whose body, not including arms, was about a foot in diameter) managed to squeeze through a tiny opening at the top of a National Aquarium of New Zealand exhibit, fall to the floor, and, although an aquatic creature, make his way on the ground into a 164-foot-long drainpipe, which fed into the ocean waters of Hawke's Bay, and disappear—never to be seen again by human eyes.[82] He accomplished this by being fully cognizant of his body state and its relationship to the environment. Inky also exercised Daniel Goleman's third criterion of emotional intelligence, self-regulation. Given the literal lengths that he went, one can imagine his tremendous pent-up passion to escape his prison and be free. Yet Inky managed these deep emotional impulses. He bided his time to plan his escape, and he acted when the right moment arrived.

As Octopuses move around their watery home, their self-awareness and empathy allow them to evade dangerous carnivores, such as Pyjama Sharks who live off the coast of South Africa, where Octopuses are plentiful. Evasion is successful only if one judges one's physical abilities to move and dart on the correct path at the right speed (self-aware), and if the pursued rightly assesses the mental and physical states of the pursuer (empathy). A more tender expression of empathy is shown in the documentary film *My Octopus Teacher,* where diver Craig Foster and an Octopus become friends and develop a trusting, loving relationship. Their interactions and expressions depict a tremendous sense of shared care and understanding.[83]

Octopuses demonstrate the fourth criterion of emotional intelligence through their ability to integrate all the other dimensions of this capacity. Inky, for example, was able to gather the necessary information derived from internal stimuli (self-aware, subjective information communicated via his version of the limbic system) and external stimuli (empathetic, objective information about the lay of the aquarium and the outlet pipe's connection to the ocean), time his actions correctly (self-regulation), and then, putting this all together, judge the appropriate strategy with a measure of confidence and self-efficacy.

For Octopuses, however, all this recent scientific attention and human discoveries bring a mixture of good and bad news. On the one hand, Octopuses and other invertebrates are now receiving greater respect and appreciation. On the other, they are also being seen as a new source for human genetic medicine research, to assess disease pathogenesis and progression.[84] This means that various species of Octopuses are, similar to other Animals, bred in captivity by the millions[85] and subjected to procedures that are ethically banned for use on human subjects. Octopuses are now being heralded as the "new lab rat," following the fates of those countless Animals who are subjected to the most heinous, painful, and obliterating experiments for the purpose of fueling Western science's insatiable appetite for information, no matter the cost to life.[86] Octopuses are yet another entry in Western science's list of profound ethical-epistemic disconnects.

If Octopuses, Rats, Cats, and Planaria are adequate models of human brains, minds, and emotions for use in experiments prohibited for our species, then nonhuman species qualify for as much protection as humans are afforded. Instead of adding another set of persons to science and society's list of victims, we would do best by adopting the Octopus's emotional and social intelligence, which is expressed less by what they do than the fact that they do not do to us what we do to them. This is another lesson from the connected companionship worldview.

Moral Commitment

Gray Wolves

THEY SAY THAT Wolves avoid anything that has been touched by a human. Even a Moose carcass left as bait, so tempting, so needed in the depth of winter, will be avoided. Perhaps it was layered snow that rendered the trap so invisible to eye and nose that it caught the female Wolf unawares. She was gripped by the steel teeth for two weeks. Her partner remained with her until the trapper came back and shot her dead. After her death, the male traveled fourteen miles back to the natal den. He then began to furiously clean out the burrows that were buried under several feet of snow. The next day, he ran back the fourteen miles to where his love had lain. After a while, he left her and trotted over to a plateau where he sat and began to howl. Over the next two months, the male returned regularly to the death site, even after he had partnered with another female. One day, the male Wolf trekked over twenty miles to return to the trapping site. His new mate could not keep up. Eventually, she left and *joined another group. Four months after his beloved's death, the Wolf continued to make his pilgrimages. In April, he connected with a second new female, but she was killed. He narrowly escaped only to die himself within the week, shot by hunters.*

What makes a society—Wolf, human, Penguin, or otherwise—livable and healthy depends on the quality of its moral commitment, the desire to respect and support the wellness and rights of others.[1] Moral commitment is a natural, integral part of child raising in companionship cultures.[2] Understanding and acquiring a moral sense is not something that you are told or that you think—it is embodied through experience in community.[3] Moral commitment must be experienced, because our neuronal systems are shaped by our culture's values, and values infuse how we live, make decisions, and interact with one another. Our neural connections are literally shaped and wired by our experiences and our natural sense-making of those experiences. They help us discern and evaluate what we know and feel internally relative to the external world.

Adult morals, which coalesce at the societal level, are highly influenced by initial brain wiring of the emotion circuitries that are set in babyhood.[4] How an infant is brought into the world and what they experience in the first years of life lay down foundational tracks of who they will be, how they will behave, and what they value in the future and as an adult. From neuroendocrinology and immune function to sociality and morality, the early years of life are strong determinants of adult mental health, physical health, and ethics—and those of society as a whole.[5]

The first moral commitment that a nested baby experiences is a *social engagement ethic*. It emerges in the loving presence of carers when a baby is met with reverent hospitality, empathy, ongoing synchrony, and mutual influence.[6] On the other hand, if a baby experiences carers who do not demonstrate nestedness and moral commitment, a wedge or gap can develop in the continuum of connection.[7] Children raised in unnested care are therefore prone to learn detachment and lack of open-hearted commitment to others because they did not experience moral commitment themselves. While moral commitment can be cultivated later in life with others, such as with a grandparent, these values may not take root as deeply as when habits of mind and heart are built from the ground up.[8] This situation is characteristic of settler-colonizing cultures that dim sensory perception and awareness, distancing all from Animal kin so that "self-interest is promoted over the interests of community and the tenor of moral authority has moved from community values to the valorisation of the globalised individual."[9]

In Nature-based cultures, however, social engagement ethics are woven into a lifestyle of collective interactions.[10] Companionship in these societies nurtures flexible relational attunement, the capacity for engaging in loving interpersonal dances with others, enabling a lifelong ethic to treat others— including nonhumans—with hospitality, respect, and reverence. Social enjoyment and interpersonal enhancement are the coins of daily life.[11]

Nature-based cultures such as the Maori are imbued with a social engagement ethic that is *ecological.* An ecological engagement ethic is one where humans "and the world are bound together by ties of kinship and people must accept the associated responsibilities . . . [and that] everything in the universe has its own *whakapapa* (genealogy), that is part of the unified whole."[12] Life takes place in a Nature-inclusive plural.[13] As New Zealand professor of outdoor education Mike Boyes describes it, "We treat the earth with the care and respect we show to a parent and are prepared to be guardians and stewards of it as we are reconnecting with the interdependent nature of our existence." This "recognition that all things have *mauri* (life essence)" undergirds respectful relationships. "As individuals, we are spiritually nourished by knowing we have a rightful place on the earth and knowing well the specific places where we belong. *Turangawaewae* (a place to stand) comes with moral commitments to take full responsibility for the well-being of the features and organisms within that place."[14]

Intergenerational, Nature-based ethical resonance sustains Nature's coherence and well-being. When looking out across a landscape at the fullness of mountains, expansive grasslands, and endless skies, we experience Nature's moral commitment to us in the generosity of her gifts and in the peace and coherence we feel. The same sense of peace and moral coherence comes from following Nature's evolved nest patterns and processes.[15] These patterns of ecological and moral shaping are found among every species, no matter their lifestyle. While most people are open to accepting that Animals such as the herbivorous Elephant possess a sense of morality, they are less apt to extend this understanding to Bears and Wolves. But, as we have previously witnessed, the true nature of Nature is often hidden by layers of human projections, and Gray Wolves are no exception.

In the form of one subspecies or another, Wolves have lived interleaved in human cultures for thousands of years throughout Europe, North America, most of Asia, and Africa's north. Many cultures identify Wolves as part of their heritage. The Celtic high king Cormac mac Airt, who was said to have been raised by a mother Wolf, is one example; the Ainu of Hokkaido, Japan, are another. The Ainu attribute the willingness of Wolves to help humans in distress to an ancestral White Wolf–goddess union. We find similar respect in Egypt, where the venerated deity Anubis is not a Jackal, as previously assumed before DNA analyses, but a Wolf.[16]

These positive cultural narratives clash with popular European and conquest North American stories told 'round the campfire and bedsides of wide-eyed children on wind-torn nights, depicting helpless Red Riding Hoods, hapless Pigs, and princesses at the mercy of menacing Wolves. Wolves in Europe and settler-colonial North America were, and still are, typically stereotyped as aggressive, competitive, vicious, and incapable of empathy for anyone but their mate or pup. When scientific and historical data are examined, however, Wolf-on-human aggression is almost nonexistent. Unprovoked attacks on humans by Wolves are extremely rare, with most committed by rabies-infected individuals.[17]

Seasoned scientists—such as Gordon Haber, who spent a half century with Alaska's Denali Wolves—describe a very different character, one threaded with themes of care and kin. Haber describes Wolf society this way: "A group of wolves is not a snarling aggregation of fighting beasts, each bent on fending only for itself, but a highly organized group of related individuals or family units, all working together in a remarkably amiable, efficient manner."[18] As this chapter's epigraph—adapted from Haber's observations—illustrates, Wolves form deep, emotional bonds and display intense grief when their mate or other family member dies.[19]

Much of the bias against Wolves comes from Europeans and settler-colonizers who saw Wolves as formidable competitors and challengers to human supremacy, an attitude that was fortified by the Christian Bible, which associates Wolves with evil.[20] The Wolf's propensity to eat other Animals, like other obligate carnivores, also has something to do with it. Wolves, however, are not that different from herbivores. Just as groups of Wolves eat Moose and Elk, groups of Elephants and Elands consume savanna Grasses. The main difference is that while herbivores travel to find their meals, they don't have to hunt them down, nor do they require help from family and friends in order to eat. Elephant nourishment is stationary, found beneath their feet or in the architecture of a Tree. An Elephant family may rely on elder wisdom to find water and food, but it does not take an entire family to secure a mouthful of Grass. Wolves also rely on matriarchal knowledge, yet in most cases they must partner with family members to achieve nourishment.[21]

Wolves have to search for, locate, and then catch moving food. Unless the meal is smaller than a Deer, the endeavor requires participation by the entire group. Wolf bodies, minds, and social organization have evolved for this purpose. Sighting, stalking, and taking down an individual, such as a Moose, is a formidable task that demands intricately choreographed physical, mental, and communicative prowess to succeed. Only approximately 5 percent of Wolf-on-Moose hunts in winter result in a successful kill.[22] Much like the evolved nest practices of our human ancestors and other Animals, an individual Wolf works with and for the many of her group.

Rick McIntyre, who has studied Yellowstone Wolves in detail for almost thirty years—including fifteen summers spent in Alaska and three in Glacier National Park—recounts a story of how a family of Wolves stole an Elk body from two young Grizzlies.[23] The two young Bears were likely siblings who had recently emerged from hibernation in need of calorie-rich sustenance. When the Wolf family spotted the young Bears at the Elk carcass, the family "worked as a team: two charged at the bears and drove them away from the calf while another ran to the carcass. The bears turned around and ran at the two wolves behind them. One swatted at a wolf with a front paw, but missed. Unable to deal with the harassment, the young bears left the area, and the five wolves took over the kill."[24]

Hunting is serious business exercised with parsimony.[25] When hunting is not required, carnivores and omnivores generally follow a "live and let live" policy. Haber relates, "I've seen moose and caribou walk right through or near a homesite with wolves present but flaked out in the daytime heat. In one case a cow moose nearly stepped on a resting Savage River wolf, but moose and wolf ignored each other."[26] Charlie Russell, who lived immersed in Grizzly and Brown Bear societies, witnessed how harming and killing in the wild functions on a must-need basis. Carnivores operate on a "I won't hunt you when I am not hungry" ethic.[27] Even European explorers, who came from countries that regarded Wolves as terrifying enemies to be persecuted and hunted down without question, were astonished when they saw Indigenous tribes, such as the Ohlone of Turtle Island, living peaceably alongside carnivores.[28]

Wolf families are well-disciplined and are generally headed by a female and her mate in a supportive leadership role (frequently referred to by biologists as an "alpha" pair). Finding food is a priority, but at its heart, the task is driven by the imperative to maintain protection and care for the group and their young.[29] Raising children is Wolf social glue.[30]

The Gray Wolf evolved nest is a social, emotional, and physical compound comprising an extended family and an associated area or territory as large as a thousand square miles.[31] The extent and definition of a viable territory depends on multiple factors, including group size, number and proximity to other Wolf families, food abundance, and availability of adequate denning sites, water, and cover, most of which vary with climate and circumstance. As Haber notes from his observations and those of Adolph Murie, which together span nearly a century: "Complex systems such as wolf societies can be expected to behave in counterintuitive, nonlinear ways, with lags and discontinuities."[32] This implies that, ideally, a territory has enough spatial flexibility to accommodate change and allow Wolves to move fluidly to obtain what they need.

In most places, however, Wolves' ability to move with Nature's metabolism has been eliminated. Yellowstone National Park, for example, is home to ten Wolf groups in thirty-five thousand square miles, which means it can get "crowded." Also, unlike modern humans, Wildlife cannot be held to jurisdictional boundaries. They have to make a living in a dynamic land-scape. The unwillingness to recognize even science's logic has created enormous pressure and challenges for Wolves. Even though Yellowstone Wolves have been protected since being reintroduced to the park, if any of them leave the park they are considered fair hunting game. In 2021 twenty-five Wolves (20 percent of the Yellowstone population) were killed because they strayed outside the narrow bounds of the park.[33] All of these dangers and restrictions trickle down into family functions.

In precolonial, preslaughter settings, a mother Wolf in Alaska bears her young in the communal den in May, after two months' gestation. In the more temperate Yellowstone, this happens in April. Pups remain within the den area for about five months. Similar to Beaver lodges, Wolf dens are part of a burrow-and-chamber complex that can reach twenty to thirty feet in length. The homesite complex is not limited to the underground. Aboveground, there is a well-laid-out design, including places where the young can play in safety and freedom, bed areas for resting, and lookouts for spotting danger. Strategically placed in hillsides and near streams, the honeycomb of homesites is often arrayed in clusters to facilitate family and interfamily connection and communication. The overall space, which can encompass up to thirty or more acres,[34] accommodates a meeting ground where the entire community can gather.[35] Some complexes are estimated to be a century or two old, a testimony to an ancient tradition and well-developed culture.[36]

Culture is not limited to the creation of cathedrals, paintings, and con-certi. At its core, culture embodies attitudes, philosophy, values, and ontologies generated and processed by ancestry, all of which inform morality. A nested culture is one that nurtures flexible capacities that cultivate a life-long engagement ethic. Central to Nature-based cultures is the interstitial transmission of values and learning through brains, behaviors, and con-sciousnesses that are morally committed to community well-being. Haber notes that the Wolf "basic social framework is programmed in the genes, but important details are 'tuned' via learning to fit available resources . . . thus providing the society with much flexibility and adaptability. These details are so adaptable that they last for generations—families therefore develop traditions. The result of this collection of traditions can be viewed as culture."[37] It is within this space that the body and mind of a young Wolf is planted and grows.

Prior to birthing and for subsequent months, Wolf family members remain close to the homesite, interrupted only by foraging outings.

> There is a group effort in raising and training [the young], the cooperative effort of many. In these and other respects, wolves, like our own human ancestors, have developed a highly effective means of coping with a wide variety of ecological conditions. . . . Life within a family group, which in most cases is an extended family of pups, parents, grandparents, uncles, and cousins, including even newcomers, is replete with ceremonies, divisions of labor, and other variations in behavior that adapt them to a variety of changing conditions.

As an example, one male Wolf stayed with the lead couple, even during their courtship and mating, and continued to remain close to help prepare the den for birthing. He effectively "performed the major duties of fatherhood," and, Haber concludes, "virtually all family members help the parents," which makes it "largely meaningless to distinguish between parent and nonparents at this time of year."[38] These relationships make up the ethical architecture of family group function, variously attended by mother, father, yearlings, and other members of the family.[39] Young developing brains map these experiences, which are rooted in cultural practices.

After birth, every infant, human and Wolf, begins an intensive and rapid journey of development. Baby brains are self-organizing systems initially governed by the brain stem and limbic system, both of which guide cognitive growth but are shaped by experience.[40] The quality of early relationships that a baby experiences also relates to one kind of quantity: the number of neuronal connections the baby develops. Every species has its own timetable of rapid brain development, which in altricial species is largely associated with the period of nursing and dependent care.

During the critical time from human conception to about six years of age, synapses—information bridges between neurons—are created at a faster rate than at any other time in the life span.[41] Between bursts of neuronal production, synapses undergo "pruning": elimination of unneeded connections. This process continues through the third decade of life.[42] An infant's experiences determine what is not needed and results in the pruning of excess synapses. The initial overabundance of synapses, however, is not for naught; that would go against Nature's waste-not-want-not parsimony. Pruning is best viewed as a process of shaping a child's internal map to match and align with those around them. A baby's neural spring "bloom" readies them for postnatal experience. Babies of all species are acutely sensitive to what they experience. Spring blooms and successive pruning are designed to optimize a baby's ability to come into limbic resonance and develop mutual empathy with those they experience in the moment. Neural and behavioral plasticity is an ingenious way of shaping a baby to fit into the precise environment in which they live.

Moment by moment, loving reactions and responses that are experienced with and promoted by the caregiver are foundational for seeding a social engagement ethic, an egalitarian, socially responsive, and flexible orientation.[43] The engagement ethic is dependent on developmentally appropriate care during infancy and childhood because the systems underlying it are epigenetically molded, requiring co-construction by experience that fosters the circuitries in the brain necessary for sociality, largely dependent on right hemisphere development.

Practices of the evolved nest foster species-normal moral development.[44] Sensory experience builds patterns of importance and differentiation, shaping attention, orientation, and the child's perceptual and experiential capacities according to their culture.[45] The culture of *Homo sapiens-amans amans* will shape a different being from the culture of *Homo sapiens-amans aggressans* or *arrogans*. The experienced patterns engrave upon the child a set of moral values—a *habitus*, "a history turned into nature"—that is carried forward into life.[46] "The characteristic ways in which one is led to focus on and attend to others can become directly incorporated into individual systems of experiencing and organizing the world" as selfways.[47] It is only certain human cultures that have denied their young nested care, violated Nature's patterns, and undermined species-normal social and moral development.

As the landmark Adverse Childhood Experiences studies have shown, when early care is toxic and traumatic, psychophysiological systems that undergird social and moral development are constrained, leading to a limited capacity for positive social engagement. Psychiatrist Sigmund Freud intuited correctly what neurobiologists would ascertain a century later when he asserted that his patients' psychological problems were physiological footprints of past experiences.[48]

Infants who experience routine stress and adversity are compelled to put their energies into surviving instead of growing according to naturally scheduled developmental needs. As Gordon Neufeld and Gabor Maté note: "Down to the very cellular level, human beings are either in defensive mode or in growth mode, but they cannot be in both at the same time."[49] In these cases, as a child matures, they are likely to react to social encounters with self-protection rather than openness and empathy.[50] Negative associations and memories experienced during early development can lead to a proliferation of negative attitudes and diminished empathetic capacities in adulthood.[51] Illness is more likely,[52] and without the moral threads that make up the evolved nest, children do not acquire a sense of social or ecological responsibility. Their sense of self is not only limited; it is disconnected from life-enhancing opportunities.

A baby's sense of self begins before birth in relationship, in their mother's womb, with or without an eggshell. An individual self-system is part of the continuity of being, gradually refined by the responsiveness of the baby's carers. Self is only known in relation to others. For 25 percent of their natural life span, young Wolves are dependent on adults.[53] Self-development involves processes embedded in the presence and context of many. This reflects, as Gordon Haber notes, "one of the hallmarks of an advanced society: prolonged dependency (or neoteny) of the young enables the society to transfer large stores of accumulated past learning to each new generation."[54] Wolf mothers and carers create a relational field of holistic support through touch and caresses—a womb of spirit through embodied love. Within this sensed knowing of safety and belonging, children build the confidence and resources to show themselves to the world and grow with assurance that their basic needs will be met.

Being present to the baby from the first awareness of their existence in the womb to moments immediately after birth is vital for developing compassionate morality.[55] Companionship caring fosters a full, healthy sense of self and self-in-relation-to-others, including the nonhuman, which includes an understanding of autonomy with responsibility.[56] Carer nurturance maintains the continuity of self-and-others by bridging the shift from womb to world.

Transitioning from union inside the mother to separation outside her requires nested support to prevent feelings of vulnerability or loneliness. Without safe birthing followed by the constant safety of nestedness, a child may withdraw into a self-protective psychophysiological shell, stunted by fear, deprivation, and even despair. Continual assurance of security ensures a child's innate affinity for connection and exploration, companionship ethics flourish, and a promising life story begins.

Self-development is an embodied experience of being and existing that expands over time. Through active, positive participation in interpersonal experiences, a child develops diverse aspects of selfhood, including autonomy, freedom, self-consciousness, and moral responsibility. Their selfhood journey begins with a *protoself*, a first coherent sense of being.[57] A *core self*, a sense of self-as-body, is fostered by the synchrony of action with affectionate carers during social play, feeding, and snuggling.[58] In time, an *autobiographical self*[59] nucleates through the knitting together of diverse, discrete events and experiences into a coherent narrative.[60]

Neurobiologically, the periaqueductal gray medial frontal cortical areas work with the reticular activating system—a set of brain stem nerve pathways connecting the spinal cord, cerebrum, and cerebellum[61]—to form a network that functions as a critical source of awareness, blending cognition and emotion.[62] These systems have evolved to develop properly through the experiences of nestedness.

The protoself and core self form what we might call a *minimal self*, or multiple minimal selves as they change, situation by situation. An *extended consciousness* knits together and brings coherence to the diverse sets of minimal selves experienced minute by minute, day by day. Processes such as interoception are performed by a minimal self in the moment, and they serve as intermediaries between the environment and the actions the youngling exerts in interactions. Over time, core self-development threads together a sense of being across past, present, and future, creating a fuller sense of self.

In the technoindustrial urbanized world, it is easy to forget how we are integral to the ecologies in which we have evolved. Humans, Beavers, Parrots, and Wolves are born into an ecology, an evolutionary environment that has coevolved with previous generations and coevolves with us as we live. Wolf, human, and Penguin ancestral senses of self are experienced by and characterize an individual, but one whose identity extends beyond the singular. It is a diffuse self, an eco-self, inclusive and reflective of the context—social and ecological—in which a child develops. With a diffuse self, instead of a static self that hobbles consciousness through greater and greater efforts to establish one's separate merit and existence, an individual is able to stay floating in heart-mind, the coupling of sensory experience and feeling, deeply connected to the whole of Nature, a common self of existence.[63]

With the building blocks of relational attunement, the natural inclination and desire to *fit in* Nature (*sensu* Russell) are seeded.[64] Early life sets up an empathic universe for the self, *empathic effectivity roots*, which constitute unconscious procedural knowledge about emotional connection to and awareness of effects on others.[65] The nested individual operates as a hub of many selves with whom she is joined and with whom she shares a mutual ethic. There is no being without shared social relations—*one lives with others in mind.*[66] Every detail of Wolf family dynamics and baby care reflects this understanding, philosophy, and practice. The Wolf natal space is filled with responsive nursing, nuzzling, and play laced with learning the nuanced ways of Wolf etiquette and wisdom. Pleasurable and joyful intersubjective attunement brings limbic resonance into relational communion. One way this natural bond is reinforced is through touch and grooming, which older Wolves provide to their pups.[67] Play is another.

As Beaver cultures beautifully demonstrate, play is a practice ground for learning body knowledge, ethics, and interpersonal skill sets; at the same time, play lays down neural networks of joy, culture, and love. As young Wolves mature, older Wolves, often yearling siblings, accompany them on "puppy walks" to "rendezvous sites" in the complex, where exploration can be undertaken in safety. In August and September, the final days of the five-month homestay, young Wolves experience a threshold event affecting self-development: they leave the natal compound with their families and step into the open world.

Infant Wolves, like the infants raised by our human nomadic-foraging ancestors, emerge from and into wholeness. They are part of an intricate tapestry woven by minds and lives into the ecology, experienced and transmitted over millions of years. Evolutionary developmental biology, the study of how organism development evolves, emphasizes this intermingled, purposeful organization within an organism that is informed by multitudinous processes and actors in space and time. Our becomings, our worldings, are intertwined. Self-development, also called *autopoiesis*, of various physiological systems is partnered with a relational world of *sympoiesis*, communal co-development.[68] Self-development does not occur in a void.

By definition, it unfolds in a relational world of *sympoietic entanglement*. While humans may sometimes feel alone, isolated in our individual bodies, such separation is an illusion. We are not alone. We do not live alone. We become-with others, developing, growing, and living symbiotically, in companionship. They cocreate us in sympoietic entanglement. For example, each individual is populated with trillions of bacteria and fungi that comprise that person's microbiome. We are host of and are hosted by many other species inside, on, and outside our bodies.[69] As Humberto Maturana and Francisco Varela say, "We have only the world that we bring forth with others, and only love helps us bring it forth."[70] The tree of life, as Charles Darwin described, is layered with sexual, parental, and social instincts, all of which lead to a moral sense.[71] Returning to our ancestral *Homo sapiens-amans amans* heritage begins with the biology of love in early life and the ethic of ecological engagement with all others in our world. Baby, carers, and ecology are partnered.

Each species evolved to want and require particular physical and psychological resources that their evolved nest provides. American psychologist Abraham Maslow identified several basic needs and ordered them in a pyramidal hierarchy.[72] But infants require them all, and more,[73] for physical and psychological support.[74] The provision of basic needs for self-actualization, and how and when they are provided, are the rain, sun, and soil nurturance required for healthy infant development. Nestedness evolved for this very purpose—to provide the buffering for any set of genetic components to ensure optimal conditions for development.

If, however, babies are not welcomed into the world, they do not intuit or feel a social multiverse. Unnestedness ungrounds children from ancestor-normative organization of the protoself. Self-development, self-esteem, self-agency, and self-fidelity are undermined.[75] This is especially visible in neglected or physically or sexually abused human children, who are generally less likely to develop a positive sense of self and can become detached from and unaware of their feelings.[76] Instead, a "false self" may be created as a shield against a perceived threatening environment.[77] One's true self may become buried and obscured under layers of false selves, thereby creating disorientation and a distorted sense of morality. A child can become separated from and unreceptive to a balanced flow of attunement and support, leading to an inner feeling of emptiness that reflects the vacuum of unresponsive care experienced during critical phases of self-development.[78] Nested care obviates these externally driven internal splits.[79]

Despite the social, emotional, and practical tuning provided by nested care, young Animals and humans are on a steep learning curve when they enter the world in which they will live as adults. In the case of young Wolves, there is a marked shift when, after spending five months at or in proximity to the natal den, they leave with their families to take part in the broader environment. Many show fearfulness when confronted with the vast newness. There is a wealth of novel, and sometimes, confusing, smells, sounds, tastes, and encounters. Young Wolves are charged with learning essential skills: how to cross a river safely, how to stalk a Moose, proper responses to Bears and humans, how to find the way home to the den, and so on.[80] They enter a surround of distinct polyphonic voices in the ecology they traverse.[81] All this, however, occurs within the embrace of the Wolf family group.

As they grow, young Wolves, like nested human children, are busy problem-solving, building and integrating self-body-mind. They are always in relationship and accompanied, whether by each other, mother, father, other elders, yearlings who have transitioned from complete dependence to partial independence, or the surrounding ever-changing ecology. Soon, by winter, young Wolves settle into apprenticeship.

Some of the most challenging and important lessons revolve around finding and catching food. Developing keen hunting skills is imperative. A lot is at stake. Hunting requires tremendous expenditure of energy, and any brash, unthoughtful action can lead to injury, which, in the wild, is often fatal. Subsequently, before any pursuit can be launched, all manner of factors need to be weighed. Not all Moose and Caribou are the same, and individual states and circumstances influence the hunt outcome. An experienced Wolf has developed hunting acumen and emotional intelligence for this purpose. Relative to their elders, young Wolves often take extra time when testing the suitability of a Moose or Caribou as a candidate for pursuit. In this learning phase, young Wolves frequently "overreact," for example, by misjudging how fast and clever a Raven is. After chasing a Raven to near exhaustion, they often end up unsuccessful, with no Raven prize in hand.[82] The youngsters are still "in school" for good reason.

Errors in judgment—along with successes—are processes and experiences that refine self-regulation and self-knowledge that began with early, responsive care. By the time they are yearlings, young Wolves have developed a much deeper sense of self, competence, and relational understanding that enable them to join the group more fully. Learning and self-development continue throughout life and are always exercised in relationship. Developing independence is not the same as individuality. A Wolf self is always relationally defined. Everything about Wolves—hunting, child-rearing, sharing knowledge, and allocare—is communal and cooperative.

Finally, after two or so years, when they near sexual maturity, a young Wolf has come into self-perception as a whole being, sympoietically with full participation in the group—that is, with self-organized social, psychological, and physical systems in an entangled "making with" others.[83] Similar to Nature-based human cultures, Wolf days and lives unfold communally. Everyone contributes in accordance to what is needed and when. When, for example, there is a need for a mother's exceptional tracking skills, artfully coordinated with her male partner and the rest of the group, others step in to help out. This "frees the mother, who is generally a more experienced hunter than any of the young helpers, to join the hunt."[84] Similar to Sperm Whales, Wolf nursing is provided by other mothers or childless females who begin to lactate so that "mothers nurse each other's pups interchangeably . . . [and] nonmothers also lactate, sometimes even one-year-olds."[85] When young Wolves begin to wean, an elder Wolf will return with regurgitated food, gifts that include fleshy morsels and body parts for the young Wolves to gnaw and feed on.

Unnested care is not found among nonhuman Animals unless they have been traumatized by human activities.[86] In parallel with their Earthcentric human neighbors, Wolves have suffered severe trauma and loss of elder wisdom. Multigenerational cords of Wolf companionship cultures have been severed and family cohesion destroyed by pernicious European and settler-colonizer mass killings. The footprint of historical trauma suffered by Indigenous peoples is echoed in Wolf cultural biographies.

By the mid-1900s, US government extermination programs had eliminated Wolves in the lower forty-eight American states, with the exception of small, isolated pockets in Wisconsin, Minnesota, and Michigan.[87] The Gray Wolf was "pursued with more determination than any other animal in United States history."[88] Until hunting resumed outside Yellowstone Park, Wolf-on-Wolf fatalities, including intraspecific, intrafamilial killing of adults and pups as well as incidents of intense intergroup attacks and killings, were the number one cause of death among Yellowstone Wolves.[89] Such incidents and behaviors appear to contrast with Denali Wolves in Alaska, who are reported as an extremely prosocial society with an absence of intraspecific violence.[90]

Unlike the Denali Wolves, who, until recently, have been relatively "unexploited" and able to maintain their traditions and culture intact,[91] the Yellowstone Wolves have experienced a history of violence. The reintroduced Yellowstone Wolves are not all related; they were imported from Alberta and British Columbia, Canada, where populations sustained intensive hunting. The reintroduction program involved further traumas: capture, crating, and being transported to the park, where they went through a period of captivity in acclimatization pens. The Wolves were finally released but were psychologically and physically vulnerable. They found themselves in a completely unfamiliar area, with no local ecological knowledge and not knowing if other Wolves were present. The next year another group of Wolves was reintroduced, with no prior history with or relationship to the first group.[92]

All of these events and circumstances took Yellowstone Wolves far outside the realm of nested care and historically normative Wolf culture. Neuropsychology predicts that the signature of these traumatic events would emerge intergenerationally. According to psychological criteria, the reintroduced Wolves are candidates for a diagnosis of complex PTSD (like the young male Elephants who also suffered a series of profound traumas). In contrast with what Haber described among Denali Wolves, Yellowstone Wolves have exhibited intraspecific aggression, infanticide, and asociality.[93] A description of systematic Wolf killing—which is still in effect outside the park and elsewhere, and which nearly extinguished the species in the United States—reads as being nearly identical to what happened to the Elephants:[94] "Picture a family group of wolves, parents, current pups, earlier offspring—together in the hills interacting in all their ebullient, highly advanced ways. Then imagine the scene transformed into panic and chaos as one or two planes suddenly appear just over a nearby ridge and, in a blast of blowing snow, swoop down ten feet over the wolves. One by one, wolves are targeted and chased to exhaustion. As they flee, they fall head over heels in the snow, crash head-first into trees, and attempt to hide in thick brush. The gunner leans out of the plane and shoots wolves, killing some, but not all, of this family of wolves, leaving the rest—often the younger, less experienced wolves—to fend for themselves."[95] Life has continued to change for Alaskan Wolves, and those elsewhere, with the proliferation of hunting and trapping. It can no longer be claimed that Wolves are unexploited.[96]

The individual Wolf is a constellation in form, mind, and purpose. All of the dramas of life—joyful, frightening, exhilarating, sorrowful—are shared. Wolves demonstrate this through speech, touch, work, and play with each other and how they monitor each other's states of minds and wellness. Their repertoire of howls and calls keep them in near-constant touch and fortify cohesion. Much of this social and ecological unity is invisible to modern human eyes. At times, however, Nature's heartbeat breaks through even the most conditioned mind.

In 2009, when Gordon Haber's plane crashed into an Alaskan mountainside, the Wolves knew that their colleague, companion, and champion had died. Friends of Haber's who were hiking in the vicinity of the crash, unaware of the accident and Haber's death, suddenly heard a chorus of Wolf howling of a strength and length they had never heard during their twenty-five years of residence in Alaska.[97] Though Haber was human, the Wolves had grown to know him as a friend, as one in the many and the many in the one of Wolves.

The Peace of
Wild Things[1]

In our exploration of Earth's breathtaking complexity, on the one hand we have obtained only a glimpse of the existential, ethical, and ontological depths of Wildlife experience. On the other hand, by using the lens of neuropsychology to focus on the heart of Wildlife cultures—namely, the rearing and care of their children—we have been graced with a more intimate entrée into the inner worlds of these remarkable beings. As it is for all Animals, it is with our children and for our children that we are most vulnerable. Our journey was undertaken with this understanding. It brings many lessons.

Each Animal, each Plant—each individual—of the Earth community evolved with its own Umwelt,[2] its unique perceptual and sensory experience of the world, whether it is the African Elephant's twinned infrasonic and seismic communiqués, Amazon Parrots' ultraviolet missives, or Sperm Whales' complex system of clicks. Much of this, as Chief Luther Standing

Bear (Teton Sioux) reflected, is beyond most human ken: "The character of the Indian's emotion left little room in his heart for antagonism toward his fellow creatures. . . . For the Lakota, mountains, lakes, rivers, springs, valleys, and woods were all finished beauty. Winds, rain, snow, sunshine, day, night, and change of seasons were endlessly fascinating. Birds, insects, and animals filled the world with knowledge that defied the comprehension of man."[3]

Yet among this diversity, there is a common theme. We share with Animals capacities for consciousness, feelings, thoughts, and dreams. Cross-species similarities are predictable because the Earth's diversity of species grows from the same substrate: Nature.[4] "That which the tree exhales, I inhale. That which I exhale, the trees inhale. Together we form a circle. When I breathe I am breathing the breath of billions of now-departed trees and plants. When trees and plants breathe they are breathing the breath of billions of now-departed humans, animals, and other peoples."[5]

Until recently, Birds, Fish, and Reptiles were regarded as lacking neural and psychological capabilities comparable to those of humans and other Mammals. Comparative neuroanatomical studies, however, show that while Mammalian and Avian brain evolution may have diverged, psychological evolution has converged. As the Cambridge Declaration notes, "Birds appear to offer, in their behavior, neurophysiology, and neuroanatomy a striking case of parallel evolution of consciousness."[6] Even those who are more remote from us on the evolutionary tree are not so distant when it comes to inner complexity.

Invertebrates such as the Octopus, with whom human ancestors parted evolutionary company hundreds of millions of years ago, share with vertebrates the same brain processes that govern experiences and abilities we cherish ourselves.[7] Core neural mechanisms are common across phyla. This is why, despite the vast diversity of outer shapes, sizes, and colors, Animal kin and their lifeways feel so familiar. But, as we have seen, we share something more.

Unless disrupted by outsiders, Animals and Plants follow evolution's path of wellness for their young in the welcome embrace of community. Everyone in Nature's gifting culture receives and gives in return. Life supports life in a constant flow of mutualism[8] and symbiosis.[9] Under the guidance of family and ancestors—and, in the language of Western science, experience and genes—young Animals learn how to live and thrive in their land, water, and skyscapes. This set of processes and structures constitutes the evolved nest.

Nestedness is integral to all of Nature. It is evolution's design for creating wellness and positive resonance across generations.[10] The evolved nest provides children with the social and ecological microenvironment harmoniously tailored for their optimal growth and health. To ensure this continuity and resilience, every species has evolved its unique niche. The physical Beaver niche, which comprises a complex of dams, lodges, canals, and ponds cohered by the social network of the Beaver family, is exquisitely suited to meet the internal and external needs of baby Beavers. The Emperor Penguin niche accomplishes the same despite the radical differences in climate and terrain. All nests evolved to meet the biological, social, and psychological needs of the young through similar child-raising practices, whether the Animals in question are Gray Wolves, Elephants, or humans. Their diversity is united by the same ethics and principles embodied in the evolved nest.

Essential Elements of the Evolved Nest

Nature gifted us with accompaniment and companionship by a host of relations beyond our own species, from the sun and moon to the Plant and Animal companions on and in our bodies and in our neighborhoods. Within this companionship, each species evolved its nest, a set of practices that represent a biology of love, love in action. The evolved nest comprises at least ten essential elements:[11]

- a welcoming social climate;
- soothing perinatal experiences;
- extensive breastfeeding;
- nearly constant touch;

- accompanied care from mother and others;

- self-directed play;

- responsive relationships;

- Nature immersion;

- connected holism; and

- routine healing practices.

From the perspective of the neurosciences, evolved nests co-construct each of us from the bottom up—from the functionality of the vagus nerve, neurotransmitters, and stress response, to numerous nonverbal skills and understandings upon which more sophisticated empathy and sociality build.[12]

As we witnessed among African Elephants, from conception onward a mother and child are supported and **welcomed into a community that accompanies them** throughout life. Children must feel an invitation to exist in our presence, exactly the way they are.[13] Commensurate with Nature's ways, humanity's heritage is similarly grounded in a gifting culture.[14] Nested communities take responsibility for a mother's body-mind support throughout gestation and child raising.[15]

For many species, a child first experiences unilateral gifting from mother, or in the case of an Emperor Penguin, father, who is accompanied by other fathers.[16] For humans, **soothing perinatal experiences** follow nine months of safety inside mother's body, succeeded by several years of intensive post-natal support by mother and others. Companionship care—for example, in the case of the father Penguin who cares for the egg that will soon become a baby—provides the necessary intersubjective scaffolding for healthy neuro-biological development.[17] **Extensive breastfeeding** is a Mammalian design for on-request feeding initiated by the infant and produced by a mothering body. Emperor Penguin fathers accomplish this without breasts, using milk generated by their crop in the protective embrace of feathered pouches.

One factor that is integral to infant brain-body nurturance is intimate, **nearly constant touch,** whether a trunk's caress, a furry nuzzle, an inquir-ing beak, or a ready nipple. Holding, touching, and caressing grows the brain toward prosociality by orienting a baby to love and safety.[18] Babies soak up loving attention through their skin, their first medium of communication with the outside world.[19] Contented babies cuddle down into and wrap around their mother's bodies, an understanding of which is reflected in the practices of many preconquest Nature-based peoples, such as the Ye'kuana, who traditionally carry their younglings with them everywhere.[20]

Elephant and Sperm Whale children are unerringly accompanied by family constellations of responsive **allomothers.** Allomothers bridge any gap to ensure that a child is never without love and positive support. We see this in our own ancestry. The evolutionary split of *Homo sapiens-amans* from other hominids coincided with a move toward communal child raising[21] to accommodate a large brain that requires extensive pre- and postnatal support from a community of carers.[22]

Self-directed, creative social play is central to body-mind self-organization[23] and social, connected development. This kind of spontaneous whole-body social play is called "original play" by O. Fred Donaldson, meaning "to engage in a metapattern of belonging that connects life forms across species and cultural barriers. Original play is a gift of Creation; it is our birthright. When we truly play, we are authenticated by all things."[24] It enables us to join a universal energy of being in the moment with one another, letting go of a limited ego-self to receive others in the unity of *no-self* with kindness, compassion, and fearless vulnerability. Play allows one to learn that life is constant birthing of new *being* in an unfolding cosmos.[25] The joy of being is also especially felt when shared with others during a sunset or other holistic sensory-emotion coupling experiences. Beavers, famed for their hardworking industry, provide a sterling example of the three togethernesses—working, living, and eating—integrated together in the accompanied pleasure of families at play.[26] Play is something that all can relearn, including parents and families.[27]

Responsive care from mothers, fathers, and others is instrumental in nurturing healthy ways of living with our social and ecological communities. In loving reciprocity and collaboration, carer and child mutually share intentions, interests, emotional exchange, and understanding.[28] Starting from birth, babies discover the relational nature of communication and of life on the whole. They are born with the expectation of partnered existence and the experience of intersubjectivity, a shared experience of being that fosters deep sociality. Evolved nest care meets these evolutionary expectations.

Nature immersion and Nature attachment are the heritages of every Animal, including human beings. As scholar Vine Deloria Jr. (Standing Rock Sioux) writes, "The Sioux people cherished their lands and treated them as if they were people who shared a common history with humans."[29] Nature-based communities "recognize that the world is full of persons, only some of whom are human, and that life is always lived in relationship with others."[30] Such communities live in diversity embedded in oneness, mutual respect, and self-responsibility. Gordon Haber witnessed this in the case of Moose and Gray Wolves. Tensions between herbivores and carnivores arise only when exigencies of survival demand it.[31]

When we align evolved nest practices with kinship or Indigenous worldviews[32] and with the maternal gift economy,[33] it is apparent that **connected holism** is central to Nature's way. In all examples of relationship and child-rearing among humans and other Animals, *connection* is central. First is connection of the child to self, the unfolding of mind in accordance with place in the world (embodied cognition). Simultaneously, there is connection to elders—mother and others. Connection is maintained through extensive physical presence, touch, responsive care, and play. Father Penguins, mother Bears, and diverse constellations of carers midwife the transition from internal to external regulation of the infant's psychological and biological development. Obedient to the needs of the growing member(s) of the community, adults do not resist meeting the child's needs; rather, they generously provide what they sense the child requires for healthy growth according to the species' supportive nest. Finally, the circle of connection extends beyond the family and species community to the world of Nature.

Connectedness to the rest of the natural world is fundamental. "The life of Native American peoples revolves around the concept of the sacredness, beauty, power and relatedness of all forms of existence."[34] Among our Animal cousins, such connection is normative because Animals and Plants live in entangled ecosystems. But we do also. We just need to recognize this fact. As nineteenth-century German philosopher F. W. J. Schelling said, "As long as I myself am identical with Nature, I understand what living Nature is as well as I understand myself."[35] Nature lies inside and outside each individual, which is why, despite hurricanes, wildfires, landslides, and other changes in the environment, Nature retains her coherence.

We witness Nature's coherence when we experience the peace and quiet in a forest or standing at a lake's edge. At these moments, Schelling reflected, "Mind is invisible Nature, while Nature is visible mind."[36] This coherence co-regulates our biology to intersubjectively connect with the beings around us. Charlie Russell describes this coexistence in relationship where "there [is] mutual respect and caring for others. You can't have a positive relationship if you want to control someone. . . . We are brainwashed to think that nature is here for humans, that nature is infinite and we can do what we want with bears and the land without any consequences. Of course, this doesn't make any sense and doesn't even agree with science. Thinking that we can get away with this, thinking that humans are stronger and smarter than nature, actually makes us weak. If you fit in with nature, you are stronger because you aren't using up all your energy fighting nature."[37]

Psychobiological attunement is the main ingredient for empathic understanding and optimal emotional and social development.[38] Initially, it is the duet of attunement of infant and carer during which the infant's sense of self is seeded and becomes known in a relational, social world. Then it extends beyond. Even semi-"precocious" Beavers, who are able to walk and swim soon after birth, require sensory attunement, which begins in their mother's womb, followed by companionship care in the intimate quarters of the family lodge with parents and siblings, before they are ready to launch out into their aquatic neighborhood. A child's embeddedness in their natal landscape is fundamental to learning how to live fully and well—so fundamental that, because of "Nature deficit disorder," numerous initiatives are underway to encourage rewilding of children.[39]

Growing one's potential takes connectedness and a *holistic becoming*. Abraham Maslow made an attempt to describe wholeness. His path to awareness gives us some insight. After being educated and published in Western experimental psychology, Maslow was transformed after spending a summer with the Blackfoot (Siksika) tribe. He was astonished at what he found: tribe members were what he described as "ego secure"—they felt at home in a benevolent psychological world—which is the opposite of being neurotic. Instead of neuroses he found a common personality of "dignity and friendliness and containing little insecurity, suspicion, envy, jealousy, antagonism and hostility or anxiety."[40] Instead, tribe members displayed "feelings of being liked and loved; the perception of the world as a warm and friendly place; a tendency to expect good to happen; feelings of calm, ease, and relaxation; self-acceptance; a desire for adequacy with respect to problems rather than for power over people; social interest; cooperative-ness; kindliness; interest in others; and sympathy."[41]

Impressed by the tribe members' psychological health, Maslow shifted his scholarly emphasis to **growing full potential.** He was seminally influenced by the actualization orientation of the Blackfoot (who did not emphasize the *self* in actualization, but rather the individual's *gift* to the community). "Each person fit and belonged and was secure. . . . Each person was valued, welcome, protected, included, taught to give back, and pro-vided the opportunity to become actualized."[42] For the Blackfoot, actualiza-tion was the foundation of becoming human, not the last achievement in a human life.[43] "To truly 'raise' a child, then, would be to bring that child to his or her full potential as a human being."[44]

Animal children, and children of human foraging communities, do not learn how to live and thrive from books. They experience life fully from observing, imitating, and being guided by community members through play and engagement.[45] They learn in embodiment, with all their senses.[46] This is another reason why it is important for children to learn about them-selves in the mother of all—Nature—and understand what it means to be integral as a part of—not *apart from*—the landscape in which they live. This encourages the building of receptive intelligence,[47] which requires deep engagement in timeless reality (ancestor-mind) and perception of deeper patterns (pattern-mind).[48] Holistic learning is rooted in right hemisphere development, which is scheduled to take place more rapidly in early childhood.[49] This involves gathering experiences from which to form a worldview and know-how for living, shaping habits and automaticity for cooperation. It is whole-body learning, building motivation-emotion-cognition-skill together.[50]

By definition, Nature-based human cultures immerse their children in community life, modeling virtuous behavior—kindness, empathy, gratitude—through ceremonies of respect and practices honoring the natural world.[51] They tell stories as guides for living and practice ceremony throughout the day. The community stands back to let the child find their way, refraining from interrupting the child's concentration, agency, or exploration.[52] Any awkward explorations, gestures, or emotions are greeted with playful, patient responses. It is understood that these are merely ways of learning and gaining balance that are tuned up by loving, attentive, and morally engaged carers.[53] A holistic approach means that the child guides their own learning with a focus less on verbal learning and adult teaching than on developing heartsense and listening to Nature's voices.[54] "Indigenous knowing," physicist David Peat asserts, "is a vision of the world that encompasses both the heart and the head, the soul and the spirit. It could no more deal with matter in isolation than the theory of relativity could fragment space from time."[55]

Among Nature-based peoples such as the Lakota Sioux and the Ye'kuana, children are nurtured to feel at home on the Earth in the human community but also to feel connected to the universe on a spiritual level.[56] As Vine Deloria Jr. (Standing Rock Sioux) underscores: "At the deepest philosophical level our universe must have as a structure a set of relationships in which all entities participate. Within this physical world, this universal structure can be best understood as a recognition of the sacredness of places."[57]

Children are encouraged to find their spiritual connections to place and to Animal and Plant peoples through traditional practices. Mourning Dove (Okanagan Salish and Colville) describes how young children were sent out at night to hunt for a guardian spirit and were encouraged to receive a vision.[58] With maturation, young people who were prepared to do so participated in deep explorations such as vision quests—several days of fasting and isolation in a high place—as a critical step in solidifying a connection with the universe beyond the ego, something sorely missing and deeply needed in modern societies.[59]

A sense of disconnection develops when components of the evolved nest are missing. Disconnection is traumatic for a baby. Separating a human infant from their carer and placing them in a pen or crib, in a room alone, are forms of solitary confinement—a severe punishment for any age. Much like the trauma of solitary confinement in prisons, relational connection is cut off, and agency curtailed.[60] For a young one, this is hell. Perhaps it is a different circle of hell for orphans who can hear other children crying in nearby cribs, but it is still the abyss. This enforced separation violates all aspects of the nest: a welcoming climate, touch, responsive care, social play. A young infant has no sense of time, of temporariness, of parents in the next room.[61] The trauma is engraved in the body-brain, remembered ever after, and the feeling of abandonment and rejection becomes a fearful shadow following just behind. The violence done toward baby reverberates through the life of the individual, the society, and the planet.

Much of the modern world has forgotten what wholeness looks like in a human being and human communities. There has been a widespread "extinction of experience"[62] of the natural world and Nature's ways. The lack of nest provision extinguishes all sorts of experiences that shape our humanity, from Nature-receptive intelligence to deep empathy roots to communally inclusive imaginations. Most modern industrialized adults lack capacities that are intrinsic to nested communities, such as intelligence receptive to a sentient Earth;[63] a humble sharing orientation to the needs of others,[64] including children; multiperspectivalism and polymorphic perception of the world;[65] and a transpersonal sense of self (kinship-mind).[66] The evolved nest enables the development and expression of these capacities that maintain moral sense.[67]

The final component of the evolved nest is a particularly acute need for our species today: **routine healing practices.** Animals display a plethora of healing practices—such as instinctively eating clay or particular herbs for stomach upset or analgesics for pain—that, along with the ability to range freely in the landscape, keep them in balanced good health despite frequent encounters with pathogens.[68] Animals help one another heal. Matabele Ants, for instance, have "paramedics" who assist wounded mates, and Deer and Rabbits groom a vulnerable friend and lick their injuries.[69] There are other, innumerable examples of other intra- and interspecies care and compassion.[70]

Healing practices are greatly needed in modern cultures. When a small group of humans stepped off the path of Nature-based wellness, they started down a trauma-inducing pathway.[71] Human minds were uprooted from the continuum of Nature's way. As Charlie Russell puts it, they ceased to "fit in" with the rest of Nature.[72] Alienated from Nature, the modern world promotes disconnection from body, heart, and spirit. Not only have many humans become divorced from Animal kin; their minds have also detached from their bodies. Life has ceased to be an embodied, inclusive celebration of mutual appreciation and care. This has led to social and ecological trauma, crises and chaos gripping the entire planet. Modern, unnested societies are deeply wounded and scarred from the primal trauma of the disconnection between self and Nature.[73]

Healing practices are needed now, especially for those who did not experience the fullness of the evolved nest or compensate with mitigating experiences. Without companionship support, fear and anxiety soak into our neurobiology from the experience of unmitigated distress and unmet needs. The individual who experiences an excessive amount of early stress can be shaped for antisociality[74]—a detour from humanity's evolution—because that person will be less able to live, thrive, reproduce, and become a well-functioning community member.

Healing practices are a part of humanity's heritage. They are often communal, holistic, and integrated into everyday life.[75] There are diverse examples of healing practices,[76] ceremonies, and methods, including those of Indigenous peoples from around the world, that can inspire individuals and communities.[77] The San People, for example, whose communities have been in existence for two hundred thousand years or more, conduct healing ceremonies nearly every week. Ju/'hoansi People practice all-night healing ceremonies to cure ill bodies and minds; mend the social fabric through a respectful, manageable release of hostility; and enhance humans' and Nature's physical, mental, and spiritual well-being.[78] Healing transformation takes place through the sharing of *n/om*, the spiritual energy that "boils over" to all through trance dancing and laying on of hands by group healers who experience *!aia,* a form of enhanced consciousness. A Ju/'hoansi elder explains: "Being at a dance makes our hearts happy,"[79] suggesting that there is a greater sense of essentiality and authenticity: "I want to have a dance soon so that I can really become myself again."[80]

Implicit in evolved nesting, and in Nature's wild, is holding presence. Only by being fully present, back in our bodies, heart-centered in feeling-with others "living out of our minds,"[81] will we be able to behold the living Earth and our place in it. "Mindful awareness can bring into consciousness those hidden, past-based perspectives so that they no longer frame our worldview. Choice begins the moment you disidentify from the mind and its conditioned patterns, the moment you become present. . . . In present awareness we are liberated from the past."[82] Other community-based healing practices common among Nature-based peoples may be needed, such as gathering in community to dance, drum, sing, and play spontaneously,[83] building *communitas*[84] and collective effervescence.[85] Individual Nature immersion through sit spots,[86] earthing, gardening, and sunning are also rejuvenating.

Nurturing Humanity Back to Nature's Ways through Lifelong Nestedness

Humanity used to be universally well integrated with Nature, with the rhythms of Earth, moon and sun, Animals and Plants, in a particular locale.[87] Our humanity was nurtured by our integration with these systems and our ability to live and dynamically change with them.[88] Although humanity's evolved nest is critically important in the first five years of life for brain-body-mind foundations, it is also critical for supporting our humanity *throughout life.* This means that even adults need welcoming social climates, responsive relationships, affectionate touch, self-directed play, Nature immersion, connected holism, and regular healing practices.[89]

The evolved nest provides the cultural commons for helping humans back to Nature's ways of building the cooperative, mindful, generous personalities visible in nested communities around the world.[90] Nested companionship has evolved to provide the appropriate nourishment and experiences that will enable and maintain perceptual, emotional, communal, aesthetic, and moral integration in body and mind. Nestedness promotes partnership—whether with other people or with the more than human—instead of domination.

Western, Nature-dissociated thinking that has generated widespread social and ecological malaise is not sufficient to solve the climate crisis and mass extinctions, nor to heal human and nonhuman hearts, minds, and bodies. By adopting and cultivating Nature-based practices that promote thriving in individuals and communities, we all can reknit and revive the vitality of our planet.[91] Instead of building technologies to escape reality and Earth, we can, like the Octopus and other Animals, direct our complex brains and minds to cultivate the beauty in which we live and care for everyone around us, all our kin. A gentle approach starts at the grassroots with changing our own actions as part of a complex system, embracing uncertainty and diversity, adjusting our actions as we go, and patiently watching for tipping points when deep change becomes viral.[92]

Nestedness is not just for children. We become fully human by "owning up to being animal, a creature of the Earth. Tuning our animal senses to the sensible terrain: blending our skin with the rain-rippled surface of rivers, mingling our ears with the thunder and the thrumming of frogs, and our eyes with the molten gray sky. Feeling the polyrhythmic pulse of this place—this huge windswept body of water and stone. This vexed being in whose flesh we're entangled. Becoming earth. Becoming animal."[93]

We can all renest and reconnect ourselves and our communities with Animal kin and the heritage of Nature-based living, where we fit into the peace of Nature, the wild, and embrace our place in the planetary community.[92]

Suggested Readings and Resources

WEBSITES

https://EvolvedNest.org
https://Kerulos.org
https://KindredMedia.org
https://naturemindfulness.org

BOOKS

Carnivore Minds: Who These Fearsome Animals Really Are by G. A. Bradshaw
Neurobiology and the Development of Human Morality: Evolution, Culture and Wisdom by Darcia Narvaez
Restoring the Kinship Worldview: Indigenous Voices Introduce 28 Precepts for Rebalancing Life on Planet Earth by Wahinkpe Topa (Four Arrows) and Darcia Narvaez
Talking with Bears: Conversations with Charlie Russell by G. A. Bradshaw

Acknowledgments

We thank the many who have mentored us on our life journeys to this time and place. To name a few: Brown Bears, Elephants, Octopuses, Beavers, Emperor Penguins, Gray Wolves, Sperm Whales, Amazon Parrots, and alphabetically:

Deeksha Agrawal	Jennifer Mather
André Ancel	Rick McIntyre
Robin Bjork	Ashley Montagu
Anne Borchardt	Jaak Panksepp
Greg Cajete	James Prescott
C. Sue Carter	Allan Schore
Lokesh Coomar	Gerhard Schwab
Olivia Crossman	Deborah Slicer
Richard and Leanna DeNeale	Barbara Smuts
Susan Donohue	Alan Sroufe
Ben Goldfarb	Elizabeth Marshall Thomas
J. Zoharah Hieronimus	Wahinkpe Topa
Marybeth Holleman	Genevieve Vaughan
Sarah Hrdy	Sam Wasser
Diana Hulet	Mary Watkins
Melvin Konner	Hal Whitehead
Tommy R. Lapin	Jenny Wiegand
Tom and Carolyn Long	Gypsy Wulff
Gabor Maté	Jon Young

With gratitude to NAB for their guidance and support throughout the process.

Notes

Foreword

1 Wade Davis, *The Wayfinders: Why Ancient Wisdom Matters in the Modern World* (Toronto: House of Anansi Press, 2009), 13.

A Note on Terminology and Sources

1 Gregory Cajete, *Native Science: Natural Laws of Interdependence* (Santa Fe, NM: Clear Light Publishers, 2000); Jessica Hernandez, *Fresh Banana Leaves: Healing Indigenous Landscapes through Indigenous Science* (Berkeley, CA: North Atlantic Books, 2022).

2 Gregory Younging, *Elements of Indigenous Style: A Guide for Writing by and about Indigenous Peoples* (Edmonton, Alberta: Brush Education, 2018).

3 Jinting Wu, Paul William Eaton, David W. Robinson-Morris, Maria F. G. Wallace, and Shaofei Han, "Perturbing Possibilities in the Postqualitative Turn: Lessons from Taoism (道) and *Ubuntu*," *International Journal of Qualitative Studies in Education* 31, no. 6 (2018): 504–19, 517.

4 G. A. Bradshaw, *Carnivore Minds: Who These Fearsome Animals Really Are* (New Haven, CT: Yale University Press, 2017).

5 Wahinkpe Topa (Four Arrows) and Darcia Narvaez, *Restoring the Kinship Worldview: Indigenous Voices Introduce 28 Precepts for Rebalancing Life on Planet Earth* (Berkeley, CA: North Atlantic Books, 2022).

6 F. David Peat, *Blackfoot Physics* (Boston: Weiser Books, 2001), 5.

7 Cajete, *Native Science*, 2.

8 Cajete, 19.

9 https://globalsocialtheory.org/concepts/settler-colonialism/; www .oxfordbibliographies.com/view/document/obo-9780190221911/obo -9780190221911-0029.xml.

1. Nature's Way

1 G. A. Bradshaw, *Carnivore Minds: Who These Fearsome Animals Really Are* (New Haven, CT: Yale University Press, 2017), 2–3; Daniela C. Rößler, Kris Kim, Massimo De Agrò, Alex Jordan, C. Giovanni Galizia, and Paul S. Shamble, "Regularly Occurring Bouts of Retinal Movements Suggest an REM Sleep-Like State in Jumping Spiders," *Proceedings of the National Academy of Sciences* 119, no. 33 (2022): e2204754119; Philip Low, Jaak Panksepp, Diana Reiss, David Edelman, Bruno Van Swinderen, and Christof Koch, "The Cambridge Declaration on Consciousness" (Francis Crick Memorial Conference, Cambridge, UK, July 7, 2012), https://fcmconference.org/img/CambridgeDeclaration OnConsciousness.pdf.

2 Darcia Narvaez, *Neurobiology and the Development of Human Morality: Evolution, Culture, and Wisdom* (New York: W. W. Norton, 2014). Also see these open access papers: Darcia Narvaez, "Getting Back on Track to Being Human," *Interdisciplinary Journal of Partnership Studies* 4, no. 1 (March 2, 2017), https://doi.org/10.24926/ijps.v4i1.151; M. Tarsha and Darcia Narvaez, "The Evolved Nest: A Partnership System That Fosters Child Wellbeing," *International Journal of Partnership Studies* 6, no. 3 (2019), https://doi.org/10.24926/ijps .v6i3.2244; Darcia Narvaez, L. Wang, A. Cheng, T. Gleason, R. Woodbury, A. Kurth, and J. B. Lefever, "The Importance of Early Life Touch for Psychosocial and Moral Development," *Psicologia: Reflexão e Crítica* 32, no. 16 (2019), https://doi.org/10.1186/s41155-019-0129-0.

3 Gilbert Gottlieb, "On the Epigenetic Evolution of Species-Specific Perception: The Developmental Manifold Concept," *Cognitive Development* 17 (2002): 1287–1300, https://doi.org/10.1016/S0885-2014(02)00120-X; Robert Lickliter and C. Harshaw, "Canalization and Malleability Reconsidered: The Developmental Basis of Phenotypic Stability and Variability," in *Handbook of Developmental Science, Behavior, and Genetics,* ed. D. E. Hood, C. T. Halpern, G. Greenberg, and R. M. Lerner (New York: Blackwell, 2010), 491–526; Karola Stotz and Darcia Narvaez, "Niche," in *Encyclopedia of Personality and Individual Differences,* ed. V. Zeigler-Hill and T. Shackelford (New York: Springer, 2018), https://doi.org/10.1007/978-3-319-28099-8_1554-1.

4 Gabor Maté and Daniel Maté, *The Myth of Normal: Trauma, Illness, and Healing in a Toxic Culture* (Garden City, NY: Avery, 2022).

5 Jean Liedloff, *The Continuum Concept: In Search of Happiness Lost* (Cambridge, MA: Perseus Books, 1977), https://continuumconcept.org/.

6 Liedloff, *Continuum Concept,* 10.

7 Liedloff, 8.

8 Vine Deloria Jr., *The World We Used to Live In: Remembering the Powers of the Medicine Men* (Wheat Ridge, CO: Fulcrum Publishing, 2006).

9 Genevieve Vaughan, "Introduction: A Radically Different Worldview Is Possible," in *Women and the Gift Economy,* ed. Genevieve Vaughan (Toronto: Ianna Publications, 2007), 1–40; Thomas Widlok, *Anthropology and the Economy of Sharing* (London: Routledge, 2017); Donald Worster, *Nature's Economy: A History of Ecological Ideas,* 2nd ed. (Cambridge, UK: Cambridge University Press, 1994).

10 Haunani-Kay Trask, *From a Native Daughter: Colonialism and Sovereignty in Hawaii,* rev. ed. (Honolulu: University of Hawaii Press, 1999), 32.

11 The term "Nature-based" refers to human communities that live according to the principles and ethics of Nature, as nonhumans do.

12 Liedloff, *Continuum Concept.*

13 Aldo Leopold, *A Sand County Almanac* (New York: Oxford University Press, 2016); Arne Naess and D. Rothenberg, *Ecology, Community and Lifestyle* (Cambridge, UK: Cambridge University Press, 1989).

14 Gregory Cajete, "Philosophy of Native Science," in *American Indian Thought: Philosophical Essays,* ed. Anne Waters (London: Wiley-Blackwell, 2004), 47–55.

15 Vine Deloria Jr., *Spirit & Reason: The Vine Deloria, Jr., Reader,* ed. Barbara Deloria, Kristen Foehner, and Samuel Scinta (Wheat Ridge, CO: Fulcrum Publishing, 1999), 46.

16 See also Geralyn Gendreau, *Jungle Jean: The Captivating Biography of Jean Liedloff* (Birmingham, UK: Precision House Publishing, 2021), www .junglejean.com.

17 Narvaez, *Neurobiology.*

18 Riane Eisler and Douglas Fry, *Nurturing Our Humanity* (New York: Oxford University Press, 2019); Douglas P. Fry, Geneviève Souillac, Larry Liebovitch, Peter T. Coleman, Kane Agan, Elliot Nicholson-Cox, Dani Mason, Frank Palma Gomez, and Susie Strauss, "Societies within Peace Systems Avoid War and Build Positive Intergroup Relationships," *Humanities and Social Sciences Communication* 8 (2021): 17, https://doi.org/10.1057/s41599-020-00692-8; Douglas P. Fry, *The Human Potential for Peace: An Anthropological Challenge to Assumptions about War and Violence* (New York: Oxford University Press, 2006).

19 Wade Davis, *The Wayfinders: Why Ancient Wisdom Matters in the Modern World* (Toronto: House of Anansi, 2009).

20 Bradshaw, *Carnivore Minds;* G. A. Bradshaw, *Talking with Bears: Conversations with Charlie Russell* (Victoria, BC: Rocky Mountain Books, 2020).

21 Four Arrows, "The Media Have Missed a Crucial Message of the UN's Biodiversity Report," *The Nation,* May 20, 2019, www.thenation.com/article /archive/biodiversity-un-report-indigenous-worldview.

22 Darcia Narvaez, "Ecocentrism: Resetting Baselines for Virtue Development," *Ethical Theory and Moral Practice* 23 (2020): 391–406, https://doi.org/10.1007 /s10677-020-10091-2.

23 Clive Ponting, *A Green History of the World: The Environment and the Collapse of Great Civilizations* (London: Penguin, 1991).

24 Narvaez, *Neurobiology.*

25 Calvin L. Martin, *In the Spirit* (Baltimore: Johns Hopkins University Press, 1992).

26 Benjamin Madley, *An American Genocide* (New Haven, CT: Yale University Press, 2016); Peter Nabokov, *Native American Testimony: A Chronicle of Indian-White Relations from Prophecy to the Present, 1492–2000* (New York: Penguin, 1999); Danilo Urzedo and Pratichi Chatterjee, "The Colonial Reproduction of Deforestation in the Brazilian Amazon: Violence against Indigenous Peoples for Land Development," *Journal of Genocide Research* 23, no. 2 (2021): 302–24; Andres J. Azuero, Dan Arreaza-Kaufman, Jeanette Coriat, Stefano Tassinari, Annette Faria, Camilo Castañeda-Cardona, and Diego Rosselli, "Suicide in the Indigenous Population of Latin America: A Systematic Review," *Revista Colombiana de Psiquiatria* 46, no. 4 (2017): 237–42.

27 G. A. Bradshaw, Allan N. Schore, Janine L. Brown, Joyce H. Poole, and Cynthia J. Moss, "Elephant Breakdown," *Nature* 433, no. 7028 (2005): 807; Survival International, "Guarani Suicides—How Mankind's Divorce from Nature Impacts the Psyche," 2022, www.survivalinternational.org/articles/3247-guarani-suicides-how-mankinds-divorce-from-nature-impacts-on-the-psyche; Madley, *American Genocide;* Nabokov, *Native American Testimony;* Urzedo and Chatterjee, "Colonial Reproduction"; Azuero et al., "Suicide."

28 "Capitalocene" is used in lieu of "Anthropocene" because not all humans have brought this about; rather, it is caused by those who promote colonialism, industrialization, capitalism, and its globalization. See Jason Moore, ed., *Anthropocene or Capitalocene: Nature, History and the Crisis of Capitalism* (Oakland, CA: PM Press, 2016).

29 E. Richard Sorenson, "Preconquest Consciousness," in *Tribal Epistemologies,* ed. Helmut Wautischer (Aldershot, UK: Ashgate, 1998), 79–115.

30 Narvaez, *Neurobiology.*

31 Andrew Garner, Michael Yogman, and Committee on Psychosocial Aspects of Child and Family Health, Section on Developmental and Behavioral Pediatrics, Council on Early Childhood, "Preventing Childhood Toxic Stress: Partnering with Families and Communities to Promote Relational Health," *Pediatrics* 148, no. 2 (2021): e2021052582.

32 Narvaez, *Neurobiology.*

33 Humberto Maturana and Gerda Verden-Zöller, *The Origin of Humanness in the Biology of Love,* ed. Pille Bunnell (Exeter, UK: Imprint Academic, 2008).

34 Maté and Maté, *Myth of Normal;* Gabor Maté, "Addiction: Childhood Trauma, Stress and the Biology of Addiction," *Journal of Restorative Medicine* 1, no. 1 (2012): 56–63; Robin Karr-Morse and Meredith S. Wiley, *Ghosts from the Nursery: Tracing the Roots of Violence* (New York: Atlantic Monthly Press, 1997);

Robin Karr-Morse and Meredith S. Wiley, *Scared Sick: The Role of Childhood Trauma in Adult Disease* (New York: Basic Books, 2012); Ruth A. Lanius, Eric Vermetten, and Clare Pain, *The Impact of Early Life Trauma on Health and Disease: The Hidden Epidemic* (New York: Cambridge University Press, 2010).

35 Maté and Maté, *Myth of Normal*.

36 Jennifer Block, *Pushed: The Painful Truth about Childbirth and Modern Maternity Care* (New York: Lifelong Books/Da Capo/Perseus, 2007).

37 Babies vary how long they stay in the womb by up to fifty-five days. Ashley Montagu, "Brains, Genes, Culture, Immaturity, and Gestation," in *Culture: Man's Adaptive Dimension,* ed. Ashley Montagu (New York: Oxford University Press, 1968), 102–13.

38 Marsden Wagner, *Born in the USA: How a Broken Maternity System Must Be Fixed to Put Women and Children First* (Berkeley: University of California Press, 2006).

39 Elysia P. Davis and Curt A. Sandman, "The Timing of Prenatal Exposure to Maternal Cortisol and Psychosocial Stress is Associated with Human Infant Cognitive Development," *Child Development* 81, no. 1 (2010): 131–48.

40 Ali B. Rodgers, Christopher P. Morgan, N. Adrian Leu, and Tracy L. Bale, "Transgenerational Epigenetic Programming via Sperm MicroRNA Recapitulates Effects of Paternal Stress," *Proceedings of the National Academy of Sciences* 112, no. 44 (2015): 13699–704.

41 Baby-Friendly USA, *Guidelines and Evaluation Criteria for Facilities Seeking Baby-Friendly Designation* (Sandwich, MA: Baby-Friendly USA, 2010).

42 US Department of Health and Human Services, *The Surgeon General's Call to Action to Support Breastfeeding* (Washington, DC: US Department of Health and Human Services, Office of the Surgeon General, 2011).

43 Stephanie Coontz, *The Way We Never Were: American Families and the Nostalgia Trap* (New York: Basic Books, 1992).

44 Bradshaw, *Carnivore Minds*.

45 Jenara Nerenberg, "Why Are So Many Adults Today Haunted by Trauma," *Greater Good Magazine,* June 8, 2017, https://greatergood.berkeley.edu/article/item/why_are_so_many_adults_today_haunted_by_trauma; Lanius et al., *Impact*.

46 Edward O. Wilson, "Biodiversity, Prosperity, and Value," in *Ecology, Economics, Ethics: The Broken Circle,* ed. F. Herbert Bormann and Stephen R. Kellert (New Haven, CT: Yale University Press, 1991), 3–10.

47 Narvaez, *Neurobiology*; Darcia Narvaez, Julia Braungart-Rieker, Laura Miller-Graff, Lee Gettler, and Paul Hastings, eds., *Contexts for Young Child Flourishing: Evolution, Family and Society* (New York: Oxford University Press, 2016); Darcia Narvaez, Kristin Valentino, James McKenna, Agustin Fuentes, and Peter Gray, eds., *Ancestral Landscapes in Human Evolution: Culture, Childrearing and Social Wellbeing* (New York: Oxford University Press, 2014); Darcia

Narvaez, Jaak Panksepp, Allan Schore, and Tracy Gleason, eds., *Evolution, Early Experience and Human Development: From Research to Practice and Policy* (New York: Oxford University Press, 2013).

48 Raj Patel and Jason W. Moore, *A History of the World in Seven Cheap Things: A Guide to Capitalism, Nature, and the Future of the Planet* (Berkeley: University of California Press, 2017), 206.

49 Alison Gopnik, *The Gardener and the Carpenter* (New York: Farrar, Straus and Giroux, 2016).

50 www.apa.org/monitor/2011/04/mind-midlife.

51 Narvaez, *Neurobiology.*

52 Liedloff, *Continuum Concept,* 163.

53 Sherri Mitchell, *Sacred Instructions* (Berkeley, CA: North Atlantic Books, 2018), 158.

54 Sarah Hrdy, *Mothers and Others: The Evolutionary Origins of Mutual Understanding* (Cambridge, MA: Belknap Press, 2009).

55 Joanna Macy and Molly Brown, *Coming Back to Life* (Gabriola Island, BC: New Society Publishers, 2014).

2. Should I Have Children? Brown Bears

1 Charles C. Schwartz, Sterling D. Miller, and Mark A. Haroldson, "Grizzly Bear," in *Wild Mammals of North America: Biology, Management, and Conservation,* ed. George A. Feldhamer, Bruce Carlyle Thompson, and Joseph A. Chapman (Baltimore: Johns Hopkins University Press, 2003), 556.

2 Charlie Russell, *Grizzly Heart: Living without Fear among the Brown Bears of Kamchatka* (Toronto: Vintage Canada, 2011).

3 G. A. Bradshaw, *Talking with Bears: Conversations with Charlie Russell* (Victoria, BC: Rocky Mountain Books, 2020), 197–98.

4 Bradshaw, *Talking with Bears,* 63.

5 Bradshaw, 34.

6 Tatsuya Sakamoto and Stephen D. McCormick, "Prolactin and Growth Hormone in Fish Osmoregulation," *General and Comparative Endocrinology* 147, no. 1 (2006): 24–30; Cornelis Groot, *Pacific Salmon Life Histories* (Vancouver, BC: UBC Press, 1991).

7 E. Toolson, "Acclimation of Osmoregulatory Function in Salmon," accessed June 1, 2022, www.unm.edu/~toolson/salmon_osmoregulation.html; Thomas P. Quinn, *The Behavior and Ecology of Pacific Salmon and Trout* (Seattle: University of Washington Press, 2018); Stephen D. McCormick and Richard L. Saunders, "Preparatory Physiological Adaptations for Marine Life of Salmonids: Osmoregulation, Growth, and Metabolism," *American Fisheries Society Symposium* 1, no. 21 (1987): 1–229.

8 Russell, *Grizzly Heart.*

9 Sarah Hrdy, *Mothers and Others: The Evolutionary Origins of Mutual Understanding* (Cambridge, MA: Belknap Press, 2009).

10 Humberto Maturana and Gerda Verden-Zöller, *The Origin of Humanness in the Biology of Love*, ed. Pille Bunnell (Exeter, UK: Imprint Academic, 2008).

11 Wenda R. Trevathan, *Human Birth: An Evolutionary Perspective*, 2nd ed. (New York: Aldine de Gruyter, 2011).

12 Judith M. Burkart, Sarah B. Hrdy, and Carel P. van Schaik, "Cooperative Breeding and Human Cognitive Evolution," *Evolutionary Anthropology* 18 (2009): 175–86.

13 Ashley Montagu, *Touching: The Human Significance of the Skin* (New York: Harper & Row, 1986).

14 Trevathan, *Human Birth*.

15 Pascal Steiner, "Brain Fuel Utilization in the Developing Brain," *Annals of Nutrition Metabolism* 75, suppl. 1 (2019): 8–18, https://doi.org/10.1159/000508054.

16 Darcia Narvaez, Jaak Panksepp, Allan Schore, and Tracy Gleason, *Evolution, Early Experience and Human Development: From Research to Practice and Policy* (New York: Oxford University Press, 2013).

17 Montagu, *Touching*.

18 Darcia Narvaez, *Neurobiology and the Development of Human Morality: Evolution, Culture and Wisdom* (New York: W. W. Norton, 2014).

19 Hrdy, *Mothers and Others*.

20 Michael J. Meaney, "Maternal Care, Gene Expression, and the Transmission of Individual Differences in Stress Reactivity across Generations," *Annual Review of Neuroscience* 24, no. 1 (2001): 1161–92.

21 Juan M. Rodríguez, Leonides Fernández, and Valerie Verhasselt, "The Gut–Breast Axis: Programming Health for Life," *Nutrients* 13, no. 2 (2021): 606; Kyoung Min Kim and Jae-Won Choi, "Associations between Breastfeeding and Cognitive Function in Children from Early Childhood to School Age: A Prospective Birth Cohort Study," *International Breastfeeding Journal* 15, no. 1 (2020): 83.

22 Edward Tronick, *The Neurobehavioral and Social-Emotional Development of Infants and Children* (New York: Norton, 2007).

23 Colwyn Trevarthen, "Stepping Away from the Mirror: Pride and Shame in Adventures of Companionship—Reflections on the Nature and Emotional Needs of Infant Intersubjectivity," in *Attachment and Bonding: A New Synthesis*, ed. C. Sue Carter, Lieselotte Ahnert, K. E. Grossmann, Sarah B. Hrdy, Michael E. Lamb, Stephen W. Porges, and Norbert Sachser (Cambridge, MA: MIT Press, 2005), 55–84.

24 Daniel Stern, *Forms of Vitality: Exploring Dynamic Experience in Psychology, the Arts, Psychotherapy, and Development* (New York: Oxford University Press, 2010).

25 Lesley Le Grange, "Ubuntu, Ukama, Environment and Moral Education," *Journal of Moral Education* 41, no. 3 (2012): 329–40.

26 Thomas R. Verny and Pamela Weintraub, *Pre-Parenting: Nurturing Your Child from Conception* (New York: Simon & Schuster, 2002).

27 Colwyn Trevarthen, "Action and Emotion in Development of the Human Self, Its Sociability and Cultural Intelligence: Why Infants Have Feelings Like Ours," in *Emotional Development,* ed. Jacqueline Nadel and Darwin Muir (Oxford: Oxford University Press, 2005), 61–91; Trevarthen, "Stepping Away."

28 Ruth Feldman, A. Weller, L. Sirota, and A. I. Eidelman, "Skin-to-Skin Contact (Kangaroo Care) Promotes Self-Regulation in Premature Infants: Sleep-Wake Cyclicity, Arousal Modulation, and Sustained Exploration," *Developmental Psychology* 38, no. 2 (2002): 194–207.

29 Isabella B. R. Scheiber, Brigitte M. Weiß, Sjouke A. Kingma, and Jan Komdeur, "The Importance of the Altricial–Precocial Spectrum for Social Complexity in Mammals and Birds—A Review," *Frontiers in Zoology* 14, no. 1 (2017): 1–20.

30 Kerstin Uvnas-Moberg, "Neuroendocrinology of the Mother-Child Interaction," *Trends in Endocrinology and Metabolism* 7 (1996): 126–31; Ruth Feldman, "Oxytocin and Social Affiliation in Humans," *Hormones and Behavior* 61, no. 3 (2012): 380–91; C. Sue Carter, "Developmental Consequences of Oxytocin," *Physiological Behavior* 79, no. 3 (2003): 383–97.

31 Kerstin Uvnas-Moberg, "Oxytocin-Linked Antistress Effects—The Relaxation and Growth Response," *Acta Psychologica Scandinavica* 161, suppl. 640 (1997): 38–42.

32 Grazyna Kochanska, "Mutually Responsive Orientation between Mothers and Their Young Children: A Context for the Early Development of Conscience," *Current Directions in Psychological Science* 11, no. 6 (2002): 191–95.

33 Charles C. Schwartz et al., "Grizzly Bear," 556–86.

34 Bradshaw, *Talking,* 180.

35 Bradshaw, *Talking.*

36 Thich Nhat Hanh and Arnold Kotler, *Being Peace* (Berkeley, CA: Parallax, 1987).

37 K. Kramer and M. Gawlick, *Martin Buber's I and Thou: Practicing Living Dialogue* (Mahwah, NJ: Paulist Press, 2003).

38 G. A. Bradshaw, *Carnivore Minds: Who These Fearsome Animals Really Are* (New Haven, CT: Yale University Press, 2017), 87.

39 Keith Basso, *Wisdom Sits in Places: Landscape and Language among the Western Apache* (Albuquerque: University of New Mexico Press, 1996); Enrique Salmon, "Kincentric Ecology: Indigenous Perceptions of the Human–Nature Relationship," *Ecological Applications* 10, no. 5 (2000): 1327–32.

40 Eric C. Hellgren, "Physiology of Hibernation in Bears," *Ursus* 10 (1998): 467–77; Alberto García-Rodríguez, Robin Rigg, I. Elguero-Claramunt, Katarzyna Bojarska, Miha Krofel, Jamshid Parchizadeh, T. Pataky, et al., "Phenology of Brown Bear Breeding Season and Related Geographical Cues," *European Zoological Journal* 87, no. 1 (2020): 552–58.

41 www.ucsfhealth.org/education/conception-how-it-works; L. Sanders, "Misconceptions Cloud Abortion Debate: Key Aspects of Pregnancy Biology Are Often Misunderstood," *Science News*, July 15 and 29, 2022, 6–7, www .sciencenews.org/article/abortion-roe-v-wade-pregnancy-biology-supreme -court-ruling.

42 Cory T. Williams, Brian Barnes, G. J. Kenagy, and C. Loren Buck, "Phenology of Hibernation and Reproduction in Ground Squirrels: Integration of Environmental Cues with Endogenous Programming," *Journal of Zoology* 292, no. 2 (2014): 112–24.

43 Kathryn Wilsterman, Mallory A. Ballinger, and Caroline M. Williams, "A Unifying, Eco-Physiological Framework for Animal Dormancy," *Functional Ecology* 35, no. 1 (2021): 11–31.

44 Michael D. Thom, Dominic D. P. Johnson, and David W. Macdonald, "The Evolution and Maintenance of Delayed Implantation in the Mustelidae (Mammalia: Carnivora)," *Evolution* 58, no. 1 (2004): 175–83.

45 Andrea Friebe, Alina L. Evans, Jon M. Arnemo, Stephane Blanc, Sven Brunberg, Gunther Fleissner, Jon E. Swenson, and Andreas Zedrosser, "Factors Affecting Date of Implantation, Parturition, and Den Entry Estimated from Activity and Body Temperature in Free-Ranging Brown Bears," *PLOS One* 9, no. 7 (2014): e101410; Mikael Sandell, "The Evolution of Seasonal Delayed Implantation," *Quarterly Review of Biology* 65, no. 1 (1990): 23–42.

46 Charles T. Robbins, Merav Ben-David, Jennifer K. Fortin, and O. Lynne Nelson, "Maternal Condition Determines Birth Date and Growth of Newborn Bear Cubs," *Journal of Mammalogy* 93, no. 2 (2012): 540–46.

47 Friebe et al., "Factors."

48 Philip Ball, *The Book of Minds: How to Understand Ourselves and Other Beings* (London: Picador, 2022).

49 Oren Lyons, "An Iroquois Perspective," in *Learning to Listen to the Land*, ed. William B. Willers (Washington, DC: Island Press, 1991), 202–5.

50 Bradshaw, *Talking with Bears*; Russell, *Grizzly Heart*.

51 Friebe et al., "Factors."

52 Peter Kropotkin, *Mutual Aid: A Factor of Evolution* (Charleston, SC: Biblio-Bazaar, 2006).

53 Friebe et al., "Factors"; Sandell, "Evolution."

54 Samuel K. Wasser, "Stress and Reproductive Failure: An Evolutionary Approach with Applications to Premature Labor," *American Journal of Obstetrics and Gynecology* 180, no. 1 (1999): S272–S274.

55 Wasser, "Stress and Reproductive Failure."

56 Narvaez, *Neurobiology*.

57 Maurizio Benazzo and Zaya Benazzo, *The Wisdom of Trauma*, film (Sebastopol, CA: Science and Nonduality, 2021), https://thewisdomoftrauma.com/; Gabor Maté and Daniel Maté, *The Myth of Normal: Trauma, Illness, and Healing in a Toxic Culture* (Garden City, NY: Avery, 2022).

58 Maté and Maté, *Myth of Normal*, 145.

3. Mutual Accompaniment: African Elephants

1 Peter Nabokov and Robert Easton, *Native American Architecture* (New York: Oxford University Press, 1990).

2 Daphne Jenkins Sheldrick, *Love, Life, and Elephants* (New York: Farrar, Straus and Giroux, 2013), 314.

3 G. A. Bradshaw, *Talking with Bears: Conversations with Charlie Russell* (Victoria, BC: Rocky Mountain Books, 2020), 49, 209.

4 Sylvia K. Sikes, *Natural History of the African Elephant* (New York: American Elsevier, 1971); https://decolonialatlas.wordpress.com/2018/03/06/comparative-latitudes.

5 Charles Siebert, "Zoos Call It 'Rescue' but Are the Elephants Really Better Off?" *New York Times Magazine*, July 9, 2019, www.nytimes.com/2019/07/09/magazine/elephants-zoos-swazi-17.html.

6 Cynthia J. Moss, *Elephant Memories: Thirteen Years in the Life of an Elephant Family* (New York: William Morrow, 1988); Cynthia J. Moss, "The Demography of an African Elephant *(Loxodonta africana)* Population in Amboseli, Kenya," *Journal of Zoology* 255, no. 2 (2001): 145–56; Cynthia J. Moss and Joyce H. Poole, "Relationships and Social Structure of African Elephants," in *Primate Social Relationships: An Integrated Approach,* ed. Robert A. Hinde (Oxford, UK: Blackwell Scientific Publications, 1983), 315–25; G. A. Bradshaw, *Elephants on the Edge: What Animals Teach Us about Humanity* (New Haven, CT: Yale University Press, 2009), 261–62.

7 Mary Watkins, *Mutual Accompaniment and the Creation of the Commons* (New Haven, CT: Yale University Press, 2019).

8 Garrett Barnwell, G. A. Bradshaw, and Mary Watkins, "Grounding Community Psychology in Practices of Ecopsychosocial Accompaniment," in *The Routledge International Handbook of Community Psychology*, ed. Carolyn Kagan, Jacqueline Akhurst, Jaime Alfaro, Rebecca Lawthom, Michael Richards, and Alba Zambrano (New York: Routledge, 2022), 60–74.

9 Christian Leroy and Ginette Leroy, *An Elephant Is Born*, film (Nariobi, Kenya: Sheldrick Wildlife Trust, 2011), www.youtube.com/watch?v=Vb5-6-BQzlI.

10 Darcia Narvaez, Jaak Panksepp, Allan N. Schore, and Tracy R. Gleason, *Evolution, Early Experience and Human Development: From Research to Practice and Policy* (New York: Oxford University Press, 2013).

11 Allan N. Schore, *The Development of the Unconscious Mind* (New York: W. W. Norton, 2019).

12 Iain McGilchrist, *The Matter with Things: Our Brains, Our Delusions, and the Unmaking of the World,* vols. I–II (London: Perspectiva Press, 2021).

13 Ron Tweedy, ed., *The Divided Therapist: Hemispheric Differences and Contemporary Psychotherapy* (London: Routledge, 2021).

14 Schore, *Development.*

15 National Scientific Council, "Excessive Stress Disrupts the Development of Brain Architecture," *Journal of Children's Services* 9, no. 2 (2014): 143–53.

16 Susan D. Calkins and Ashley Hill, "Caregiver Influences on Emerging Emotion Regulation: Biological and Environmental Transactions in Early Development," in *Handbook of Emotion Regulation,* ed. James J. Gross (New York: Guilford Press, 2007), 229–48.

17 Daniel L. Everett, "Concentric Circles of Attachment in the Pirahã: A Brief Survey," in *Different Faces of Attachment: Cultural Variations on a Universal Human Need,* ed. H. Otto and H. Keller (Cambridge, UK: Cambridge University Press, 2014), 169–86.

18 Thomas Widlok, *Anthropology and the Economy of Sharing* (London: Routledge, 2017).

19 Donald W. Winnicott, *Mother and Child: A Primer of First Relationships* (New York: Basic Books, 1957); Donald W. Winnicott, *Babies and Their Mothers* (Reading, MA: Addison-Wesley, 1987).

20 www.washington.edu/uwired/outreach/cspn/Website/Classroom%20Materials/Reading%20the%20Region/Texts%20by%20and%20about%20Natives/Commentary/9.html.

21 Mourning Dove, quotation in *The Spirit of Indian Women,* ed. Judith Fitzgerald and Michael O. Fitzgerald (Bloomington, IN: World Wisdom, 2005), 81.

22 Dennis H. McPherson and J. Douglas Rabb, *Indian from the Inside: Native American Philosophy and Cultural Renewal,* 2nd ed. (Jefferson, NC: MacFarland, 2011); Amy Bombay, Kimberly Matheson, and Hymie Anisman, "The Intergenerational Effects of Indian Residential Schools: Implications for the Concept of Historical Trauma," *Transcultural Psychiatry* 51, no. 3 (2014): 320–38, https://doi.org/10.1177/1363461513503380.

23 www.sheldrickwildlifetrust.org/.

24 Sheldrick, *Love.*

25 Sheldrick, 231.

26 Sheldrick, 236.

27 Sheldrick, 307.

28 Sheldrick Wildlife Trust, "Keeper's Diaries, January 2022," www.sheldrickwildlifetrust.org/keepers-diaries/january-2022/nursery-unit#23796.

29 Global Sanctuary for Elephants, "Pocha and Guillermina," accessed November 1, 2022, https://globalelephants.org/pocha-and-guillermina/.

30 Bradshaw, *Elephants*.

31 Global Sanctuary, "Pocha and Guillermina."

32 Bradshaw, *Elephants*.

33 Darcia Narvaez, *Neurobiology and the Development of Human Morality: Evolution, Culture and Wisdom* (New York: W. W. Norton, 2014).

34 Heide Goettner-Abendroth, *Matriarchal Societies: Studies on Indigenous Cultures across the Globe* (New York: Peter Lang, 2013); Genevieve Vaughan, *The Maternal Roots of the Gift Economy* (Toronto: Inanna, 2019).

35 Gerda Lerner, *The Creation of Patriarchy* (Oxford, UK: Oxford University Press, 1986); Calvin L. Martin, *The Way of the Human Being* (New Haven, CT: Yale University Press, 1999).

36 Roxanne Dunbar-Ortiz, *An Indigenous People's History of the United States* (Boston: Beacon Press, 2014); Karl Polanyi, *The Great Transformation: The Political and Economic Origins of Our Time* (Boston: Beacon Press, 2001); Darcia Narvaez, Four Arrows, Eugene Halton, Brian S. Collier, and Georges Enderle, eds., *Indigenous Sustainable Wisdom: First Nation Know-How for Global Flourishing* (New York: Peter Lang, 2019).

37 McPherson and Rabb, *Indian*; Bombay et al., "Intergenerational Effects."

38 Mary Annette Pember, "Death by Civilization," *The Atlantic*, March 8, 2019, www.theatlantic.com/education/archive/2019/03/traumatic-legacy-indian-boarding-schools/584293/.

39 Pember, "Death."

40 Darcia Narvaez, Angela M. Kurth, and Mary S. Tarsha, "The Centrality of Mothering for Human Flourishing," in *Matriarchal Values, Free Maternal Gift-Giving and Child-Rearing*, ed. E. Shadmi and K. Kailo (Oulu, Finland: Kaarina Kailo, 2020), 161–71.

41 Narvaez et al., "Centrality."

42 Angela Braden and Darcia Narvaez, *Primal Parenting* (New York: Oxford University Press, forthcoming).

43 Angela Sheldrick, "The Work of Generations," Sheldrick Wildlife Trust, April 28, 2022, www.sheldrickwildlifetrust.org/news/fieldnotes/work-of-generations.

44 Sheldrick Wildlife Trust, "Olmeg," accessed November 1, 2022, www.sheldrickwildlifetrust.org/orphans/olmeg.

45 Sheldrick, *Love*, 266.

46 Gabor Maté, *In the Realm of Hungry Ghosts: Close Encounters with Addiction* (New York: Random House, 2008).

47 Darcia Narvaez, "Beyond Trauma-Informed: Returning to Indigenous, Wellness-Informed Practices," *International Journal of Existential Positive Psychology* 11,

no. 1 (2022), www.meaning.ca/ijepp-article/vol11-no1/beyond-trauma
-informed-returning-to-indigenous-wellness-informed-practices/.

48 Peter D. Gluckman and Mark A. Hanson, *Fetal Matrix: Evolution, Development and Disease* (New York: Cambridge University Press, 2005); Mark Wolynn, *It Didn't Start with You* (New York: Penguin, 2017); Resmaa Menakem, *My Grandmother's Hands: Racialized Trauma and the Pathway to Mending Our Hearts and Bodies* (Las Vegas: Central Recovery Press, 2017).

49 Marsden Wagner, *Born in the USA: How a Broken Maternity System Must Be Fixed to Put Women and Children First* (Berkeley: University of California Press, 2006).

50 Marshall H. Klaus, J. H. Kennell, S. S. Robertson, and R. Sosa, "Effects of Social Support during Parturition on Maternal and Infant Morbidity," *British Medical Journal* 283 (1986): 585–87.

51 W. F. Liu, S. Laudert, B. Perkins, E. MacMillan-York, S. Martin, and S. Graven for the NIC/Q 2005 Physical Environment Exploratory Group, "The Development of Potentially Better Practices to Support the Neurodevelopment of Infants in the NICU," *Journal of Perinatology* 27 (2007): S48–S74.

52 Ashley Montagu, "Brains, Genes, Culture, Immaturity, and Gestation," in *Culture: Man's Adaptive Dimension,* ed. Ashley Montagu (New York: Oxford University Press, 1968), 102–13.

53 Tiffany Field, *Touch,* 2nd ed. (Cambridge, MA: MIT Press, 2014).

54 Sarah B. Hrdy, *Mothers and Others: The Evolutionary Origins of Mutual Understanding* (Cambridge, MA: Belknap Press, 2009).

55 Center on the Developing Child at Harvard University, *Maternal Depression Can Undermine the Development of Young Children: Working Paper No. 8* (Cambridge, MA: Harvard University, 2009), https://developingchild.harvard
.edu/resources/maternal-depression-can-undermine-the-development-of
-young-children/.

56 New York State Department of Health, "What Is Maternal Depression?" revised January 2015, www.health.ny.gov/community/pregnancy/health_care/perinatal
/maternal_depression/providers/what_is_maternal_depression.htm.

57 Center on the Developing Child, *Maternal Depression.*

58 National Scientific Council on the Developing Child, *Excessive Stress Disrupts the Architecture of the Developing Brain: Working Paper 3,* updated edition (Cambridge, MA: Harvard University, 2014), developingchild.harvard.edu
/wp-content/uploads/2005/05/Stress_Disrupts_Architecture_Developing
_Brain-1.pdf.

59 National Scientific Council, *Excessive Stress.*

60 Center on the Developing Child, *Maternal Depression.*

61 Schore, *Development.*

62 Humberto Maturana and Gerda Verden-Zöller, *The Origin of Humanness in the Biology of Love,* ed. Pille Bunnell (Exeter, UK: Imprint Academic, 2008).

63 Martha G. Welch, "Calming Cycle Theory: The Role of Visceral/Autonomic Learning in Early Mother and Infant/Child Behaviour and Development," *Acta Pædiatrica* 105, no. 11 (2016): 1266–74.

64 Bradshaw, *Elephants*.

65 G. A. Bradshaw and Allan N. Schore, "How Elephants Are Opening Doors: Developmental Neuroethology, Attachment and Social Context," *Ethology* 113, no. 5 (2007): 426–36.

66 Bradshaw and Schore, "Elephants."

67 Anna M. Whitehouse, "Tusklessness in the Elephant Population of the Addo Elephant National Park, South Africa," *Journal of Zoology* 257, no. 2 (2002): 249–54; Bradshaw, *Elephants*, 268.

68 Allan N. Schore, "All Our Sons: The Developmental Neurobiology and Neuroendocrinology of Boys at Risk," *Infant Mental Health Journal* 38, no. 1 (2017): 15–52.

4. Breastfeeding: Sperm Whales

1 Roger Searle, "Tectonic Pattern of the Azores Spreading Centre and Triple Junction," *Earth and Planetary Science Letters* 51, no. 2 (1980): 415–34.

2 Studies show that an Orca cerebellum makes up approximately 14 percent of the total brain mass, while the cerebellum of a Sperm Whale accounts for 7 percent of brain mass. See Sam H. Ridgway and Alisa C. Hanson, "Sperm Whales and Killer Whales with the Largest Brains of All Toothed Whales Show Extreme Differences in Cerebellum," *Brain, Behavior and Evolution* 83, no. 4 (2014): 266–74.

3 Megan F. McKenna et al., "Morphology of the Odontocete Melon and Its Implications for Acoustic Function," *Marine Mammal Science* 28, no. 4 (2011): 690–713.

4 Linda Weilgart, Hal Whitehead, and Katharine Payne, "A Colossal Convergence," *American Scientist* 84, no. 3 (1996): 278–87.

5 Hal Whitehead, *Sperm Whales: Social Evolution in the Ocean* (Chicago: University of Chicago Press, 2003), 286; Hal Whitehead, "Sperm Whale: *Physeter macrocephalus*," in *Encyclopedia of Marine Mammals*, 3rd ed., ed. Bernd Wursig, J. G. M. Thewissen, and Kit M. Kovacs (London: Academic Press, 2019), 919–25.

6 Hal Whitehead, personal communication, July 2, 2022.

7 Gilda Morelli, Paula Ivey Henry, and Steffen Foerster, "Relationships and Resource Uncertainty: Cooperative Development of Efe Hunter-Gatherer Infants and Toddlers," in *Ancestral Landscapes in Human Evolution: Culture, Childrearing and Social Wellbeing*, ed. Darcia Narvaez, Kristin Valentino, Agustin Fuentes, James McKenna, and Peter Gray (New York: Oxford University Press, 2014), 69–103.

8 Barry S. Hewlett and Michael E. Lamb, *Hunter-Gatherer Childhoods: Evolutionary, Developmental and Cultural Perspectives* (New Brunswick, NJ: Aldine, 2005).

9 Whitehead, personal communication.

10 Weilgart et al., "Colossal," 282.

11 Weilgart et al.

12 Whitehead, personal communication.

13 Christine M. Konrad, Timothy R. Frasier, Hal Whitehead, and Shane Gero, "Kin Selection and Allocare in Sperm Whales," *Behavioral Ecology* 30, no. 1 (2019): 194–201; Whitehead, personal communication.

14 The normal length of breastfeeding for human infants before industrialization was two and a half to seven years. See Katherine A. Dettwyler, "A Time to Wean: The Hominid Blueprint for the Natural Age of Weaning in Modern Human Populations," in *Breastfeeding: Biocultural Perspectives,* ed. Patricia Stuart-Macadma and Katherine A. Dettwyler (New York: Aldine de Gruyter, 1997), 39–74.

15 Weilgart et al., "Colossal," 282.

16 Valeria Teloni et al., "Shallow Food for Deep Divers: Dynamic Foraging Behavior of Male Sperm Whales in a High-Latitude Habitat," *Journal of Experimental Marine Biology and Ecology* 354, no. 1 (2008): 119–31.

17 Hayao Kobayashi, Hal Whitehead, and Masao Amano, "Long-Term Associations among Male Sperm Whales *(Physeter macrocephalus),*" *PLOS One* 15, no. 12 (2020): e0244204.

18 www.darewin.org/page2/.

19 Robert L. Pitman et al., "Killer Whale Predation on Sperm Whales: Observations and Implications," *Marine Mammal Science* 17, no. 3 (2001): 494–507.

20 Pitman et al., "Killer Whale."

21 Anonymous, personal communication, 2009.

22 Daphne Sheldrick, *Love, Life, and Elephants* (New York: Farrar, Straus and Giroux, 2012), 313.

23 D. H. Lawrence, "Whales Weep Not," *The Complete Poems of D. H. Lawrence* (Stansted, UK: Wordsworth Editions, 1957).

24 G. Johnson et al., "Evidence That Sperm Whale *(Physeter macrocephalus)* Calves Suckle through Their Mouth," *Marine Mammal Science* 26, no. 4 (2010): 990–96.

25 Michael L. Power and Jay Schulkin, *Milk: The Biology of Lactation* (Baltimore: Johns Hopkins University Press, 2016); Jeremiah S. Doody, Vladimir Dinets, and Gordon M. Burghardt, *The Secret Social Lives of Reptiles* (Baltimore: John Hopkins University Press, 2021).

26 Ben Shaul, "The Composition of the Milk of Wild Animals," *International Zoo Yearbook* 4 (1962): 333–42.

27 R. Jenness, "The Composition of Human Milk," *Semin Perinatol* 3, no. 3 (1979): 225–39, https://pubmed.ncbi.nlm.nih.gov/392766/.

28 Shaul, "Composition."

29 www.fisheries.noaa.gov/species/harbor-seal.

30 Power and Schulkin, *Milk*.

31 Theo Tacail, Jeremy E. Martin, Florent Arnaud-Godet, J. Francis Thackeray, Thure E. Cerling, Jose Braga, and Vincent Balter, "Calcium Isotopic Patterns in Enamel Reflect Different Nursing Behaviors among South African Early Hominins," *Science Advances* 5, no. 8 (2019): eaax3250, https://doi.org/10.1126/sciadv.aax3250.

32 Power and Schulkin, *Milk*.

33 Lars Hanson, *Immunobiology of Human Milk* (New York: Raven Press, 1988).

34 Katherine A. Dettwyler, "When to Wean: Biological versus Cultural Perspectives," *Clinical Obstetrics and Gynecology* 47, no. 3 (1997): 712–23.

35 James Akre, "From Grand Design to Change on the Ground: Going to Scale with a Global Feeding Strategy," in *Infant and Young Child Feeding—Challenges to Implementing a Global Strategy,* ed. Fiona Dykes and Victoria Hall Moran (Chichester, UK: Wiley-Blackwell, 2009), 1–31.

36 Power and Schulkin, *Milk*.

37 Ashley Montagu, *Touching: The Human Significance of the Skin* (New York: Harper & Row, 1986).

38 Armond S. Goldman, "The Immune System of Human Milk: Antimicrobial, Anti-inflammatory and Immunomodulating Properties," *Pediatric Infectious Disease Journal* 12, no. 8 (1993): 664–71.

39 Jennifer T. Smilowitz, Carlito B. Lebrilla, David A. Mills, J. Bruce German, and Samara L. Freeman, "Breast Milk Oligosaccharides: Structure-Function Relationships in the Neonate," *Annual Review of Nutrition* 34 (2014): 143–69.

40 Akre, "Grand Design."

41 Barry M. Lester, Elisabeth Conradt, Linda L. LaGasse, Edward Z. Tronick, James F. Padbury, and Carmen J. Marsit, "Epigenetic Programming by Maternal Behavior in the Human Infant," *Pediatrics* 142, no. 8 (2018): e20171890, https://doi.org/10.1542/peds.2017-1890.

42 Jessica G. Woo et al., "Human Milk Adiponectin Affects Infant Weight Trajectory during the Second Year of Life," *Journal of Pediatric Gastroenterology and Nutrition* 54, no. 4 (2012): 532–39; Christian Rosas-Salazar et al., "Exclusive Breast-Feeding, the Early-Life Microbiome and Immune Response, and Common Childhood Respiratory Illnesses," *Journal of Allergy and Clinical Immunology* S0091-6749 (2022): 00292-5.

43 Akre, "Grand Design."

44 Kathryn B. H. Clancy, Katie Hinde, and Julienne N. Rutherford, *Building Babies: Primate Development in Proximate and Ultimate Perspective* (New York: Springer, 2013); Smilowitz et al., "Breast Milk."

45 Mohammadbagher Hosseini, Einollah Valizadeh, Nafiseh Hosseini, Shirin Khatibshahidi, and Sina Raeisi, "The Role of Infant Sex on Human Milk Composition," *Breastfeeding Medicine* 15, no. 5 (2020): 341–46.

46 Merel F. Italianer, "Circadian Variation in Human Milk Composition: A Systematic Review," *Nutrients* 12, no. 8 (2020): 2328.

47 K. Iigaya et al., "An Effect of Serotonergic Stimulation on Learning Rates for Rewards Apparent after Long Intertrial Intervals," *Nature Communications* 9, no. 1 (2018): 2477, https://doi.org/10.1038/s41467-018-04840-2.

48 The microbiome in the gastrointestinal tract ("gut") is involved in the development and function of our immune, metabolic, and nervous systems. It is closely connected with the brain through bidirectional biochemical communication, referred to as the "gut-brain axis." See: Fei Huang and Xiaojun Wu, "Brain Neurotransmitter Modulation by Gut Microbiota in Anxiety and Depression," *Frontiers in Cell and Developmental Biology* 9 (2021): https://doi.org/10.3389/fcell.2021.649103; Jeremy Appleton, "The Gut-Brain Axis: Influence of Microbiota on Mood and Mental Health," *Integrative Medicine* 17, no. 4 (2018): 28–32.

49 C. M. Hibberd et al., "Variation in the Composition of Breast Milk during the First 5 Weeks of Lactation: Implications for the Feeding of Preterm Infants," *Archives of Diseases in Childhood* 57, no. 9 (1981): 658–62.

50 Goldman, "Immune System."

51 Italianer, "Circadian Variation"; Power and Schulkin, *Milk*.

52 Glenn O'Malley, *Shelley and Synesthesia* (Evanston, IL: Northwestern University Press, 1964).

53 Nils Bergman, quoted in Akre, "Grand Design," 13.

54 Montagu, *Touching*.

55 https://developingchild.harvard.edu/science/key-concepts/brain-architecture/.

56 https://onezero.medium.com/our-skulls-are-out-evolving-us-and-that-could-mean-a-public-health-crisis-f950faed696d.

57 Tamer Rizk, "Breast Milk versus Formula Milk and Neuropsychological Development and Sleep," *Journal of Pediatrics and Neonatal Care* 1, no. 2 (2014): 00005.

58 Joan Stiles, *The Fundamentals of Brain Development: Integrating Nature and Nurture* (Cambridge, MA: Harvard University Press, 2008).

59 James J. McKenna, *Safe Infant Sleep* (Washington, DC: Platypus Media, 2020).

60 Montagu, *Touching*.

61 Montagu.

62 McKenna, *Safe*.

63 Lena Tschiderer, Lisa Seekircher, Setor K. Kunutsor, Sanne A. E. Peters, Linda M. O'Keeffe, and Peter Willeit, "Breastfeeding Is Associated with a Reduced

Maternal Cardiovascular Risk: Systematic Review and Meta-Analysis Involving Data from 8 Studies and 1,192,700 Parous Women," *Journal of the American Heart Association* 11, no. 2 (2022): e022746, https://doi.org/10.1161/JAHA.121.022746.

64 Erica P. Gunderson, Cora E. Lewis, Ying Lin, Mike Sorel, Myron Gross, Stephen Sidney, David R. Jacobs, James M. Shikany, and Charles P. Quesenberry, "Lactation Duration and Progression to Diabetes in Women across the Childbearing Years," *JAMA Internal Medicine* 178, no. 3 (2018): 328–37, https://doi.org/10.1001/jamainternmed.2017.7978.

65 Lisette T. Jacobson et al., "Breastfeeding History and Risk of Stroke among Parous Postmenopausal Women in the Women's Health Initiative," *Journal of the American Heart Association* 7, no. 17 (2018): e008739, https://doi.org/10.1161/JAHA.118.008739.

66 Molly Fox, Prabha Siddarth, Hanadi Ajam Oughli, Sarah A. Nguyen, Michaela M. Milillo, Yesenia Aguilar, Linda Ercoli, and Helen Lavretsky, "Women Who Breastfeed Exhibit Cognitive Benefits after Age 50," *Evolution, Medicine, and Public Health* 9, no. 1 (2021): 322–31, https://doi.org/10.1093/emph/eoab027.

67 Wenda R. Trevathan, *Human Birth: An Evolutionary Perspective*, 2nd ed. (New York: Aldine de Gruyter, 2011).

68 Montagu, *Touching*.

69 Jay Schulkin, *The Neuroendocrine Regulation of Behavior* (New York: Cambridge University Press, 1999).

70 Jennifer M. Weaver et al., "Breastfeeding Duration Predicts Greater Maternal Sensitivity over the Next Decade," *Developmental Psychology* 54, no. 2 (2017): 220–27, https://doi.org/10.1037/dev0000425.

71 Gianluca Malatesta et al., "The Left-Cradling Bias and Its Relationship with Empathy and Depression," *Scientific Reports* 9, no. 1 (2019): 1–9.

72 Irena Rot-Nikcevic, Christopher N. Taylor, and Richard J. Wassersug, "The Role of Images of Conspecifics as Visual Cues in the Development and Behavior of Larval Anurans," *Behavioral Ecology and Sociobiology* 60, no. 1 (2006): 19–25.

73 Karina Karenina et al., "Lateralization of Mother–Infant Interactions in a Diverse Range of Mammal Species," *Nature Ecology and Evolution* 1, no. 2 (2017): 1–4.

74 Ann M. Zoidis and Kate S. Lomac-MacNair, "A Note on Suckling Behavior and Laterality in Nursing Humpback Whale Calves from Underwater Observations," *Animals* 7, no. 7 (2017): 51; Frances M. D. Gulland, Linda J. Lowenstine, and Terry R. Spraker, "Noninfectious Diseases," in *CRC Handbook of Marine Mammal Medicine,* ed. Leslie A. Dierauf and Frances M. D. Gulland (Boca Raton, FL: CRC Press, 2001), 530–31.

75 Shane Gero and Hal Whitehead, "Suckling Behavior in Sperm Whale Calves: Observations and Hypotheses," *Marine Mammal Science* 23, no. 2 (2007): 398–413; Whitehead, personal communication.

76 E. Richard Sorenson, "Preconquest Consciousness," in *Tribal Epistemologies,* ed. Helmut Wautischer (Aldershot, UK: Ashgate, 1998), 79–115.

77 Kerstin Uvnas-Moberg and Danielle K. Prime, "Oxytocin Effects in Mothers and Infants during Breastfeeding," *Infant* 9, no. 6 (2013): 201–6.

78 Hewlett and Lamb, *Hunter-Gatherer Childhoods.*

79 American mothers in particular can struggle to breastfeed. Researchers are starting to examine the many interacting factors that may affect breastfeeding success; see www.nationalgeographic.com/science/article/many-women -struggle-to-breastfeed-scientists-are-starting-to-ask-why.

80 World Health Organization, "Infant and Young Child Feeding," June 9, 2021, www.who.int/news-room/fact-sheets/detail/infant-and-young-child -feeding.

81 Cesar G. Victora, Rajiv Bahl, Aluísio J. D. Barros, Giovanny V. A. França, Susan Horton, Julia Krasevec, Simon Murch, Mari Jeeva Sankar, Neff Walker, and Nigel C. Rollins for The Lancet Breastfeeding Series Group, "Breastfeeding in the 21st Century: Epidemiology, Mechanisms, and Lifelong Effect," *The Lancet* 387, no. 10017 (2016): 475–90. For a longer list, see Akre, "Grand Design"; see also Zahara Sulaiman, Lisa H. Amir, and Pranee Liamputtong, "Infant Feeding Practices: Rates, Risks of Not Breastfeeding, and Factors Influencing Breast-feeding," in *Evolution, Early Experience and Human Development: From Research to Practice and Policy,* ed. Darcia Narvaez, Jaak Panksepp, Allan N. Schore, and Tracy R. Gleason (New York: Oxford University Press, 2013), 277–98.

82 Dettwyler, "When to Wean."

83 www.babyfriendlyusa.org/about/.

84 US Department of Health and Human Services, *The Surgeon General's Call to Action to Support Breastfeeding* (Washington, DC: US Department of Health and Human Services, Office of the Surgeon General, 2011).

85 www.babyfriendlyusa.org/.

86 The United States was the only country to vote against the Code; World Health Organization, *International Code of Marketing of Breast-Milk Substitutes* (Geneva: World Health Organization, 1981), www.who.int/publications/i/ item/9241541601.

87 Lori Wallach and Patrick Woodall, *Whose Trade Organization? The Comprehensive Guide to the WTO* (New York: The New Press, 2004).

88 www.who.int/news/item/22-02-2022-more-than-half-of-parents-and-pregnant -women-exposed-to-aggressive-formula-milk-marketing-who-unicef; www.who .int/news/item/28-04-2022-who-reveals-shocking-extent-of-exploitative-formula -milk-marketing.

89 Akre, "Grand Design."

90 Adelota Louis-Jacques and Alison Stuebe, "Long-Term Maternal Benefits of Breastfeeding," *Contemporary OB/GYN* 63, no. 7 (2018): 26–29; Chinelo

Ogbuanu et al., "The Effect of Maternity Leave Length and Time of Return to Work on Breastfeeding," *Pediatrics* 127, no. 6 (2011): e1414–e1427.

91 Carla Moquin, *Babies at Work: Bringing New Life to the Workplace* (self-published, 2008).

92 https://europeanmilkbanking.com/joint-emba-and-hmbana-statement -on-milk-sharing-has-been-released/.

93 Kelley L. Baumgartel, Larissa Sneeringer, and Susan M. Cohen, "From Royal Wet Nurses to Facebook: The Evolution of Breastmilk Sharing," *Breastfeeding Review* 24, no. 3 (2016): 25–32.

94 www.bellybelly.com.au/baby-sleep/babywise-dangers-warnings-parents -need-to-know/.

95 Montagu, *Touching*, 129.

96 Penelope Leach, *Children First: What Our Society Must Do—and Is Not Doing— for Our Children Today* (New York: Vintage, 1995).

97 Sara A. Quandt, "Sociocultural Aspects of the Lactation Process," in *Breastfeeding: Biocultural Perspectives,* ed. Patricia Stuart-Macadma and Katherine A. Dettwyler (New York: Aldine de Gruyter, 1997), 127–43.

98 www.llli.org/breastfeeding-info/mastitis/.

99 Madison S. Andrew, Roshan J. Selvaratnam, Miranda Davies-Tuck, Kim Holwand, and Mary-Ann Davey, "The Association between Intrapartum Interventions and Immediate and Ongoing Breastfeeding Outcomes: An Australian Retrospective Population-Based Cohort Study," *International Breastfeeding Journal* 17, no. 48 (2022), https://doi.org/10.1186/s13006-022-00492-7.

100 Christine Greenway, "Hungry Earth and Vengeful Stars: Soul Loss and Identity in the Peruvian Andes," *Social Science and Medicine* 47, no. 8 (1998), 993.

5. Sharing Care: Emperor Penguins

1 André Ancel, Michaël Beaulieu, Yvon Le Maho, and Caroline Gilbert, "Emperor Penguin Mates: Keeping Together in the Crowd," *Proceedings of the Royal Society B: Biological Sciences* 276, no. 1665 (2009): 2163–69.

2 André Ancel, personal communication, June 23, 2022.

3 "The lowest recorded Antarctic temperature was taken at Vostok Station in July 1983: –89.2°C (–128.6°F). . . . The highest wind speeds recorded in Antarctica were at Dumont d'Urville station in July 1972: 327km/h (199 mph)." IceCube, "Antarctic Weather," accessed November 1, 2022, https://icecube .wisc.edu/pole/weather/.

4 Bernard Stonehouse, *The Emperor Penguin (Aptenodytes forsteri, Gray): I. Breeding Behaviour and Development* (London: HMSO, 1953); Cristopher B. Sturdy and Richard Mooney, "Communication: Two Voices Are Better Than One," *Current Biology* 10, no. 17 (2000): R634–R636.

5 Ancel, personal communication.

6 André Ancel, Michaël Beaulieu, and Caroline Gilbert, "The Different Breeding Strategies of Penguins: A Review," *Comptes Rendus Biologies* 336, no. 1 (2013): 1–12.

7 Yves Cherel and Gerald L. Kooyman, "Food of Emperor Penguins *(Aptenodytes forsteri)* in the Western Ross Sea, Antarctica," *Marine Biology* 130, no. 3 (1998): 335–44.

8 Barbara Wienecke, Graham Robertson, Roger Kirkwood, and Kieran Lawton, "Extreme Dives by Free-Ranging Emperor Penguins," *Polar Biology* 30, no. 2 (2007): 133–42.

9 Kimberly T. Goetz, Birgitte I. McDonald, and Gerald L. Kooyman, "Habitat Preference and Dive Behavior of Non-Breeding Emperor Penguins in the Eastern Ross Sea, Antarctica," *Marine Ecology Progress Series* 593 (2018): 155–71.

10 Ancel, personal communication.

11 Hervee Lormee, Pierre Jouventin, Olivier Chastel, and Robert Mauget, "Endocrine Correlates of Parental Care in an Antarctic Winter Breeding Seabird, the Emperor Penguin, *Aptenodytes forsteri*," *Hormones and Behavior* 35, no. 1 (1999): 9–17.

12 Ancel, personal communication.

13 André Ancel, Caroline Gilbert, Nicolas Poulin, Michael Beaulieu, and Bernard Thierry, "New Insights into the Huddling Dynamics of Emperor Penguins," *Animal Behaviour* 110 (2015): 91–98.

14 Ancel, personal communication.

15 Ancel et al., "New Insights."

16 Daniel P. Zitterbart, Barbara Wienecke, James P. Butler, and Ben Fabry, "Coordinated Movements Prevent Jamming in an Emperor Penguin Huddle," *PLOS One* 6, no. 6 (2011): e20260.

17 Sasan Harifi, Madjid Khalilian, Javad Mohammadzadeh, and Sadoullah Ebrahimnejad, "Emperor Penguins Colony: A New Metaheuristic Algorithm for Optimization," *Evolutionary Intelligence* 12, no. 2 (2019): 211–26.

18 Thierry Aubin and Pierre Jouventin, "How to Vocally Identify Kin in a Crowd: The Penguin Model," *Advances in the Study of Behavior* 31 (2002): 243–77.

19 Aubin and Jouventin, "Vocally Identify."

20 Stephanie Pappas, "Mama Dolphins Sing Their Name to Babies in the Womb," Live Science, August 9, 2016, www.livescience.com/55699-mother-dolphins -teach-babies-signature-whistle.html.

21 Ancel, personal communication.

22 Ancel et al., "Different Breeding."

23 William Goldfarb, "Psychological Privation in Infancy and Subsequent Adjustment," *American Journal of Orthopsychiatry* 15, no. 2 (1945): 247–55.

24 Harry Bakwin, "Loneliness in Infants," *American Journal of Diseases in Children* 63, no. 1 (1942): 30–40.

25 René A. Spitz, "Hospitalism: An Inquiry into the Genesis of Psychiatric Conditions in Early Childhood," *Psychoanalytic Study of the Child* 1 (1945): 53–74, https://doi.org/10.1080/00797308.1945.11823126.

26 Frank C. P. van der Horst and René van der Veer, "Loneliness in Infancy: Harry Harlow, John Bowlby and Issues of Separation," *Integrative Psychological and Behavioral Science* 42, no. 4 (2008): 325–35.

27 John Bowlby, *Attachment and Loss: Volume I: Attachment* (London: The Hogarth Press and the Institute of Psycho-Analysis, 1969); John Bowlby, *Attachment and Loss: Volume II: Separation, Anxiety and Anger* (London: The Hogarth Press and the Institute of Psychoanalysis, 1973); John Bowlby, *Attachment and Loss: Volume III: Loss, Sadness and Depression* (London: The Hogarth Press and the Institute of Psychoanalysis, 1980).

28 Bowlby, *Volume I*; Bowlby, *Volume II*; Bowlby, *Volume III*; John Bowlby, *Maternal Care and Mental Health* (New York: Schocken, 1951).

29 Jude Cassidy and Phillip Shaver, eds., *Handbook of Attachment: Theory, Research, and Clinical Applications*, 3rd ed. (New York: Guilford Press, 2016).

30 David C. Bell, "Evolution of Parental Caregiving," *Personality and Social Psychology Review* 5, no. 3 (2001): 216–29.

31 John Bowlby, *Attachment and Loss: Volume I: Attachment*, 2nd ed. (London: The Hogarth Press and the Institute of Psycho-Analysis, 1969; New York: Basic Books, 1982).

32 For a personal take on the development of attachment research by one of its leaders, see L. Alan Sroufe, *A Compelling Idea: How We Become the Persons We Are* (Brandon, VT: Safer Society Press, 2020).

33 Humberto Maturana and Gerda Verden-Zöller, *The Origin of Humanness in the Biology of Love*, ed. Pille Bunnell (Exeter, UK: Imprint Academic, 2008).

34 Colwyn Trevarthen, "Stepping Away from the Mirror: Pride and Shame in Adventures of Companionship—Reflections on the Nature and Emotional Needs of Infant Intersubjectivity," in *Attachment and Bonding: A New Synthesis*, ed. C. Sue Carter, Lieselotte Ahnert, K. E. Grossmann, Sarah B. Hrdy, Michael E. Lamb, Stephen W. Porges, and Norbert Sachser (Cambridge, MA: MIT Press, 2005), 55–84.

35 Bowlby, *Volume I*.

36 Colin M. Turnbull, *The Human Cycle* (New York: Simon & Schuster, 1984).

37 Susan W. Coates, "John Bowlby and Margaret S. Mahler: Their Lives and Theories," *Journal of the American Psychoanalytic Association* 52, no. 2 (2004): 571–601.

38 Jeremy Holmes, *John Bowlby and Attachment Theory* (London: Routledge, 1993), 17.

39 Alex Renton, "Boarding School Syndrome Review—Education and the Pain of Separation," *The Guardian*, June 8, 2015, www.theguardian.com/books/2015

/jun/08/boarding-school-syndrome-joy-schaverien-review; Joy Schaverien, *Boarding School Syndrome: The Psychological Trauma of the "Privileged" Child* (London: Routledge, 2015). Characteristics include unresolved grief; a false masculinity; a sense of entitlement; broken family attachments; distorted emotions, emotional expression, and sexuality; loneliness and inability to form lasting intimate relationships; greed and disturbed appetites; and PTSD from abuse and neglect.

40 Wade Davis, *Schooling the World* (Vancouver, BC: TEDxVancouverED, 2014), lecture, www.youtube.com/watch?v=hwk2w-9aekA&t.

41 Donald T. Jacobs and Jessica Jacobs-Spencer, *Teaching Virtues: Building Character across the Curriculum* (Lanham, MD: Scarecrow Education, 2001).

42 Carol Black, *Schooling the World: The White Man's Last Burden,* film, accessed December 5, 2022, http://carolblack.org/schooling-the-world.

43 Dennis H. McPherson and J. Douglas Rabb, *Indian from the Inside: Native American Philosophy and Cultural Renewal,* 2nd ed. (Jefferson, NC: MacFarland, 2011).

44 Iain McGilchrist, *The Matter with Things: Our Brains, Our Delusions, and the Unmaking of the World,* vols. I–II (London: Perspectiva Press, 2021); Darcia Narvaez, *Neurobiology and the Development of Human Morality: Evolution, Culture and Wisdom* (New York: W. W. Norton, 2014).

45 Tyson Yunkaporta, *Sand Talk: How Indigenous Thinking Can Save the World* (New York: HarperCollins, 2020).

46 Winona LaDuke, "Honor the Earth: Our Native American Legacy" (lecture, Ninth Annual Westheimer Peace Symposium, Wilmington College, Wilmington, OH, October 20, 1999).

47 Emily Oster, *Cribsheet: A Data-Driven Guide to Better, More Relaxed Parenting, from Birth to Preschool* (New York: Penguin Press, 2019).

48 F. David Peat, *Blackfoot Physics* (Boston: Weiser Books, 2001), 65.

49 William Easterly, *The White Man's Burden: Why the West's Efforts to Aid the Rest Have Done So Much Ill and So Little Good* (London: Penguin, 2007).

50 Bowlby, *Volume I;* Bowlby, *Volume II;* Bowlby, *Volume III.*

51 Konrad Lorenz, *The Foundations of Ethology* (New York: Springer-Verlag, 1981).

52 Bowlby, *Volume I.*

53 G. A. Bradshaw, *Carnivore Minds: Who These Fearsome Animals Really Are* (New Haven, CT: Yale University Press, 2017).

54 Hiltrud Otto and Heidi Keller, eds., *Different Faces of Attachment: Cultural Variations on a Universal Human Need* (Cambridge, UK: Cambridge University Press, 2014); Naomi Quinn and Jeannette Marie Mageo, eds., *Attachment Reconsidered: Cultural Perspectives on a Western Theory* (New York: Palgrave-Macmillan, 2013).

55 Otto and Keller, *Different Faces of Attachment.*

56 Paul Shepard, *Coming Home to the Pleistocene,* ed. F. R. Shepard (Washington, DC: Island Press/Shearwater Books, 1998).

57 Suzanne Gaskins, Marjorie Beeghly, Kim A. Bard, Ariane Gernhardt, Cindy H. Liu, Douglas M. Teti, Ross A. Thompson, Thomas S. Weisner, and Relindis D. Yovsi, "Meaning and Methods in the Study and Assessment of Attachment," in *The Cultural Nature of Attachment: Contextualizing Relationships and Development*, ed. Heidi Keller and Kim A. Bard (Cambridge, MA: MIT Press, 2017), 195–230.

58 Bruce S. McEwen and E. Stellar, "Stress and the Individual: Mechanism Leading to Disease," *Archives of Internal Medicine* 153, no. 18 (1993): 2093–101.

59 Allan N. Schore, *The Development of the Unconscious Mind* (New York: W. W. Norton, 2019), 10.

60 Daniel J. Siegel, *The Developing Mind: How Relationships and the Brain Interact to Shape Who We Are* (New York: Guilford Press, 1999).

61 Martha G. Welch, "Calming Cycle Theory: The Role of Visceral/Autonomic Learning in Early Mother and Infant/Child Behaviour and Development," *Acta Pædiatrica* 105, no. 11 (2016): 1266–74.

62 Thomas Lewis, Fari Amini, and Richard Lannon, *A General Theory of Love* (New York: Vintage, 2000).

63 Schore, *Development*, 10.

64 Marilia Carabotti, Annunziata Scirocco, Maria Antonietta Maselli, and Carola Severi, "The Gut-Brain Axis: Interactions between Enteric Microbiota, Central and Enteric Nervous Systems," *Annals of Gastroenterology* 28, no. 2 (2015): 203; Jeremy Appleton, "The Gut-Brain Axis: Influence of Microbiota on Mood and Mental Health," *Integrative Medicine* 17, no. 4 (2018): 28–32.

65 Welch, "Calming."

66 Colwyn Trevarthen, "Musicality and the Intrinsic Motive Pulse: Evidence from Human Psychobiology and Infant Communication," *Musicae Scientiae* special issue 3, no. 1 (1999): 157–213; Colwyn Trevarthen, "Action and Emotion in Development of the Human Self, Its Sociability and Cultural Intelligence: Why Infants Have Feelings Like Ours," in *Emotional Development*, ed. Jacqueline Nadel and Darwin Muir (Oxford, UK: Oxford University Press, 2005), 61–91.

67 Wenda R. Trevathan, *Human Birth: An Evolutionary Perspective*, 2nd ed. (New York: Aldine de Gruyter, 2011).

68 Stephen Malloch and Colwyn Trevarthen, eds., *Communicative Musicality: Exploring the Basis of Human Companionship* (Oxford, UK: Oxford University Press, 2009).

69 Mylene M. Mariette, David F. Clayton, and Katherine L. Buchanan, "Acoustic Developmental Programming: A Mechanistic and Evolutionary Framework," *Trends in Ecology and Evolution* 36, no. 8 (2021): 722–36.

70 Mariette et al., "Acoustic."

71 Allan N. Schore, "Attachment and the Regulation of the Right Brain," *Attachment and Human Development* 2, no. 1 (2000): 23–47.

72 C. Sue Carter and Stephen W. Porges, "Neurobiology and the Evolution of Mammalian Social Behavior," in *Evolution, Early Experience and Human Development: From Research to Practice and Policy,* ed. Darcia Narvaez, Jaak Panksepp, Allan N. Schore, and Tracy Gleason (New York: Oxford University Press, 2013), 132–51.

73 Wendy Middlemiss, D. A. Granger, W. A. Goldberg, and L. Nathans, "Asynchrony of Mother-Infant Hypothalamic-Pituitary-Adrenal Axis Activity following Extinction of Infant Crying Responses Induced during the Transition to Sleep," *Early Human Development* 88, no. 4 (2012): 227–32, https://doi.org/10.1016/j.earlhumdev.2011.08.010.

74 Daphne Blunt Bugental, Gabriela Martorell, and Veronica Barraza, "The Hormonal Costs of Subtle Forms of Infant Maltreatment," *Hormones and Behaviour* 43, no. 1 (2003): 237–44; Megan R. Gunnar and Bonny Donzella, "Social Regulation of the Cortisol Levels in Early Human Development," *Psychoneuroendocrinology* 27, no. 1–2 (2002): 199–220.

75 Naomi I. Eisenberger, Matthew D. Lieberman, and Kipling D. Williams, "Does Rejection Hurt? An FMRI Study of Social Exclusion," *Science* 302, no. 5643 (2003): 290–92; Jaak Panksepp, "Feeling the Pain of Social Loss," *Science* 302, no. 5643 (2003): 237–39; Jon-Kar Zubieta, Terrence A. Ketter, Joshua A. Bueller, Yanjun Xu, Michael R. Kilbourn, Elizabeth A.Young, and Robert A. Koeppe, "Regulation of Human Affective Responses by Anterior Cingulate and Limbic and Mu-opioid Neurotransmission," *General Psychiatry* 60, no. 11 (2003): 1037–172.

76 Douglas F. Watt and Jaak Panksepp, "Depression: An Evolutionarily Conserved Mechanism to Terminate Separation Distress? A Review of Aminergic, Peptidergic, and Neural Network Perspectives," *Neuropsychoanalysis* 11, no. 1 (2009): 5–48.

77 Christian Caldji, Darlene Francis, Shakti Sharma, Paul M. Plotsky, and Michael Meaney, "The Effects of Early Rearing Environment on the Development of $GABA_A$ and Central Benzodiazepine Receptor Levels and Novelty-Induced Fearfulness in the Rat," *Neuropsychopharmacology* 22 (2000): 219–29; Fu-Chun Hsu, Guo-Jun Zhang, Yogendra Sinh H. Raol, Rita J. Valentino, Douglas A. Coulter, and Amy R. Brooks-Kayal, "Repeated Neonatal Handling with Maternal Separation Permanently Alters Hippocampal $GABA_A$ Receptors and Behavioural Stress Responses," *Proceedings of the National Academy of Sciences* 100, no. 21 (2003): 12213–18.

78 Ruth A. Lanius, Eric Vermetten, and Clare Pain, *The Impact of Early Life Trauma on Health and Disease: The Hidden Epidemic* (New York: Cambridge University Press, 2010); D. Niehoff, *The Biology of Violence: How Understanding the Brain, Behavior, and Environment Can Break the Vicious Circle of Aggression* (New York: Free Press, 1999).

79 Jaak Panksepp, "How Primary-Process Emotional Systems Guide Child Development: Ancestral Regulators of Human Happiness, Thriving, and Suffering," in *Evolution, Early Experience and Human Development: From*

Research to Practice and Policy, ed. Darcia Narvaez, Jaak Panksepp, Allan N. Schore, and Tracy Gleason (New York: Oxford University Press, 2013), 74–94.

80 Schore, *Development,* 10.

81 Hans Seyle, *The Stress of Life* (New York: McGraw Hill, 1973).

82 Lanius et al., *Impact.*

83 Peter A. Levine and Maggie Kline, *Trauma through a Child's Eyes* (Berkeley, CA: North Atlantic Books, 2019).

84 Bowlby, *Volume I.*

85 Stephen Porges, *The Polyvagal Theory* (New York: Norton, 2011).

86 Gabor Maté and Daniel Maté, *The Myth of Normal: Trauma, Illness, and Healing in a Toxic Culture* (Garden City, NY: Avery, 2022).

87 József Haller, G. Harold, Carmen Sandi, and I. D. Neumann, "Effects of Adverse Early-Life Events on Aggression and Anti-social Behaviours in Animals and Humans," *Journal of Neuroendocrinology* 26, no. 10 (2014): 724–38.

88 James P. Henry and Sheila Wang, "Effects of Early Stress on Adult Affiliative Behavior," *Psychoneuroendocrinology* 23, no. 8 (1998): 863–75; Darcia Narvaez, "The Ethics of Early Life Care: The Harms of Sleep Training," *Clinical Lactation* 4, no. 2 (2013): 66–70.

89 Michael J. Meaney, "Maternal Care, Gene Expression, and the Transmission of Individual Differences in Stress Reactivity across Generations," *Annual Review of Neuroscience* 24, no. 1 (2001): 1161–92.

90 John Bowlby, *Child Care and the Growth of Love* (Harmondsworth, UK: Penguin, 1955).

91 Patricia M. Crittenden, "Attachment and Psychopathology," in *Attachment Theory: Social, Developmental, and Clinical Perspectives,* ed. Susan Goldberg, Roy Muir, and John Kerr (Hillsdale, NJ: Analytic Press, 1995), 367–406. Note that Crittenden used the term "feeling" instead of "emoting," but as Alan Sroufe has pointed out (personal communication, July 10, 2022), there is no infant who does not feel. Emoting refers to emotional expression.

92 Phillip R. Shaver and Mario Mikulincer, "Adult Attachment Strategies and the Regulation of Emotion," in *Handbook of Emotion Regulation,* ed. James J. Gross (New York: Guilford Press, 2007), 446–65.

93 Shaver and Mikulincer, "Adult."

94 Bruce D. Perry, R. A. Pollard, T. L. Blakely, W. L. Baker, and D. Vigilante, "Childhood Trauma, the Neurobiology of Adaptation, and 'Use-Dependent' Development of the Brain: How 'States' Become 'Traits,'" *Infant Mental Health Journal* 16, no. 4 (1995): 271–91.

95 Melvin Konner, *The Evolution of Childhood* (Cambridge, MA: Belknap Press, 2010).

6. Free Play: Beavers

1 Gordon M. Burghardt, *The Genesis of Animal Play: Testing the Limits* (Cambridge, MA: MIT Press, 2005).

2 Sarah Zylinski, "Fun and Play in Invertebrates," *Current Biology* 25, no. 1 (2015): R10–R12.

3 Burghardt, *Genesis*.

4 Burghardt.

5 Jaak Panksepp, *Affective Neuroscience: The Foundations of Human and Animal Emotions* (New York: Oxford University Press, 1998).

6 Panksepp, *Affective Neuroscience.*

7 Jaak Panksepp, "Can PLAY Diminish ADHD and Facilitate the Construction of the Social Brain?" *Journal of the Canadian Academy of Child and Adolescent Psychiatry* 16, no. 2 (2007): 57; Marek Spinka, Ruth C. Newberry, and Marc Bekoff, "Mammalian Play: Training for the Unexpected," *Quarterly Review of Biology* 76, no. 2 (2001): 141–68; Marc Bekoff, "Comparative Studies of Social Play, Fairness, and Fitness: What We Know and Where We Should Be Heading," in *Ancestral Landscapes in Human Evolution: Culture, Childrearing and Social Wellbeing,* ed. Darcia Narvaez, Kristin Valentino, Agustin Fuentes, James J. McKenna, and Peter Gray (New York: Oxford University Press, 2014), 214–17.

8 J. Burgdorf, R. A. Kroes, M. C. Beinfeld, J. Panksepp, and J. R. Moskal, "Uncovering the Molecular Basis of Positive Affect Using Rough-and-Tumble Play in Rats: A Role for Insulin-Like Growth Factor I," *Neuroscience* 168, no. 3 (2010): 769–77.

9 Burghardt, *Genesis*.

10 Panksepp, *Affective Neuroscience.*

11 Burgdorf et al., "Uncovering."

12 Burghardt, *Genesis;* Douglas P. Fry, "The Environment of Evolutionary Adaptedness, Rough-and-Tumble Play, and the Selection of Restraint in Human Aggression," in *Ancestral Landscapes in Human Evolution: Culture, Childrearing and Social Wellbeing,* ed. Darcia Narvaez, Kristin Valentino, Agustin Fuentes, James J. McKenna, and Peter Gray (New York: Oxford University Press, 2014), 167–86; Peter Gray, "The Play Theory of Hunter-Gatherer Egalitarianism," in *Ancestral Landscapes in Human Evolution: Culture, Childrearing and Social Wellbeing,* ed. Darcia Narvaez, Kristin Valentino, Agustin Fuentes, James J. McKenna, and Peter Gray (New York: Oxford University Press, 2014), 190–213.

13 US Fish and Wildlife Service, "Beaver Conservation Strategy," accessed November 2, 2022, www.fws.gov/project/beaver-conservation-strategy.

14 Roxanne Dunbar-Ortiz, *An Indigenous People's History of the United States* (Boston: Beacon Press, 2014).

15 B. W. Baker and E. P. Hill, "Beaver *(Castor canadensis),*" in *Wild Mammals of North America: Biology, Management, and Conservation,* 2nd ed., ed. George A. Feldhamer, Bruce C. Thompson, and Joseph A. Chapman (Baltimore: Johns Hopkins University Press, 2003), 288–310.

16 Wirgiliusz Żurowski, "Building Activity of Beavers," *Acta Theriologica* 37, no. 4 (1992): 403–11.

17 Baker and Hill, "Beaver."

18 Baker and Hill.

19 Brian G. Slough, "Beaver Food Cache Structure and Utilization," *Journal of Wildlife Management* 42, no. 3 (1978): 644–46.

20 Ellen Wohl, "Legacy Effects of Loss of Beavers in the Continental United States," *Environmental Research Letters* 16, no. 2 (2021): 025010.

21 Dietland Müller-Schwarze, *The Beaver: Natural History of a Wetlands Engineer* (Ithaca, NY: Comstock Publishing Associates, 2011).

22 Hope Ryden, *Lily Pond: Four Years with a Family of Beavers* (New York: HarperCollins, 1990), 50–51.

23 J. Matthias Starck and Robert E. Ricklefs, eds., *Avian Growth and Development: Evolution within the Altricial-Precocial Spectrum* (Oxford, UK: Oxford University Press on Demand, 1998).

24 Françoise Patenaude, "The Ontogeny of Behavior of Free-Living Beavers *(Castor canadensis),*" *Zeitschrift für Tierpsychologie* 66, no. 1 (1984): 33–44.

25 Barbara Rogoff, *Apprenticeship in Thinking: Cognitive Development in Social Context* (New York: Oxford University Press, 1990); Barbara Rogoff and Jean Lave, *Everyday Cognition: Its Development in Social Context* (Cambridge, MA: Harvard University Press, 1984).

26 Dorothy Richards and Hope Sawyer Buyukmihci, *Beaversprite: My Years Building an Animal Sanctuary* (San Francisco: Chronicle Books, 1977).

27 Enos Mills, *In Beaver World* (Boston: Houghton Mifflin, 1913).

28 Sherri Mitchell, *Sacred Instructions* (Berkeley, CA: North Atlantic Books, 2018), 158.

29 Fry, "Environment"; Gray, "Play Theory."

30 Daniel J. Siegel, *The Developing Mind: How Relationships and the Brain Interact to Shape Who We Are* (New York: Guilford Press, 1999).

31 Allan N. Schore, *The Development of the Unconscious Mind* (New York: W. W. Norton, 2019).

32 Jaak Panksepp and Lucy Biven, *The Archaeology of Mind: Neuroevolutionary Origins of Human Emotions* (New York: Norton, 2012).

33 Eric Scott and Jaak Panksepp, "Rough-and-Tumble Play in Human Children," *Aggressive Behavior* 29, no. 6 (2003): 539–51; Stuart Brown, "Play as an Organizing Principle: Clinical Evidence and Personal Observations," in *Animal Play:*

Evolutionary, Comparative, and Ecological Perspectives, ed. Marc Bekoff and J. A. Beyer (Cambridge, UK: Cambridge University Press, 1998), 242–51.

34 Bessel A. van der Kolk and Rita E. Fisler, "Childhood Abuse and Neglect and Loss of Self-Regulation," *Bulletin of the Menninger Clinic* 58, no. 2 (1994): 145–68.

35 Allan Schore, "The Experience-Dependent Maturation of a Regulatory System in the Orbital Prefrontal Cortex and the Origin of Development Psychopathology," *Development and Psychopathology* 8, no. 1 (1996): 59–87.

36 Ruth Feldman, "Parent-Infant Synchrony and the Construction of Shared Timing: Physiological Precursors, Developmental Outcomes, and Risk Conditions," *Journal of Child Psychology and Psychiatry* 48, no. 3–4 (2007): 329–54; Ruth Feldman, "Parent-Infant Synchrony: Biological Foundations and Developmental Outcomes," *Current Directions in Psychological Science* 16, no. 6 (2007): 340–45.

37 Joanna J. Cemore and Joan E. Herwig, "Delay of Gratification and Make-Believe Play of Preschoolers," *Journal of Research in Childhood Education* 19, no. 3 (2005): 251–66.

38 Peter LaFreniere, "Evolutionary Functions of Social Play: Life Histories, Sex Differences, and Emotion Regulation," *American Journal of Play* 3, no. 4 (2011): 464–88; Eric W. Lindsey and Malinda J. Colwell, "Pretend and Physical Play: Links to Preschoolers' Affective Social Competence," *Merrill-Palmer Quarterly* 59, no. 3 (2013): 330–60.

39 Tracy R. Gleason, Mary S. Tarsha, Darcia Narvaez, and Angela Kurth, "Opportunities for Free Play and Young Children's Autonomic Regulation," *Developmental Psychobiology* 63, no. 6 (2021): e22134.

40 Gleason et al., "Opportunities."

41 Michael Yogman et al., "The Power of Play: A Pediatric Role in Enhancing Development in Young Children," *Pediatrics* 142, no. 3 (2018): e20182058.

42 Ryden, *Lily Pond,* 60–62.

43 Darcia Narvaez, *Neurobiology and the Development of Human Morality: Evolution, Culture and Wisdom* (New York: W. W. Norton, 2014).

44 Plato, *The Republic,* trans. D. Lee (London: Penguin Books, 1974).

45 E. T. Seton, *Lives of Game Animals,* vol. 4, part 2, *Rodents* (New York: Doubleday, 1929); Baker and Hill, "Beaver."

46 Bart A. Nolet and Frank Rosell, "Comeback of the Beaver *Castor fiber:* An Overview of Old and New Conservation Problems," *Biological Conservation* 83, no. 2 (1998): 165–73.

47 Baker and Hill, "Beaver."

48 Ben Goldfarb, *Eager: The Surprising, Secret Life of Beavers and Why They Matter* (White River Junction, VT, and London: Chelsea Green Publishing, 2018), 18–19.

49 Laura Wagner, "Long-Lost Parachuting Beaver Footage from 1950," NPR, October 22, 2015, www.npr.org/sections/thetwo-way/2015/10/22/450958213/watch-long-lost-parachuting-beaver-footage-from-1950.

50 V. G. Schwab and M. Schmidbauer, "Beaver (*Castor fiber* L., Castoridae) Management in Bavaria," *Denisia 9, Neue Serie 2* (2003): 99–106.

51 Kent Nerburn, ed., *The Wisdom of the Native Americans* (Novato, CA: New World Library, 1999), 36–37.

52 Social anthropologist Robert Redfield identified two worldviews, one that considers the cosmos unified, sacred, and moral, and the other that considers the cosmos fragmented, disenchanted, and amoral. Robert Redfield, *The Primitive World and Its Transformations* (Ithaca, NY: Cornell University Press, 1953).

53 Gregory Cajete, *Native Science: Natural Laws of Interdependence* (Santa Fe, NM: Clear Light Publishers, 2000); Wahinkpe Topa (Four Arrows) and Darcia Narvaez, *Restoring the Kinship Worldview: Indigenous Voices Introduce 28 Precepts for Rebalancing Life on Planet Earth* (Berkeley, CA: North Atlantic Books, 2022).

54 Eduardo S. Brondizio, Josef Settele, Sandra Díaz, and Hien T. Ngo, eds., *Global Assessment Report on Biodiversity and Ecosystem Services of the Intergovernmental Science-Policy Platform on Biodiversity and Ecosystem Services* (Bonn, Germany: IPBES, 2019), https://ipbes.net/global-assessment.

55 Joni Mitchell, "Big Yellow Taxi," track 10 on *Ladies of the Canyon*, Reprise Records, 1970.

56 Derrick Jensen, "When I Dream of the Planet in Recovery," *YES!*, April 6, 2016, www.yesmagazine.org/issue/life-after-oil/2016/04/06/when-i-dream-of-the-planet-in-recovery.

7. Touch: Amazon Parrots

1 Ashley Montagu, *Touching: The Human Significance of the Skin* (New York: Harper & Row, 1986).

2 G. A. Bradshaw, *Carnivore Minds: Who These Fearsome Animals Really Are* (New Haven, CT: Yale University Press, 2017), 169.

3 Yaara Endevelt-Shapira, Emir Djalovski, Guillaume Dumas, and Ruth Feldman, "Maternal Chemosignals Enhance Infant-Adult Brain-to-Brain Synchrony," *Science Advances* 7, no. 50 (2021): eabg6867, https://doi.org/10.1126/sciadv.abg6867.

4 Darcia Narvaez, *Neurobiology and the Development of Human Morality: Evolution, Culture and Wisdom* (New York: W. W. Norton, 2014).

5 Tiffany Field, *Touch in Early Development* (New York: Psychology Press, 1995); Tiffany Field and Martin Reite, *The Psychobiology of Attachment and Separation* (New York: Academic Press, 1985).

6 Gabor Maté, *When the Body Says No: The Hidden Cost of Stress* (New York: Wiley, 2011).

7 Robin D. Bjork, *Delineating Pattern and Process in Tropical Lowlands: Mealy Parrot Migration Dynamics as a Guide for Regional Conservation Planning* (Corvallis: Oregon State University, 2004).

8 Franziska Hausmann, Kathryn E. Arnold, N. Justin Marshall, and Ian P. F. Owens, "Ultraviolet Signals in Birds Are Special," *Proceedings of the Royal Society of London Series B: Biological Sciences* 270, no. 1510 (2003): 61–67.

9 Mike Parr and Tony Juniper, *Parrots: A Guide to Parrots of the World* (New York: Bloomsbury Publishing, 2010); John and Pat Stoodley, *Genus Amazona* (Portsmouth, UK: Bezels Publications, 1990).

10 Field, *Touch.*

11 Montagu, *Touching,* 7.

12 Elisabeth Young-Bruehl and Faith Bethelard, *Cherishment: A Psychology of the Heart* (New York: Free Press, 2000).

13 Donald W. Winnicott, *The Maturational Processes and the Facilitating Environment* (Madison, WI: International University Press, 1960).

14 Montagu, *Touching.*

15 Sarah J. Buckley, "Executive Summary of Hormonal Physiology of Childbearing: Evidence and Implications for Women, Babies, and Maternity Care," *Journal of Perinatal Education* 24, no. 3 (2015): 145–53.

16 Wenda R. Trevathan, *Human Birth: An Evolutionary Perspective,* 2nd ed. (New York: Aldine de Gruyter, 2011).

17 Heng Ou, *The First Forty Days: The Essential Art of Nourishing the New Mother* (New York: Abrams, 2016).

18 David J. Linden, *Touch: The Science of the Hand, Heart, and Mind* (New York: Penguin Books, 2016).

19 George Lakoff and Mark Johnson, *Philosophy in the Flesh: The Embodied Mind and Its Challenge to Western Thought* (New York: HarperCollins, 1999).

20 Ken Nerburn, ed., *The Wisdom of the Native Americans* (Novato, CA: New World Library, 1999), 5.

21 Margaret Ribble, *The Rights of Infants* (New York: Columbia University Press, 1943).

22 Ribble, *Rights.*

23 Margaret Ribble, "Disorganizing Factors of Infant Personality," *American Journal of Psychiatry* 98 (1941): 459–63.

24 Bruce Taubman, "Clinical Trial of the Treatment of Colic by Modification of Parent-Infant Interaction," *Pediatrics* 74, no. 6 (1984): 998–1003.

25 Barry Hewlett and Michael Lamb, *Hunter-Gatherer Childhoods: Evolutionary, Developmental and Cultural Perspectives* (New Brunswick, NJ: Aldine, 2005).

26 Stephen Porges, *The Polyvagal Theory: Neurophysiological Foundations of Emotions, Attachment, Communication, and Self-Regulation* (New York: W. W. Norton, 2011).

27 Jacek Kolacz, Gregory F. Lewis, and Stephen W. Porges, "The Integration of Vocal Communication and Biobehavioral State Regulation in Mammals: A Polyvagal Hypothesis," in *Handbook of Ultrasonic Vocalization: A Window into the Emotional Brain*, ed. S. M. Brudzynski (Cambridge, MA: Elsevier Academic Press, 2018), 23–34, https://doi.org/10.1016/B978-0-12-809600-0.00003-2.

28 Montagu, *Touching*, 3.

29 Porges, *Polyvagal*; Montagu, *Touching*.

30 Hewlett and Lamb, *Hunter-Gatherer Childhoods*; E. Richard Sorenson, "Preconquest Consciousness," in *Tribal Epistemologies*, ed. Helmut Wautischer (Aldershot, UK: Ashgate, 1998), 79–115; Gilda Morelli, Paula Ivey Henry, and Steffen Foerster, "Relationships and Resource Uncertainty: Cooperative Development of Efe Hunter-Gatherer Infants and Toddlers," in *Ancestral Landscapes in Human Evolution: Culture, Childrearing and Social Wellbeing*, ed. Darcia Narvaez, Kristin Valentino, Agustin Fuentes, James McKenna, and Peter Gray (New York: Oxford University Press, 2014), 69–103.

31 Evan Thompson, "Life and Mind: From Autopoiesis to Neurophenomenology," in *Emergence and Embodiment*, ed. Bruce Clarke and Mark B. N. Hansen (Durham, NC: Duke University Press, 2009), 77–93.

32 Neville Owen, Geneviève N. Healy, Charles E. Matthews, and David W. Dunstan, "Too Much Sitting: The Population-Health Science of Sedentary Behavior," *Exercise Sport Science Review* 38, no. 3 (2010): 105–13.

33 Infant brains expect to be held and carried with movement in order to grow well. See William A. Mason and Gershon Berkson, "Effects of Maternal Mobility on the Development of Rocking and Other Behaviors in Rhesus Monkeys: A Study with Artificial Mothers," *Developmental Psychobiology* 8, no. 3 (1975): 197–221; John Zahovsky, "Discard of the Cradle," *Journal of Pediatrics* 4 (1934): 660–67.

34 F. J. Varela, E. Thompson, and E. Rosch, *The Embodied Mind: Cognitive Science and Human Experience* (Cambridge, MA: MIT Press, 1991); Jaak Panksepp, *Affective Neuroscience: The Foundations of Human and Animal Emotions* (New York: Oxford University Press, 1998).

35 M. Suzanne Zeedyk, *What's Life in a Baby Buggy Like? The Impact of Buggy Orientation on Parent-Infant Interaction and Infant Stress* (London: National Literacy Trust, 2008), https://literacytrust.org.uk/documents/114/2008_01_01_free_research_-_whats_life_in_a_buggy_like_2008_iHvVXnx.pdf.

36 Gilda A. Morelli, Barbara Rogoff, David Oppenheim, and Denise Goldsmith, "Cultural Variation in Infants' Sleeping Arrangements: Questions of Independence," *Developmental Psychology* 28, no. 4 (1992): 604–13.

37 Henrik Norholt, "Revisiting the Roots of Attachment: A Review of the Biological and Psychological Effects of Maternal Skin-to-Skin Contact and Carrying of Full-Term Infants," *Infant Behavioral Development* 60 (2020): 101441.

38 James W. Prescott, "The Origins of Human Love and Violence," *Pre- and Perinatal Psychology Journal* 10, no. 3 (1996): 143–88.

39 John Bowlby, *Attachment and Loss: Volume I: Attachment,* 2nd ed. (London: The Hogarth Press and the Institute of Psycho-Analysis, 1969; New York: Basic Books, 1982).

40 Kevin N. Ochsner and James J. Gross, "The Neural Architecture of Emotion Regulation," in *Handbook of Emotion Regulation,* ed. James J. Gross (New York: Guilford Press, 2007), 87–108.

41 C. Sue Carter and Stephen W. Porges, "Neurobiology and the Evolution of Mammalian Social Behavior," in *Evolution, Early Experience and Human Development: From Research to Practice and Policy,* ed. Darcia Narvaez, Jaak Panksepp, Allan Schore, and Tracy R. Gleason (New York: Oxford University Press, 2013), 132–51; Peter Kirsch, Christine Esslinger, Qiang Chen, Daniela Mier, Stefanie Lis, Sarina Siddhanti, Harald Gruppe, Venkata S. Mattay, Bernd Gallhofer, and Andreas Meyer-Lindenberg, "Oxytocin Modulates Neural Circuitry for Social Cognition and Fear in Humans," *Journal of Neuroscience* 25, no. 49 (2005): 11489–93; Predrag Petrovic, Raffael Kalisch, Tania Singer, and Raymond J. Dolan, "Oxytocin Attenuates Affective Evaluations of Conditioned Faces and Amygdala Activity," *Journal of Neuroscience* 28, no. 26 (2008): 6607–15; Kerstin Uvnas-Moberg, Linda Handlin, and Maria Petersson, "Neuroendocrine Mechanisms Involved in the Physiological Effects Caused by Skin-to-Skin Contact—With a Particular Focus on the Oxytocinergic System," *Infant Behavior & Development* 61 (2020): 101482.

42 Ruth Feldman, "Oxytocin and Social Affiliation in Humans," *Hormonal Behavior* 61, no. 3 (2012): 380–91.

43 C. Sue Carter, "Love as Embodied Medicine," *International Body Psychotherapy Journal* 18, no. 1 (2019): 21.

44 Carter and Porges, "Neurobiology."

45 Alison B. Wismer Fries, Toni E. Ziegler, Joseph R. Kurian, Steve Jacoris, and Seth D. Pollak, "Early Experience in Humans Is Associated with Changes in Neuropeptides Critical for Regulating Social Behaviour," *Proceedings of the National Academy of Sciences* 102, no. 47 (2005): 17237–40; Anna T. Smyke, Sebastian F. Koga, Dana E. Johnson, Nathan A. Fox, Peter J. Marshall, Charles A. Nelson, Charles H. Zeanah, and BEIP Core Group, "The Caregiving Context in Institution-Reared and Family-Reared Infants and Toddlers in Romania," *Journal of Child Psychology and Psychiatry* 48, no. 2 (2007): 210–18.

46 Myron A. Hofer, "Hidden Regulators in Attachment, Separation, and Loss," in *The Development of Emotion Regulation: Behavioral and Biological Considerations,*

Monographs of the Society for Research in Child Development, ed. Nathan A. Fox (Chicago: University of Chicago Press, 1994), 192–207.

47 Nami Ohmura, Lana Okuma, Anna Truzzi, Kazutaka Shinozuka, Atsuko Saito, Susumu Yokota, Andrea Bizzego, et al., "A Method to Soothe and Promote Sleep in Crying Infants Utilizing the Transport Response," *Current Biology* 32, no. 20 (2022): 4521–29.e4, https:doi.org/10.1016/j.cub.2022.08.041.

48 Field, *Touch.*

49 Sonia J. Lupien, Bruce S. McEwen, Megan R. Gunnar, and Christine Heim, "Effects of Stress throughout the Lifespan on the Brain, Behaviour and Cognition," *Nature Reviews Neuroscience* 10, no. 6 (2009): 434–45.

50 Christopher L. Coe, "Psychosocial Factors and Immunity in Nonhuman Primates: A Review," *Psychosomatic Medicine* 55, no. 3 (1993): 298–308, https://doi.org/10.1097/00006842-199305000-00007.

51 António A. Freitas and Benedita B. Rocha, "Lymphocyte Lifespans: Homeostasis, Selection, and Competition," *Immunology Today* 14, no. 1 (1993): 25–29; G. R. Lubach, C. L. Coe, and W. B. Ershler, "Effects of Early Rearing on Immune Responses in Infant Rhesus Monkeys," *Brain and Behavioral Immunology* 9, no. 1 (1995): 31–46.

52 B. Crary et al., "Decrease in Mitogen Responsiveness of Mononuclear Cells from Peripheral Blood after Epinephrine Administration in Humans," *Journal of Immunology* 130, no. 2 (1983): 694–97.

53 B. Crary et al., "Decrease."

54 Frances A. Champagne, Ian C. G. Weaver, Josie Diorio, Sergiy Dymov, Moshe Szyf, and Michael J. Meaney, "Maternal Care Associated with Methylation of the Estrogen Receptor-alpha1b Promoter and Estrogen Receptor-alpha Expression in the Medial Preoptic Area of Female Offspring," *Endocrinology* 147, no. 6 (2006): 2909–15; Yuliya S. Nikolova and Ahmad R. Hariri, "Can We Observe Epigenetic Effects on Human Brain Function?" *Trends in Cognitive Sciences* 19, no. 7 (2015): 366–73.

55 Marija Kundakovic and Frances A. Champagne, "Early-Life Experience, Epigenetics, and the Developing Brain," *Neuropsychopharmacology* 40, no. 1 (2015): 141–53, https://doi.org/10.1038/npp.2014.140; C. Murgatroyd and D. Spengler, "Epigenetic Programming of the HPA Axis: Early Life Decides," *Stress* 14, no. 6 (2011): 581–89, https://doi.org/10.3109/10253890.2011.602146.

56 "Talking Glossary of Genomic and Genetic Terms," s.v. "Epigenome," updated May 10, 2022, www.genome.gov/genetics-glossary/Epigenome.

57 "Talking Glossary," s.v. "Epigenome."

58 Eva Jablonka and Marion J. Lamb, *Evolution in Four Dimensions: Genetic, Epigenetic, Behavioral, and Symbolic Variation in the History of Life* (Cambridge, MA: MIT Press, 2005).

59 Humberto Maturana and Gerda Verden-Zöller, *The Origin of Humanness in the Biology of Love*, ed. Pille Bunnell (Exeter, UK: Imprint Academic, 2008).

60 Isabella Lucia, Chiara Mariani Wigley, Eleonora Mascheroni, Sabrina Bonichini, and Rosario Montirosso, "Epigenetic Protection: Maternal Touch and DNA-Methylation in Early Life," *Current Opinion in Behavioral Sciences* 43 (2022): 111–17.

61 Kathleen M. Krol, Robert G. Moulder, Travis S. Lillard, Tobias Grossmann, and Jessica J. Connelly, "Epigenetic Dynamics in Infancy and the Impact of Maternal Engagement," *Science Advances* 5, no. 10 (2019): eaay0680.

62 Montagu, *Touching.*

63 Steven R. H. Beach, Gene H. Brody, Alexandre A. Todorov, Tracy D. Gunter, and Robert A. Philibert, "Methylation at SLC6A4 Is Linked to Family History of Child Abuse: An Examination of the Iowa Adoptee Sample," *American Journal of Medical Genetics Part B, Neuropsychiatric Genetics* 153B (2010): 710–13; Hee-Ju Kang, Jae-Min Kim, Robert Stewart, Seon-Young Kim, Kyung-Yeol Bae, Sung-Wan Kim, Il-Seon Shin, Myung-Geun Shin, and Jin-Sang Yoon, "Association of SLC6A4 Methylation with Early Adversity, Characteristics and Outcomes in Depression," *Progress in Neuro-Psychopharmacology and Biological Psychiatry* 44 (2013): 23–28; Monica Uddin, Allison E. Aiello, Derek E. Wildman, Karestan C. Koenen, Graham Pawelec, Regina de Los Santos, Emily Goldmann, and Sandro Galea, "Epigenetic and Immune Function Profiles Associated with Posttraumatic Stress Disorder," *Proceedings of the National Academy of Sciences* 107 (2010): 9470–75.

64 Bruce S. Cushing and Kristin M. Kramer, "Mechanisms Underlying Epigenetic Effects of Early Social Experience: The Role of Neuropeptides and Steroids," *Neuroscience and Biobehavioral Reviews* 29, no. 7 (2005): 1089–105; Helena Palma-Gudiel, A. Córdova-Palomera, Elisenda Eixarch, Michael Deuschle, and Lourdes Fañanás, "Maternal Psychosocial Stress during Pregnancy Alters the Epigenetic Signature of the Glucocorticoid Receptor Gene Promoter in Their Offspring: A Meta-analysis," *Epigenetics* 10 (2015): 893–902; Sarah R. Moore, Lisa M. McEwen, Jill Quirt, Alex Morin, Sarah M. Mah, Ronald G. Barr, W. Thomas Boyce, and Michael S. Kobor, "Epigenetic Correlates of Neonatal Contact in Humans," *Development and Psychopathology* 29, no. 5 (2017): 1517; Ian C. G. Weaver, Nadia Cervoni, Frances A. Champagne, Ana C. D'Alessio, Shakti Sharma, Jonathan R. Seckl, Sergiy Dymov, Moshe Szyf, and Michael J. Meaney, "Epigenetic Programming by Maternal Behavior," *National Neuroscience* 7, no. 8 (2004): 847–54.

65 Moshe Szyf, "Nongenetic Inheritance and Transgenerational Epigenetics," *Trends in Molecular Medicine* 21, no. 2 (2015): 134–44; Peter D. Gluckman and Mark Hanson, *Fetal Matrix: Evolution, Development and Disease* (New York: Cambridge University Press, 2005).

66 Matthew D. Anway, "Epigenetic Transgenerational Actions of Endocrine Disruptors and Male Fertility," *Science* 308, no. 5727 (2005): 1466–69; Johannes Bohacek and Isabelle M. Mansuy, "Epigenetic Inheritance of Disease and Disease Risk," *Neuropsychopharmacology* 38, no. 1 (2013): 220–36.

67 Ali B. Rodgers, Christopher P. Morgan, N. Adrian Leu, and Tracy L. Bale, "Transgenerational Epigenetic Programming via Sperm MicroRNA Recapitulates Effects of Paternal Stress," *Proceedings of the National Academy of Sciences* 112, no. 44 (2015): 13699–704; Rachel Yehuda, Nikolaos P. Daskalakis, Amy Lehrner, Frank Desarnaud, Heather N. Bader, Iouri Makotkine, Janine D. Flory, Linda M. Bierer, and Michael J. Meaney, "Influences of Maternal and Paternal PTSD on Epigenetic Regulation of the Glucocorticoid Receptor Gene in Holocaust Survivor Offspring," *American Journal of Psychiatry* 171 (2014): 872–80.

68 Elysia P. Davis and Curt A. Sandman, "The Timing of Prenatal Exposure to Maternal Cortisol and Psychosocial Stress Is Associated with Human Infant Cognitive Development," *Child Development* 81, no. 1 (2010): 131–48.

69 Katherine Gudsnuk and Frances A. Champagne, "Epigenetic Influence of Stress and the Social Environment," *Institute for Laboratory Animal Research Journal* 53, no. 3–4 (2012): 279–88.

70 Sue Grand and Jill Salberg, "Trans-generational Transmission of Trauma," in *Social Trauma—An Interdisciplinary Textbook*, ed. Andreas Hamburger, Camellia Hancheva, and Vamik D. Volkan (Cham, Switzerland: Springer, 2021), 209–15.

71 G. A. Bradshaw, *Elephants on the Edge: What Animals Teach Us about Humanity* (New Haven, CT: Yale University Press, 2009), 210.

72 Ryan D. Hubbard and Clayton K. Nielsen, "White-Tailed Deer Attacking Humans during the Fawning Season: A Unique Human–Wildlife Conflict on a University Campus," *Human-Wildlife Conflicts* 3, no. 1 (2009): 129–35.

73 Shane C. Campbell-Staton, Brian J. Arnold, Dominique Gonçalves, Petter Granli, Joyce Poole, Ryan A. Long, and Robert M. Pringle, "Ivory Poaching and the Rapid Evolution of Tusklessness in African Elephants," *Science* 374, no. 6566 (2021): 483–87.

74 Lucia et al., "Epigenetic Protection"; Darcia Narvaez, L. Wang, A. Cheng, T. Gleason, R. Woodbury, A. Kurth, and J. B. Lefever, "The Importance of Early Life Touch for Psychosocial and Moral Development," *Psicologia: Reflexão e Crítica* 32, no. 16 (2019), https://doi.org/10.1186/s41155-019-0129-0.

8. Emotions: Octopuses

1 Philip Low, "Cambridge Declaration of Consciousness," in *Francis Crick Memorial Conference on Consciousness in Human and Non-human Animals*, ed. Jaak Panksepp, Diana Reiss, David Edelman, Bruno Van Swinderen, Philip Low, and

Christof Koch (Cambridge, UK: 2012). See also: www.egg-truth.com/egg-blog/2019/5/13/the-cambridge-declaration-on-consciousness.

2 G. A. Bradshaw, *Carnivore Minds: Who These Fearsome Animals Really Are* (New Haven, CT: Yale University Press, 2017).

3 https://en.wikipedia.org/wiki/Paul_the_Octopus.

4 Edward J. Steele et al., "Cause of Cambrian Explosion—Terrestrial or Cosmic?" *Progress in Biophysics and Molecular Biology* 136 (2018): 3–23.

5 Peter Godfrey-Smith, *Other Minds: The Octopus, the Sea, and the Deep Origins of Consciousness* (New York: Farrar, Straus and Giroux, 2016), 47.

6 M. D. Norman and F. G. Hochberg, "The Current State of Octopus Taxonomy," *Phuket Marine Biological Center Research Bulletin* 66 (2005): 127–54.

7 George E. Liu, Lakshmi K. Matukumalli, Tad S. Sonstegard, Larry L. Shade, and Curtis P. Van Tassell, "Genomic Divergences among Cattle, Dog and Human Estimated from Large-Scale Alignments of Genomic Sequences," *BMC Genomics* 7, no. 1 (2006): 1–13.

8 Godfrey-Smith, *Other Minds*, 5, 6, 8. The last common ancestor between *Mollusca* and *Chordata* was identified at 570 million years ago; see Mark E. Hahn, Sibel I. Karchner, and Rebeka R. Merson, "Diversity as Opportunity: Insights from 600 Million Years of AHR Evolution," *Current Opinion in Toxicology* 2 (2017): 58–71.

9 Anton Reiner et al., "The Avian Brain Nomenclature Forum: Terminology for a New Century in Comparative Neuroanatomy," *Journal of Comparative Neurology* 473 (2004): E1; Bradshaw, *Carnivore Minds.*

10 Nicolas Di-Poï and Michel C. Milinkovitch, "The Anatomical Placode in Reptile Scale Morphogenesis Indicates Shared Ancestry among Skin Appendages in Amniotes," *Science Advances* 2, no. 6 (2016): e1600708; Robert C. Berwick, Gabriël J. L. Beckers, Kazuo Okanoya, and Johan J. Bolhuis, "A Bird's Eye View of Human Language Evolution," *Frontiers in Evolutionary Neuroscience* 4 (2012): 5, https://doi.org/10.3389/fnevo.2012.00005.

11 Susan E. Orosz and G. A. Bradshaw, "Avian Neuroanatomy Revisited: From Clinical Principles to Avian Cognition," *Veterinary Clinics of North America: Exotic Animal Practice* 10, no. 3 (2007): 775–802.

12 Jon Ablett, "How Brainy Is an Octopus?" Natural History Museum, October 8, 2018, www.youtube.com/watch?v=2x1dxoNA3k0.

13 Peter Godfrey-Smith, "The Mind of an Octopus," *Scientific American Mind* 28, no. 1 (2017): 62–69.

14 Godfrey-Smith, *Other Minds*, 50–51.

15 Jennifer A. Mather and Ludovic Dickel, "Cephalopod Complex Cognition," *Current Opinion in Behavioral Sciences* 16 (2017): 131–37.

16 Godfrey-Smith, *Other Minds*, 75.

17 "To say that cognition is embodied means that it arises from bodily inter-actions with the world. From this point of view, cognition depends on the kinds of experiences that come from having a body with particular perceptual and motor capacities that are inseparably linked and that together form the matrix within which memory, emotion, language, and all other aspects of life are meshed." Esther Thelen, Gregor Schoner, Christian Scheier, and Linda B. Smith, "The Dynamics of Embodiment: A Field Theory of Infant Perseverative Reaching," *Behavioral and Brain Sciences* 24, no. 1 (2001): 1.

18 Godfrey-Smith, *Other Minds*, 4; Roland C. Anderson, Jennifer A. Mather, and James B. Wood, *Octopus: The Ocean's Intelligent Invertebrate* (Portland, OR: Timber Press, 2010).

19 Anna Di Cosmo, Valeria Maselli, and Gianluca Polese, "*Octopus vulgaris:* An Alternative in Evolution," *Marine Organisms as Model Systems in Biology and Medicine* (2018): 585–98; Roland C. Anderson, Jennifer A. Mather, and James B. Wood, *Octopus: The Ocean's Intelligent Invertebrate: A Natural History* (New York: Workman Publishing, 1992), 13.

20 Willemijn M. Gommans, Sean P. Mullen, and Stefan Maas, "RNA Editing: A Driving Force for Adaptive Evolution?" *Bioessays* 31, no. 10 (2009): 1137–45.

21 Richard Lewontin, September 30, 2010, in response to Colin Wells's comment on "Not So Natural Selection," *New York Review of Books*, www.nybooks.com /articles/2010/09/30/what-darwin-got-wrong/.

22 Ilkka Kronholm, "Adaptive Evolution and Epigenetics," in *Handbook of Epigenetics*, ed. Trygve Tollefsbol (New York: Academic Press, 2017), 427–38.

23 Claudia L. Kleinman, Véronique Adoue, and Jacek Majewski, "RNA Editing of Protein Sequences: A Rare Event in Human Transcriptomes," *RNA* 18, no. 9 (2012): 1586–96.

24 Khatuna Gagnidze, Violeta Rayon-Estrada, Sheila Harroch, Karen Bulloch, and F. Nina Papavasiliou, "A New Chapter in Genetic Medicine: RNA Editing and Its Role in Disease Pathogenesis," *Trends in Molecular Medicine* 24, no. 3 (2018): 294–303.

25 Noa Liscovitch-Brauer, Shahar Alon, Hagit T. Porath, Boaz Elstein, Ron Unger, Tamar Ziv, Arie Admon, Erez Y. Levanon, Joshua J. C. Rosenthal, and Eli Eisenberg, "Trade-off between Transcriptome Plasticity and Genome Evolution in Cephalopods," *Cell* 169, no. 2 (2017): 191–202.

26 Sandra Garrett and Joshua J. C. Rosenthal, "RNA Editing Underlies Temperature Adaptation in K+ Channels from Polar Octopuses," *Science* 335, no. 6070 (2012): 848–51.

27 DNA mutates in two ways: by germline variants or by somatic variants. The former are inherited from parents, whereas the latter are changes that occur during a person's lifetime as a result of exposure to toxins or other environmental insults.

28 Garrett and Rosenthal, "RNA Editing."

29 Eric Kreit, "Biological versus Electronic Adaptive Coloration: How Can One Inform the Other?" *Journal of The Royal Society Interface* 10, no. 78 (2013): 20120601.

30 Jennifer A. Mather and D. Lynn Mather, "Apparent Movement in a Visual Display: The 'Passing Cloud' of Octopus Cyanea *(Mollusca: Cephalopoda),*" *Journal of Zoology* 263, no. 1 (2004): 89–94.

31 Godfrey-Smith, *Other Minds,* 109–12.

32 Lydia M. Mäthger, Alexandra Barbosa, Simon Miner, and Roger T. Hanlon, "Color Blindness and Contrast Perception in Cuttlefish *(Sepia officinalis)* Determined by a Visual Sensorimotor Assay," *Vision Research* 46, no. 11 (2006): 1746–53.

33 Alexander L. Stubbs and Christopher W. Stubbs, "Spectral Discrimination in Color Blind Animals via Chromatic Aberration and Pupil Shape," *Proceedings of the National Academy of Sciences* 113, no. 29 (2016): 8206–11.

34 Mather and Mather, "Apparent Movement."

35 Martin Moynihan and Arcadio F. Rodaniche, "The Behavior and Natural History of the Caribbean Reef Squid *Sepioteuthis sepioidea* with a Consideration of Social, Signal, and Defensive Patterns for Difficult and Dangerous Environments," *Fortschritte der Verhaltensforschung* 25 (1982): 9–150.

36 Robyn J. Crook, "Behavioral and Neurophysiological Evidence Suggests Affective Pain Experience in Octopus," *Iscience* 24, no. 3 (2021): 102229; Marc Bekoff, *Minding Animals: Awareness, Emotions and Heart* (Oxford, UK: Oxford University Press, 2002); Frans De Waal, *Are We Smart Enough to Know How Smart Animals Are?* (New York: W. W. Norton, 2017).

37 Jonathan Birch, Charlotte Burn, Alexandra Schnell, Heather Browning, and Andrew Crump, "Review of the Evidence of Sentience in Cephalopod Molluscs and Decapod Crustaceans" (London: LSE Consulting, 2021), www.lse .ac.uk/News/News-Assets/PDFs/2021/Sentience-in-Cephalopod-Molluscs -and-Decapod-Crustaceans-Final-Report-November-2021.pdf; Martha Henriques, "The Mysterious Inner Life of Octopuses," BBC Future, July 24, 2022, www.bbc.com/future/article/20220720-do-octopuses-feel-pain.

38 Sezgi Goksan et al., "fMRI Reveals Neural Activity Overlap between Adult and Infant Pain," *eLife* 4 (2015): e06356, https://doi.org/10.7554 /eLife.06356.

39 Charles R. Darwin, *The Expression of the Emotions in Man and Animals* (London: John Murray, 1872).

40 Joel Marks, "Emotion East and West: Introduction to a Comparative Philosophy," *Philosophy East and West* 41, no. 1 (1991): 1–30.

41 Lorraine Daston and Peter Galison, *Objectivity* (New York: Zone Books, 2007).

42 Melvin Konner, *The Tangled Wing* (New York: Owl Books, 2002), 139, 141.

43 Richard E. Nisbett, *The Geography of Thought: How Asians and Westerners Think Differently . . . and Why* (New York: Free Press, 2003).

44 Catherine Keller, *From a Broken Web: Separation, Sexism, and Self* (New York: Beacon Press, 1986).

45 Michael Polanyi, *Personal Knowledge: Towards a Post-Critical Philosophy* (Chicago: University of Chicago Press, 1958).

46 Daston and Galison, *Objectivity*.

47 Antonio Damasio, *Descartes' Error: Emotion, Reason and the Human Brain* (New York: Avon, 1996).

48 Jaak Panksepp, *Affective Neuroscience: The Foundations of Human and Animal Emotions* (Oxford, UK: Oxford University Press, 2004).

49 Antoine Bechara, Hanna Damasio, and Antonio R. Damasio, "Emotion, Decision Making and the Orbitofrontal Cortex," *Cerebral Cortex* 10, no. 3 (2000): 295–307.

50 Alan Fogel, *Infancy* (Cornwall-on-Hudson, NY: Sloan Publishing, 2011).

51 Elena Geangu, Hiroko Ichikawa, Junpeng Lao, So Kanazawa, Masam K.Yamaguchi, Roberto Caldara, and Chiara Turati, "Culture Shapes 7-Month-Olds' Perceptual Strategies in Discriminating Facial Expressions of Emotion," *Current Biology* 26, no. 14 (2016): R663–R664; Nangyeon Lim, "Cultural Differences in Emotion: Differences in Emotional Arousal Level between the East and the West," *Integrative Medicine Research* 5, no. 2 (2016): 105–9.

52 Panksepp, *Affective Neuroscience*.

53 Mark D. Lewis, "Bridging Emotion Theory and Neurobiology through Dynamic Systems Modelling," *Behavioral and Brain Sciences* 28, no. 2 (2005): 169–245.

54 Konner, *Tangled*.

55 Amy G. Halberstadt and Fantasy T. Lozada, "Emotion Development in Infancy through the Lens of Culture," *Emotion Review* 3, no. 2 (2011): 158–68.

56 Allan N. Schore, *Affect Dysregulation and Disorders of the Self* (New York: Norton, 2003); Allan N. Schore, *Affect Regulation and the Repair of the Self* (New York: Norton, 2003).

57 Schore, *Dysregulation*.

58 Steven W. Anderson, Antoine Bechara, Hanna Damasio, Daniel Tranel, and Antonio R. Damasio, "Impairment of Social and Moral Behavior Related to Early Damage in Human Prefrontal Cortex," *Nature Neuroscience* 2 (1999): 1032–37.

59 Jaak Panksepp, "How Primary-Process Emotional Systems Guide Child Development: Ancestral Regulators of Human Happiness, Thriving, and Suffering," in *Evolution, Early Experience and Human Development: From Research to Practice and Policy*, ed. Darcia Narvaez, Jaak Panksepp, Allan N. Schore, and Tracy Gleason (New York: Oxford University Press, 2013), 74–94.

60 Elkhonon Goldberg, *The Executive Brain: Frontal Lobes and the Civilized Brain* (New York: Oxford University Press, 2002).

61 Colwyn Trevarthen, "Intimate Contact from Birth: How We Know One Another by Touch, Voice, and Expression in Movement," in *Touch, Attachment and the Body*, ed. Kate White (London: Karnak, 2004), 1–15; Colwyn Trevarthen, "The Neurobiology of Early Communication: Intersubjective Regulations in Human Brain Development," in *Handbook on Brain and Behavior in Human Development*, ed. Alex Fedde Kalverboer and Albertus Arend Gramsbergen (Dordrecht, the Netherlands: Kluwer, 2001), 841–82.

62 Panksepp, *Affective Neuroscience*.

63 Colwyn Trevarthen, "Action and Emotion in Development of the Human Self, Its Sociability and Cultural Intelligence: Why Infants Have Feelings Like Ours," in *Emotional Development*, ed. Jacqueline Nadel and Darwin Muir (Oxford, UK: Oxford University Press, 2005), 61–91.

64 Trevarthen, "Action and Emotion."

65 Allan N. Schore, "The Experience-Dependent Maturation of a Regulatory System in the Orbital Prefrontal Cortex and the Origin of Development Psychopathology," *Development and Psychopathology* 8, no. 1 (1996): 59–87.

66 Allan N. Schore, "Early Organization of the Nonlinear Right Brain and Development of a Predisposition to Psychiatric Disorders," *Development and Psychopathology* 9, no. 4 (1997): 595–631.

67 Robin M. Hogarth, *Educating Intuition* (Chicago: University of Chicago Press, 2001); Arthur S. Reber, *Implicit Learning and Tacit Knowledge: An Essay on the Cognitive Unconscious* (New York: Oxford University Press, 1993).

68 Allan N. Schore, *The Development of the Unconscious Mind* (New York: W. W. Norton, 2019).

69 Allan N. Schore, *The Science of the Art of Psychotherapy* (New York: W. W. Norton, 2017).

70 Maurice J. Elias, May Kranzler, Sarah J. Parker, V. Megan Kash, and Roger P. Weissberg, "The Complementary Perspectives of Social and Emotional Learning, Moral Education, and Character Education," in *Handbook of Moral and Character Education*, 2nd ed., ed. Larry Nucci, Darcia Narvaez, and Tobias Krettenauer (New York: Routledge, 2014), 272–89; Pamela Qualter, Kathryn J. Gardner, and Helen E. Whiteley, "Emotional Intelligence: Review of Research and Educational Implications," *Pastoral Care in Education* 25, no. 1 (2007): 11–20; Marc A. Brackett, "The Emotional Intelligence We Owe Students and Educators," *Educational Leadership* 76, no. 2 (2018): 12–18.

71 Schore, *Development*.

72 Darcia Narvaez, *Neurobiology and the Development of Human Morality: Evolution, Culture and Wisdom* (New York: W. W. Norton, 2014).

73 Daniel N. Stern, *The Interpersonal World of the Infant* (New York: Basic Books, 1985).

74 Stanley Greenspan and Stuart Shanker, *The First Idea* (Cambridge, MA: Da Capo, 2004), 46.

75 Bradshaw, *Carnivore Minds.*

76 Ed Yong, *An Immense World: How Animal Senses Reveal the Hidden Realms around Us* (New York: Random House, 2022).

77 Daniel Goleman, *Emotional Intelligence* (New York: Bantam Books, 2006); Bradshaw, *Carnivore Minds*, 292.

78 Ronald E. Walker and Jeanne M. Foley, "Social Intelligence: Its History and Measurement," *Psychological Reports* 33, no. 3 (1973): 839–64.

79 Mylene M. Mariette, David F. Clayton, and Katherine L. Buchanan, "Acoustic Developmental Programming: A Mechanistic and Evolutionary Framework," *Trends in Ecology and Evolution* 36, no. 8 (2021): 722–36.

80 Pippa Ehrlich and James Reed, *My Octopus Teacher*, 2020, film, Netflix, 85 min.

81 Alexandra K. Schnell, Markus Boeckle, Micaela Rivera, Nicola S. Clayton, and Roger T. Hanlon, "Cuttlefish Exert Self-Control in a Delay of Gratification Task," *Proceedings of the Royal Society B* 288, no. 1946 (2021): 20203161; Elena Tricarico, Luciana Borrelli, Francesca Gherardi, and Graziano Fiorito, "I Know My Neighbour: Individual Recognition in *Octopus vulgaris*," *PLOS One* 6, no. 4 (2011): e18710.

82 Dan Bilefsky, "Inky the Octopus Escapes from a New Zealand Aquarium," *New York Times,* last modified April 14, 2016, www.nytimes.com/2016/04/14/world/asia/inky-octopus-new-zealand-aquarium.html.

83 Ehrlich and Reed, *Octopus.*

84 Gagnidze et al., "New Chapter."

85 Mićo Tatalović, "The Science and Ethics of Turning Octopuses into 'Lab Rats,'" EuroScientist, February 24, 2022, www.euroscientist.com/the-science-and-ethics-of-turning-octopuses-into-lab-rats/.

86 Emily Greenhalgh, "Team Succeeds in Culturing the Pygmy Zebra Octopus," Phys.org, last modified December 22, 2021, https://phys.org/news/2021-12-team-culturing-pygmy-zebra-octopus.html.

9. Moral Commitment: Gray Wolves

1 Ann Swidler, Richard Madsen, Robert N. Bellah, Steven Tipton, and William Sullivan, *Habits of the Heart: Individualism and Commitment in American Life* (Berkeley: University of California Press, 2007).

2 Darcia Narvaez, *Embodied Morality: Protectionism, Engagement and Imagination* (New York: Palgrave-Macmillan, 2016).

3 Darcia Narvaez, *Neurobiology and the Development of Human Morality: Evolution, Culture and Wisdom* (New York: W. W. Norton, 2014).

4 Narvaez, *Neurobiology.*

5 Narvaez.
6 Narvaez.
7 Jean Liedloff, *The Continuum Concept: In Search of Happiness Lost* (Cambridge, MA: Perseus Books, 1977).
8 Darcia Narvaez, "Baselines for Virtue," in *Developing the Virtues: Integrating Perspectives*, ed. Julia Annas, Darcia Narvaez, and Nancy Snow (New York: Oxford University Press, 2016), 14–33; Allan N. Schore, *The Development of the Unconscious Mind* (New York: W. W. Norton, 2019).
9 Mike Boyes, "Re-envisioning Nature from a New Zealand Māori Perspective," in *Encountering, Experiencing and Exploring Nature in Education* (Rateče-Planica, Slovenia: European Institute for Outdoor Adventure Education and Experiential Learning, in partnership with the Centre for School and Outdoor Education Slovenia, 2010), 94–99.
10 Morna Finnegan, "The Politics of Eros: Ritual Dialogue and Egalitarianism in Three Central African Hunter-Gatherer Societies," *Journal of the Royal Anthropological Institute* 19, no. 4 (2013): 697–715.
11 E. Richard Sorenson, "Preconquest Consciousness," in *Tribal Epistemologies*, ed. Helmut Wautischer (Aldershot, UK: Ashgate, 1998), 79–115.
12 Boyes, "Re-envisioning"; Finnegan, "Politics."
13 Boyes, "Re-envisioning."
14 Boyes, "Re-envisioning"; Sorenson, "Preconquest."
15 Narvaez, "Baselines."
16 Mona Farid, Magdi Fekri, Magdi Abd-Elaal, and Hesham Ezz-eldin Zaki, "Archeological Study of Wild Animals in the New Kingdom," *Journal of the Faculty of Tourism and Hotels-University of Sadat City* 2, no. 2 (2018): 58–77.
17 John Linnell et al., *The Fear of Wolves: A Review of Wolf Attacks on Humans* (Trondheim, Norway: NINA NIKU Stiftelsen for naturforskning og kulturminneforskning, 2002), www.researchgate.net/publication/236330045_The_fear_of_wolves_A_review_of_wolf_attacks_on_humans.
18 Gordon Haber and Marybeth Holleman, *Among Wolves: Gordon Haber's Insights into Alaska's Most Misunderstood Animal* (Fairbanks: University of Alaska Press, 2013), 35.
19 Haber and Holleman, *Among Wolves*, 110.
20 Valerie M. Fogleman, "American Attitudes towards Wolves: A History of Misperception," *Environmental Review* 13, no. 1 (1989): 63–94.
21 But see the remarkable story of Takaya, the lone male Wolf surviving on unnamed islands off the coast of British Columbia: Cheryl Alexander, *Takaya: Lone Wolf* (Victoria, BC: Rocky Mountain Books, 2020).
22 Haber and Holleman, *Among Wolves*, 133.
23 Rick McIntyre, *The Rise of Wolf 8: Witnessing the Triumph of Yellowstone's Underdog* (Vancouver, BC: Greystone Books, 2019), 22.

24 McIntyre, *Rise*, 83.
25 Enos A. Mills, *Watched by Wild Animals* (New York: Doubleday, 1923).
26 Haber and Holleman, *Among Wolves*, 92.
27 G. A. Bradshaw, *Talking with Bears: Conversations with Charlie Russell* (Victoria, BC: Rocky Mountain Books, 2020).
28 Matthew Margolin, *The Ohlone Way: Indian Life in the San Francisco-Monterey Bay Area* (Berkeley, CA: Heyday, 1978).
29 Haber and Holleman, *Among Wolves*, 37.
30 Haber and Holleman, 92.
31 www.nwf.org/Educational-Resources/Wildlife-Guide/Mammals/Gray-Wolf.
32 Haber and Holleman, *Among Wolves*, 232.
33 Nick Mott, "A Record Number of Yellowstone Wolves Have Been Killed. Conservationists Are Worried," NPR, April 13, 2022, www.npr.org/2022/04/13/1092366933/a-record-number-of-yellowstone-wolves-have-been-killed-conservationists-are-worr.
34 Haber and Holleman, *Among Wolves*, 63.
35 Haber and Holleman, 49–51.
36 Haber and Holleman, 52.
37 Haber and Holleman, 25.
38 Haber and Holleman, 36, 59.
39 Rick McIntyre, personal communication over several conversations, May and June 2022.
40 Jaak Panksepp, *Affective Neuroscience: The Foundations of Human and Animal Emotions* (New York: Oxford University Press, 1998).
41 www.zerotothree.org/early-development/brain-development.
42 Zdravko Petanjek, Milos Judaš, Goran Šimic, Mladen R. Rasin, Harry B. M. Uylings, Pasko Rakic, and Ivica Kostovic, "Extraordinary Neoteny of Synaptic Spines in the Human Prefrontal Cortex," *Proceedings of the National Academy of Sciences* 108, no. 32 (2011): 13281–86, https://doi.org/10.1073/pnas.1105108108.
43 Narvaez, *Neurobiology*.
44 Narvaez, "Baselines."
45 Kathryn L. Geurts, *Culture and the Senses: Bodily Ways of Knowing in an African Community* (Berkeley: University of California Press, 2002).
46 Pierre Bourdieu, *Outline of a Theory of Practice* (Cambridge, UK: Cambridge University Press, 1977).
47 Richard A. Shweder, Jackie Goodnow, G. Hatano, Robert LeVine, Helen Markus, and Patricia Miller, "The Cultural Psychology of Development: One Mind, Many Mentalities," in *Handbook of Child Psychology*, vol. 1, *Theoretical Models of Human Development*, ed. William Damon and Richard M. Lerner (New York: John Wiley & Sons, 2006), 716–92.

48 Vincent J. Felitti and Robert F. Anda, *The Adverse Childhood Experiences (ACE) Study* (Atlanta: Centers for Disease Control and Prevention and Kaiser Permanente, 2005); Vincent J. Felitti, "Adverse Childhood Experiences and Their Relation to Adult Health and Well-Being: Turning Gold into Lead" (symposium lecture, Human Nature and Early Experience: Addressing the Environment of Evolutionary Adaptedness, University of Notre Dame, Notre Dame, IN, October 2010).

49 Gordon Neufeld and Gabor Maté, *Hold On to Your Kids: Why Parents Need to Matter More Than Peers* (New York: Ballantine, 2006), 109.

50 Narvaez, *Neurobiology.*

51 Narvaez, *Neurobiology.*

52 Gabor Maté and Daniel Maté, *The Myth of Normal: Trauma, Illness, and Healing in a Toxic Culture* (Garden City, NY: Avery, 2022).

53 Haber and Holleman, *Among Wolves,* 25.

54 Haber and Holleman, 26.

55 Thomas R. Verny and Pamela Weintraub, *Pre-Parenting: Nurturing Your Child from Conception* (New York: Simon & Schuster, 2002).

56 Narvaez, *Neurobiology.*

57 Donald W. Winnicott, *The Maturational Processes and the Facilitating Environment* (New York: International Universities Press; London: Hogarth Press, 1965).

58 Antonio Damasio, *Self Comes to Mind* (New York: Vintage Press, 2010).

59 Ulrich Neisser, "Five Kinds of Self-Knowledge," *Philosophical Psychology* 1, no. 1 (1988): 35–39; William W. Seeley and Bruce L. Miller, "Disorders of the Self in Dementia," in *The Lost Self: Pathologies of Brain and Identity,* ed. Todd E. Feinberg and Julian Paul Keenan (New York: Oxford University Press, 2005), 147–65.

60 Endel Tulving, Shitu Kapur, Fergus I. M. Craik, Morris Moscovitch, and Sylvain Houle, "Hemispheric Encoding/Retrieval Asymmetry in Episodic Memory: Positron Emission Tomography Findings," *Proceedings of the National Academy of Sciences* 91, no. 6 (1994): 2016–20; Mark A. Wheeler, T. Donald Stuss, and Endel Tulving, "Toward a Theory of Episodic Memory: The Frontal Lobes and Autonoetic Consciousness," *Psychological Bulletin* 121, no. 3 (1997): 331–54.

61 Rodolfo R. Llinas, *I of the Vortex: From Neurons to Self* (Cambridge, MA: MIT Press, 2002).

62 Jaak Panksepp, "Affective Consciousness: Core Emotional Feelings in Animals and Humans," *Consciousness and Cognition* 14 (2005): 19–69; Jaak Panksepp, "On the Embodied Neural Nature of Core Emotional Affects," *Journal of Consciousness Studies* 12, no. 8–10 (2005): 161–87.

63 Leath Tonino, "The Egret Lifting from the River: David Hinton on the Wisdom of Ancient Chinese Poets," *The Sun,* January 2015, 4–13.

64 Bradshaw, *Talking*.

65 Narvaez, *Neurobiology*.

66 Marshall Sahlins, *The Western Illusion of Human Nature with Reflections on the Long History of Hierarchy, Equality and the Sublimation of Anarchy in the West, and Comparative Notes on Other Conceptions of the Human Condition* (Chicago: Prickly Paradigm Press, 2008).

67 Rick McIntyre, personal communication, May 29, 2022.

68 Humberto Maturana and Francisco Varela, *Autopoiesis and Cognition: The Realization of the Living* (Boston: Reidel, 1980).

69 Priscilla Kelly, Gemma Alderton, Seth Thomas Scanlon, and Caroline Ash, "A Multiplicity of Microbiomes," *Science* 376, no. 6596 (2022): 932.

70 Humberto Maturana and Francisco Varela, *The Tree of Knowledge* (Boston: Shambhala, 1998), 248.

71 Charles Darwin, *The Descent of Man* (London: Penguin Classics, 2004); Howard E. Gruber and Paul H. Barrett, *Darwin on Man: A Psychological Study of Scientific Creativity Together with Darwin's Early and Unpublished Notebooks* (London: Wildwood House, 1974); David Loye, *Darwin's Lost Theory* (Carmel, CA: Benjamin Franklin Press, 2000); David Loye, "The Moral Brain," *Brain and Mind* 3 (2002): 133–50.

72 Abraham Maslow, *Motivation and Personality*, 2nd ed. (New York: Harper & Row, 1970).

73 Darcia Narvaez, "Beyond Trauma-Informed: Returning to Indigenous, Wellness-Informed Practices," *International Journal of Existential Positive Psychology* 11, no. 1 (2022), www.meaning.ca/ijepp-article/vol11-no1/beyond -trauma-informed-returning-to-indigenous-wellness-informed-practices/.

74 Mary S. Tarsha and Darcia Narvaez, "The Developmental Neurobiology of Moral Mindsets: Basic Needs and Childhood Experience," in *Motivation and Morality: A Biopsychosocial Approach*, ed. Martha Berg and Edward Chang (Washington, DC: APA Books, forthcoming).

75 Peter Fonagy, Gyorgy Gergely, Elliot Jurist, and Mary Target, *Affect Regulation, Mentalization, and the Development of the Self* (New York: Other Press, 2004).

76 Dante Cicchetti and Sheree Toth, "Child Maltreatment," *Annual Review of Clinical Psychology* 1 (2005): 409–38.

77 Grazyna Kochanska, Nazan Aksan, and Amy L. Koenig, "A Longitudinal Study of the Roots of Preschoolers' Conscience: Committed Compliance and Emerging Internalization," *Child Development* 66, no. 6 (1995): 1752–69.

78 Bernadette Grosjean and Guochuan E. Tsai, "NMDA Neurotransmission as a Critical Mediator of Borderline Personality Disorder," *Journal of Psychiatry and Neuroscience* 32, no. 2 (2007): 103–15.

79 G. A. Bradshaw, *Elephants on the Edge: What Animals Teach us about Humanity* (New Haven, CT: Yale University Press, 2009).

80 Berne Krause, *The Great Animal Orchestra: Finding the Origins of Music in the World's Wild Places* (New York: Little & Brown, 2012).

81 Krause, *Orchestra.*

82 Haber and Holleman, *Among Wolves,* 73.

83 Donna J. Haraway, *Staying with the Trouble: Making Kin in the Chthulucene* (Durham, NC: Duke University Press, 2016). The term "sympoietic" comes from: Beth Dempster, "Sympoietic and Autopoietic Systems: A New Distinction for Self-Organizing Systems," in *Proceedings of the World Congress of the Systems Sciences and ISSS 2000,* ed. J. K. Allen and J. Wilby (Toronto: International Society for Systems Studies Annual Conference, 2000).

84 Haber and Holleman, *Among Wolves,* 59–61.

85 Haber and Holleman, 59.

86 Bradshaw, *Elephants.*

87 Karen Jones, "From Big Bad Wolf to Ecological Hero: *Canis lupus* and the Culture(s) of Nature in the American–Canadian West," *American Review of Canadian Studies* 40, no. 3 (2010): 338–50.

88 Tori Peglar, "1995 Reintroduction of Wolves in Yellowstone," Yellowstone National Park Trips, May 13, 2022, www.yellowstonepark.com/park /conservation/yellowstone-wolves-reintroduction/.

89 Rick McIntyre, personal communication, June 20, 2022; Rick McIntyre, *The Reign of Wolf 21: The Saga of Yellowstone's Legendary Druid Pack* (Vancouver, BC: Greystone Books, 2020); McIntyre, *Rise.*

90 Haber and Holleman, *Among Wolves.*

91 Haber and Holleman, 24.

92 Mark S. Boyce, "Wolves for Yellowstone: Dynamics in Time and Space," *Journal of Mammalogy* 99, no. 5 (2018): 1021–31.

93 Bradshaw, *Elephants;* G. A. Bradshaw, Allan N. Schore, Janine L. Brown, Joyce H. Poole, and Cynthia J. Moss, "Elephant Breakdown," *Nature* 433, no. 7028 (2005): 807.

94 Douglas H. Chadwick, *The Fate of the Elephant* (San Francisco: Sierra Club Books for Children, 1994), 431–32.

95 Haber and Holleman, *Among Wolves,* 210.

96 G. A. Bradshaw, "Our Common Blood," *Ecology* 99, no. 2 (2018): 505–7.

97 Barbara Brease quoted in Haber and Holleman, *Among Wolves,* 248.

10. The Peace of Wild Things

1 Wendell Berry, *The Peace of Wild Things* (New York: Penguin, 2018).

2 Jakob von Uexküll, "A Stroll through the Worlds of Animals and Men: A Picture Book of Invisible Worlds," in *Instinctive Behavior: The Development of a Modern Concept,* ed. Claire H. Schiller (New York: International Universities Press, 1957), 5–80.

3 Kent Nerburn, ed., *The Wisdom of the Native Americans* (Novato, CA: New World Library, 1999).

4 G. A. Bradshaw, *Carnivore Minds: Who These Fearsome Animals Really Are* (New Haven, CT: Yale University Press, 2017).

5 Jack D. Forbes, *Columbus and Other Cannibals: The Wétiko Disease of Exploitation, Imperialism, and Terrorism*, rev. ed. (New York: Seven Stories Press, 2008), 185.

6 Philip Low, "Cambridge Declaration of Consciousness," in *Francis Crick Memorial Conference on Consciousness in Human and Non-Human Animals*, ed. Jaak Panksepp, Diana Reiss, David Edelman, Bruno Van Swinderen, Philip Low, and Christof Koch (Cambridge, UK: 2012); Jonathan Birch, Charlotte Burn, Alexandra Schnell, Heather Browning, and Andrew Crump, "Review of the Evidence of Sentience in Cephalopod Molluscs and Decapod Crustaceans" (London: LSE Consulting, 2021), www.lse.ac.uk/News/News-Assets/PDFs/2021/Sentience-in-Cephalopod-Molluscs-and-Decapod-Crustaceans-Final-Report-November-2021.pdf. See also: www.egg-truth.com/egg-blog/2019/5/13/the-cambridge-declaration-on-consciousness.

7 Low, "Cambridge."

8 Judith L. Bronstein, ed., *Mutualism* (New York: Oxford University Press, 2015).

9 Surindar Paracer and Vernon Ahmadjian, *Symbiosis*, 2nd ed. (New York: Oxford University Press, 2000).

10 Darcia Narvaez, Lee Gettler, Julia Braungart-Rieker, Laura Miller-Graff, and Paul Hastings, "The Flourishing of Young Children: Evolutionary Baselines," in *Contexts for Young Child Flourishing: Evolution, Family and Society*, ed. Darcia Narvaez, Julia Braungart-Rieker, Laura Miller-Graff, Lee Gettler, and Paul Hastings (New York: Oxford University Press, 2016), 3–27.

11 Darcia Narvaez, "Beyond Trauma-Informed: Returning to Indigenous, Wellness-Informed Practices," *International Journal of Existential Positive Psychology* 11, no. 1 (2022), www.meaning.ca/ijepp-article/vol11-no1/beyond-trauma-informed-returning-to-indigenous-wellness-informed-practices/.

12 Daniel Stern, *Forms of Vitality: Exploring Dynamic Experience in Psychology, the Arts, Psychotherapy, and Development* (New York: Oxford University Press, 2010).

13 Gordon Neufeld, "The Keys to Well-Being in Children and Youth: The Significant Role of Families" (keynote address, European Parliament, Brussels, Belgium, November 13, 2012), quoted in Gabor Maté and Daniel Maté, *The Myth of Normal: Trauma, Illness, and Healing in a Toxic Culture* (Garden City, NY: Avery, 2022), 127.

14 Thomas Widlok, *Anthropology and the Economy of Sharing* (London: Routledge, 2017); Genevieve Vaughan, "Introduction: A Radically Different Worldview Is Possible," in *Women and the Gift Economy*, ed. Genevieve Vaughan (Toronto: Inanna Publications, 2007), 1–40.

15 Sarah Hrdy, *Mothers and Others: The Evolutionary Origins of Mutual Understanding* (Cambridge, MA: Belknap Press, 2009).

16 Genevieve Vaughan, *The Gift in the Heart of Language: The Maternal Source of Meaning* (Milan: Mimesis International, 2015).

17 Ashley Montagu, *Touching: The Human Significance of the Skin* (New York: Harper & Row, 1986).

18 Eric E. Nelson and Jaak Panksepp, "Brain Substrates of Infant–Mother Attachment: Contributions of Opioids, Oxytocin, and Norepinephrine," *Neuroscience and Biobehavioral Reviews* 22, no. 3 (1998): 437–52.

19 Montagu, *Touching*.

20 E. Richard Sorenson, "Preconquest Consciousness," in *Tribal Epistemologies*, ed. Helmut Wautischer (Aldershot, UK: Ashgate, 1998), 79–115.

21 Judith M. Burkart, Sarah B. Hrdy, and Carel P. van Schaik, "Cooperative Breeding and Human Cognitive Evolution," *Evolutionary Anthropology* 18 (2009): 175–86.

22 Darcia Narvaez, Jaak Panksepp, Allan Schore, and Tracy Gleason, eds., *Evolution, Early Experience, and Human Development: From Research to Practice and Policy* (New York: Oxford University Press, 2013); Thomas R. Verny and Pamela Weintraub, *Pre-Parenting: Nurturing Your Child from Conception* (New York: Simon & Schuster, 2002).

23 Nakia Gordon, Sharon Burke, Huda Akil, Stanley J. Watson, and Jaak Panksepp, "Socially-Induced Brain 'Fertilization': Play Promotes Brain Derived Neurotrophic Factor Transcription in the Amygdala and Dorsolateral Frontal Cortex in Juvenile Rats," *Neuroscience Letters* 341, no. 1–24 (2003): 17–20.

24 O. Fred Donaldson, *Playing by Heart: The Vision and Practice of Belonging* (Deer Beach, FL: Health Communications, 1993), xv. See also: https://originalplay.eu/.

25 Leath Tonino, "The Egret Lifting from the River: David Hinton on the Wisdom of Ancient Chinese Poets," *The Sun*, January 2015, 4–13.

26 Thich Nhat Hanh, *Fragrant Palm Leaves: Journals 1962–1966* (Berkeley, CA: Parallax Press, 2020).

27 Michael Mendizza and Joseph Chilton Pearce, *Magical Parent, Magical Child: The Art of Joyful Parenting* (Berkeley, CA: North Atlantic Books, 2004); Lawrence J. Cohen, *Playful Parenting: An Exciting New Approach to Raising Children That Will Help You Nurture Close Connections, Solve Behavior Problems, and Encourage Confidence* (New York: Ballantine Books, 2002); Anthony T. DeBenedet and Lawrence J. Cohen, *The Art of Roughhousing: Good Old-Fashioned Horseplay and Why Every Kid Needs It* (Philadelphia: Quirk Books, 2010).

28 Barbara Nicholson and Lysa Parker, *Attached at the Heart: Eight Proven Parenting Principles for Raising Connected and Compassionate Children* (Deerfield Beach, FL: Health Communications, 2013).

29 Vine Deloria, *God Is Red: A Native View of Religion* (Wheat Ridge, CO: Fulcrum Publishing, 2003), 1.

30 Graham Harvey, *Animism: Respecting the Living World* (London: C. Hurst, 2017).

31 Gordon Haber and Marybeth Holleman, *Among Wolves: Gordon Haber's Insights into Alaska's Most Misunderstood Animal* (Fairbanks: University of Alaska Press, 2013), 92.

32 Wahinkpe Topa (Four Arrows) and Darcia Narvaez, *Restoring the Kinship Worldview: Indigenous Voices Introduce 28 Precepts for Rebalancing Life on Planet Earth* (Berkeley, CA: North Atlantic Books, 2022).

33 Genevieve Vaughan, *The Maternal Roots of the Gift Economy* (Toronto: Inanna, 2019); Vaughan, "Introduction."

34 Forbes, *Columbus.*

35 Andrea Wulf, *Magnificent Rebels: The First Romantics and the Invention of the Self* (New York: Alfred A. Knopf, 2022), 195.

36 Wulf, *Magnificent Rebels,* 195.

37 G. A. Bradshaw, *Talking with Bears: Conversations with Charlie Russell* (Victoria, BC: Rocky Mountain Books, 2020), 121.

38 Tiffany Field and Martin Reite, *The Psychobiology of Attachment and Separation* (New York: Academic Press, 1985); Tiffany Field, *Touch in Early Development* (New York: Psychology Press, 1995).

39 Richard Louv, *Last Child in the Woods: Saving Our Children from Nature Deficit Disorder* (New York: Workman, 2005); Scott D. Sampson, *How to Raise a Wild Child: The Art and Science of Falling in Love with Nature* (New York: Houghton Mifflin Harcourt, 2015); Angela J. Hanscom, *Balanced and Barefoot* (Oakland, CA: New Harbinger, 2016); Rebecca P. Cohen, *15 Minutes Outside: 365 Ways to Get Out of the House and Connect with Your Kids* (Naperville, IL: Sourcebooks, 2011); Katy Bowman, *Grow Wild: The Whole-Child, Whole-Family Nature-Rich Guide to Moving More* (Carlsborg, WA: Propriometrics Press, 2021).

40 Abraham H. Maslow, *The Psychology of the Northern Blackfoot Indians* (Brooklyn, NY: Department of Psychology, Brooklyn College, 1938; unpublished draft held at the Center for the History of Psychology, University of Akron, Akron, OH), reprinted in Sidney Stone Brown, *Transformation beyond Greed: Native Self-Actualization* (Scottsdale, AZ: Book Patch, 2014), 35.

41 Abraham H. Maslow and John J. Honigmann, *Northern Blackfoot Culture and Personality* (Brooklyn, NY: Department of Psychology, Brooklyn College, 1938; unpublished draft held at the Center for the History of Psychology, University of Akron, Akron, OH), reprinted in Sidney Stone Brown, *Transformation beyond Greed: Native Self-Actualization* (Scottsdale, AZ: Book Patch, 2014), 6.

42 Brown, *Transformation,* 44–45.

43 Brown, *Transformation;* Mary S. Tarsha and Darcia Narvaez, "The Developmental Neurobiology of Moral Mindsets: Basic Needs and Childhood Experience," in *Motivation and Morality: A Biopsychosocial Approach,* ed. Martha Berg and Edward Chang (Washington, DC: APA Books, 2023), 187–204.

44 Neufeld, "Keys."

45 Barbara Rogoff and Jean Lave, *Everyday Cognition: Its Development in Social Context* (Cambridge, MA: Harvard University Press, 1984); Barbara Rogoff, *The Cultural Nature of Human Development* (New York: Oxford University Press, 2005).

46 Aidan J. MacFarlane, "Olfaction in the Development of Social Preferences in the Human Neonate," *CIBA Foundation Symposium* 33 (1975): 103–17; Robert Coopersmith and Michael Leon, "Enhanced Neural Response by Adult Rats to Odors Experienced Early in Life," *Brain Research* 371 (1986): 400–403.

47 Darcia Narvaez, *Neurobiology and the Development of Human Morality: Evolution, Culture and Wisdom* (New York: W. W. Norton, 2014).

48 Tyson Yunkaporta, *Sand Talk: How Indigenous Thinking Can Save the World* (New York: HarperCollins, 2020).

49 Allan N. Schore, *The Development of the Unconscious Mind* (New York: W. W. Norton, 2019).

50 Maria Montessori, *The Secret of Childhood* (New York: Ballantine Books, 1966).

51 Topa and Narvaez, *Kinship.*

52 Darcia Narvaez, "Original Practices for Becoming and Being Human," in *Indigenous Sustainable Wisdom: First Nation Know-How for Global Flourishing,* ed. Darcia Narvaez, Four Arrows, Eugene Halton, Brian Collier, and Georges Enderle (New York: Peter Lang, 2019), 90–110.

53 Barry S. Hewlett and Michael E. Lamb, *Hunter-Gatherer Childhoods: Evolutionary, Developmental and Cultural Perspectives* (New Brunswick, NJ: Aldine, 2005).

54 Jon Young, Ellen Haas, and Evan McGown, *Coyote's Guide to Connecting with Nature,* 2nd ed. (Santa Cruz, CA: Owlink Media, 2010).

55 F. David Peat, *Blackfoot Physics* (Boston: Weiser Books, 2001), 8.

56 Topa and Narvaez, *Kinship.*

57 Deloria, *God,* 1–2.

58 Mourning Dove, *Mourning Dove: A Salishan Autobiography,* American Indian Lives, ed. Jay Miller (Lincoln: University of Nebraska Press, 2014).

59 Paul Shepard, *Coming Home to the Pleistocene,* ed. F. R. Shepard (Washington, DC: Island Press/Shearwater Books, 1998).

60 Keri Blakinger, *Corrections in Ink: A Memoir* (New York: Macmillan, 2022).

61 Donald W. Winnicott, *Babies and Their Mothers* (Reading, MA: Addison-Wesley, 1987).

62 Masashi Soga and Kevin J. Gaston, "Extinction of Experience: The Loss of Human–Nature Interactions," *Frontiers in Ecology and the Environment* 14, no. 2 (2016): 94–101.

63 Narvaez, *Neurobiology.*

64 Widlok, *Anthropology.*

65 Marvin Bram, *A History of Humanity* (Delhi: Primus Books, 2018); Philippe Descola, *Beyond Nature and Culture,* trans. J. Lloyd (Chicago: University of Chicago Press, 2013); Darcia Narvaez and Mary S. Tarsha, "The Missing Mind: Contrasting Civilization with Non-civilization Development and Functioning," in *Psychology and Cognitive Archaeology: An Interdisciplinary Approach to the Study of the Human Mind,* ed. T. Henley and M. Rossano (London: Routledge, 2021), 55–69.

66 Yunkaporta, *Sand.*

67 Narvaez, *Neurobiology.*

68 Cindy Engel, *Wild Health: Lessons in Natural Wellness from the Animal Kingdom* (New York: Houghton Mifflin, 2003); *Animal Doctors: How Do They Heal Themselves?* Wocomo WILDLIFE, documentary, 2014, www.youtube.com /watch?v=zbvENEzZzcA.

69 Eric T. Frank, Marten Wehrhahn, and K. Eduard Linsenmair, "Wound Treatment and Selective Help in a Termite-Hunting Ant," *Proceedings of the Royal Society B* 285 (2018): 2457, http://dx.doi.org/10.1098/rspb.2017.2457.

70 G. A. Bradshaw, "Leopard Seal Compassion," Omere, August 31, 2021, https://omere.ca/essays/leopard-seal-compassion/.

71 Narvaez, "Trauma-Informed."

72 Bradshaw, *Talking.*

73 Gabor Maté, *In the Realm of Hungry Ghosts* (Berkeley, CA: North Atlantic Books, 2010).

74 Carmen Sandi and Jozsef Haller, "Stress and the Social Brain: Behavioural Effects and Neurobiological Mechanisms," *Nature Reviews Neuroscience* 16, no. 5 (2015): 290–304.

75 Richard Katz, *Indigenous Healing Psychology: Honoring the Wisdom of the First Peoples* (Rochester, VT: Healing Arts Press, 2017); Rupert Ross, *Indigenous Healing: Exploring Traditional Paths* (Toronto: Penguin Canada, 2014).

76 Katz, *Indigenous.*

77 Joanna Macy and Molly Brown, *Coming Back to Life* (Gabriola Island, BC: New Society Publishers, 2014).

78 Richard Katz, "Synergy and Empowerment: Renewing and Expanding the Community's Healing Resources," in *Synergy, Healing, and Empowerment: Insights from Cultural Diversity,* ed. Richard Katz and Stephen Murphy-Shigematsu (Calgary: Brush Education, 2012), 21–48.

79 Richard Katz, Megan Biesele, and Verna St. Denis, *Healing Makes Our Hearts Happy: Spirituality and Cultural Transformation among the Kalahari Ju/'huansi* (Rochester, VT: Inner Traditions, 1997).

80 Katz, "Synergy," 31.

81 G. A. Bradshaw, "Living Out of Our Minds," in *The Rediscovery of the Wild,* ed. Peter H. Kahn Jr. and Patricia H. Hasbach (Cambridge, MA: MIT Press, 2013), 119–38.

82 Maté, *Hungry Ghosts,* 371.

83 Katz, *Indigenous.*

84 Edith Turner, *Communitas: The Anthropology of Collective Joy* (New York: Palgrave Macmillan, 2012).

85 Émile Durkheim, *The Elementary Forms of the Religious Life* (New York: The Free Press, 1965).

86 Young et al., *Coyote's Guide.*

87 Camilla Power, Morna Finnegan, and Hilary Callan, eds., *Human Origins: Contributions from Social Anthropology* (New York: Berghahn, 2017). For practical advice on how to do this, see Tom Brown's extensive work: www.trackerschool.com/.

88 Riane Eisler and Douglas P. Fry, *Nurturing Our Humanity* (New York: Oxford University Press, 2019).

89 Katz, *Indigenous.*

90 Darcia Narvaez, "The 99%—Development and Socialization within an Evolutionary Context: Growing Up to Become 'A Good and Useful Human Being,'" in *War, Peace and Human Nature: The Convergence of Evolutionary and Cultural Views,* ed. Douglas Fry (New York: Oxford University Press, 2018), 643–72; Tim Ingold, "On the Social Relations of the Hunter-Gatherer Band," in *The Cambridge Encyclopedia of Hunters and Gatherers,* ed. Richard B. Lee and Richard Daly (New York: Cambridge University Press, 2005), 399–410.

91 Bill Plotkin, *Wild Mind: A Field Guide to the Human Psyche* (Novato, CA: New World Library, 2013).

92 F. David Peat, *Gentle Action: Bringing Creative Change to a Turbulent World* (Siena, Italy: Pari Publishing, 2008).

93 David Abram, *Becoming Animal: An Earthly Cosmology* (New York: Pantheon, 2010), 3.

94 Macy and Brown, *Life;* Peter Wohlleben, *The Secret Wisdom of Nature* (Vancouver, BC: Greystone Books, 2017).

Index

About the Authors

Darcia Narvaez is professor emerita of psychology at the University of Notre Dame. She is a fellow of the American Psychological Association, the American Educational Research Association, the Association for Psychological Science, and the American Association for the Advancement of Science. She studies moral development and human flourishing from an interdisciplinary perspective, integrating anthropology, neuroscience, and clinical, developmental, and educational sciences. She has published hundreds of papers and has authored over twenty books, including the multiple-award-winning book *Neurobiology and the Development of Human Morality: Evolution, Culture and Wisdom,* and more recently *Restoring the Kinship Worldview: Indigenous Voices Introduce 28 Precepts for Rebalancing Life on Planet Earth* with Wahinkpe Topa. She serves as president of Kindred World (www .KindredWorld.org) and hosts the website www.EvolvedNest.org.

G. A. Bradshaw is the founder and director of The Kerulos Center for Nonviolence (Kerulos.org). She holds doctoral degrees in ecology and psychology, and she was the first scientist to recognize and diagnose PTSD in Elephants, Chimpanzees, Orcas, and other Animals. Her books include the Pulitzer-nominated *Elephants on the Edge: What Animals Teach Us about Humanity; Carnivore Minds: Who These Fearsome Animals Really Are; Talking with Bears: Conversations with Charlie Russell;* and *The Elephant Letters: The Story of Billy and Kani.* She is the director and primary carer for rescued domesticated Animals and Indigenous Wildlife at Grace Village (formerly the Tortoise and the Hare Sanctuary) in the mountains of southern Oregon, located on the traditional lands of the Grizzly Bear, Takelma, Gray Wolf , and Coho Salmon.

About North Atlantic Books

North Atlantic Books (NAB) is an independent, nonprofit publisher committed to a bold exploration of the relationships between mind, body, spirit, and nature. Founded in 1974, NAB aims to nurture a holistic view of the arts, sciences, humanities, and healing. To make a donation or to learn more about our books, authors, events, and newsletter, please visit www.northatlanticbooks.com.